MW00464080

'New technologies, especially AI, are opening up entrepreneurial opportunities everywhere. This timely book covers how we can best navigate this new world of work and the challenges it presents.'

Suranga Chandratillake OBE, Partner at Balderton and Member of the Prime Minister's Council for Science and Technology

'A fascinating book, bursting with bold and practical ideas for how we can flourish in the 21st century, from one of the great technological minds of our time.'

Daniel Susskind, Author of A World Without Work *and* Growth: A Reckoning

'In this fascinating book, James explains why entrepreneurship has never been more prevalent – or more important. An in-depth analysis and useful guide to what's causing this shift, it's also a powerful rallying cry for why start-ups are so essential to our future. The next few decades will be driven by builders rather than big companies. *Start-Up Century* shows why.'

Mustafa Suleyman, Co-founder and CEO of Inflection AI and Author of The Coming Wave

JAMES WISE

START-UP CENTURY

Why we're all becoming entrepreneurs – and how to make it work for everyone

BLOOMSBURY BUSINESS

LONDON • OXFORD • NEW YORK • NEW DELHI • SYDNEY

BLOOMSBURY BUSINESS
Bloomsbury Publishing Plc
50 Bedford Square, London, WC1B 3DP, UK
29 Earlsfort Terrace, Dublin 2, Ireland

A catalogue record for this book is available from the British Library

Library of Congress Cataloguing-in-Publication data has been applied for

ISBN: 978-1-3994-1059-5; eBook: 978-1-3994-1058-8

2 4 6 8 10 9 7 5 3 1

Typeset by Deanta Global Publishing Services, Chennai, India
Printed and bound in Great Britain by CPI Group (UK) Ltd, Croydon CR0 4YY

To find out more about our authors and books visit www.bloomsbury.com
and sign up for our newsletters

For Elizabeth & William

Contents

'Ignite the mind's spark to rise the sun in you.'
FLORENCE NIGHTINGALE

Introduction: A view from the kitchen table

Does it feel like everyone you know is starting a business? That's because they are. Over the last few years, the number of people starting new companies, launching side projects, or going solo as a freelancer or gig worker has surged, breaking records across the world. Some of this has been driven by short-term shocks to our lives, with the pandemic and ensuing global economic slowdown leaving many people without any other option but to find new ways of working. At the same time, the rise of remote working and the rapid adoption of digital tools has made many people realize they no longer need the baggage that came with their old job, office and boss, leaving them to ask themselves, *Why not go it alone?*

The sudden rise in entrepreneurship is not a momentary phenomenon; it's an accelerating change in the way we live and work which has been in motion for decades. As this movement continues, fewer people will have the desire or opportunity to work in a large company, with a stable and traditional career ahead of them. Instead, more people than ever will be self-employed, learning skilled trades, providing care or using new tools to build things that used to take hundreds if not thousands of people to produce. Over the coming decades, it will become the norm for people to work alone or in small teams in start-ups, with huge implications for our way of life. This is the start of the start-up century.

Over the last 15 years, working in start-ups and as a venture capitalist, I've been fortunate to meet many thousands of entrepreneurs, from Silicon Valley-based billionaires to people working on a dream in their spare rooms. Throughout this career I've had a ringside seat to two intertwined revolutions: the invention of new technologies that empower individuals to be more productive than ever, and a rise in the number of people starting their own businesses. I've watched in real time as scientific breakthroughs have been transformed into products by start-ups that have upended industries. And I've worked with many people who have either decided to, or had to, leave traditional, stable careers and professions to start something new.

Working with entrepreneurs, and seeing them deal with the trials and tribulations of building a business, isn't something new to me. Growing up, I didn't know many people in stable careers. Outside of public servants – friends and family who were nurses or carers – almost everyone I knew was self-employed or working in very small local businesses. Their success was varied, some struggling to make ends meet, some very comfortably off. And they ranged in skills, working as odd-jobbers, tradespeople, freelance mechanics, travelling salespeople, recruitment professionals or property developers. They were all used to the roller coaster that comes with running your own business, of months of famine and months of plenty, and of the stress but also pride gained from building something yourself. Back in the 1990s, almost none of these people would have described themselves as entrepreneurs; blue-collar workers never seem to be described this way despite the risks they take. But they were to their core. Most of what I know about entrepreneurship comes from these people as much as the famous CEOs you will read about in this book.

Similarly, while working with cutting-edge technology companies for the last decade has opened my eyes to the immense change these new tools can bring about, the clearest view I've had of the impact of the software revolution was as a kid, at a kitchen table in Manchester, in the north of England. My dad, a motocross racer turned mechanic turned second-hand car salesman, ran his business from our kitchen and two-car garage. Until the late 1990s, he and his business partner relied on a landline phone, a copy of *Auto Trader* magazine and a book of car parts and prices 7.5cm (3 inches) thick, published every three months. The main tool of his trade was his decades of experience building cars and motorbikes, a head for hard negotiation, and his network of friends in the auto industry.

With the arrival of our home computer in 1999, though, things changed fast. In just a few years, every aspect of how this two-man business operated was transformed. It no longer took a morning on the phone to find that odd car part – just a few seconds on the internet. Buyers for my dad's second-hand motors came from all over the country, lured in by *Auto Trader*'s shiny new website. The business thrived, but jobs disappeared as well. The photographer who used to pitch up every week to take shots of the cars for sale was no longer needed in the age of the digital camera. The chunky *Auto Trader* magazine that landed like clockwork with a thud on our doormat vanished, replaced by a continuously updated online catalogue. And car engines, which had been the tinkerer's dream, now came with integrated circuit boards running proprietary software, putting many local car mechanics out of work. Nonetheless, my dad and his business partner were able to strike out on their own, adapt to this new world and run a successful small business from our home, doing the work of photographers, mechanics and advertisers themselves, thanks to that personal computer and the World Wide Web.

STICKS AND STONES

Humanity and technology advance together. From our earliest experiments with stone and flint tools, mastery of new technologies has been a key factor in determining which peoples and civilizations have thrived and which have failed. Historically, technological advantages were often kept in the hands of the powerful and the privileged. The Ancient Egyptians jealously guarded their advanced irrigation know-how, the key to their mastery over the banks of the Nile. English soldiers in the Hundred Years War infamously cut off the fingers of captured Frenchmen so they couldn't use their technologically superior longbows. In the late 1930s, Britain kept the details of its newly developed radar system secret, even from its allies, to maintain its military advantage.

In the twentieth century, new tools were developed and adopted faster than ever before, improving the lives of billions of people as radio, antibiotics, the combustion engine and air travel were democratized. But it was still politics, and the state's control of industry, advanced weaponry, energy and communication technologies that shaped the lives of billions of people under the conflicting banners of liberalism, capitalism, fascism and communism.

Today, though, the tools that most people on the planet can access, from smartphones to cloud computing, online learning and social media, are having a different impact to those of the twentieth century. They are wresting power away from governments and capital owners, and giving huge leverage to individuals. Those who have mastered this new generation of tools are already shaping the twenty-first century. In just its second decade, we have seen centuries-old political parties overthrown by political movements started with little more than Twitter accounts. Huge financial institutions have been brought to their knees by bedroom investors using internet forums, mobile investing apps and their pocket money. College dropouts have made billions launching businesses from their garages with a tiny fraction of the resources needed a few years ago, while entertainers have attracted legions of fans by releasing content online – without signing a record deal or setting foot on stage.

For some people, this change has been revelatory, giving them the superpower of *extreme productivity*; for others it's been devastating. The science fiction author William Gibson famously wrote back in 1993, 'The future is already here, it's just not evenly distributed.' For many people the future feels like it's already here, 'it's just not doing much for me'.

A clear digital divide has emerged. This is despite the fact that this period of technological change has been far more open than in the past. Today's new technologies have been shared across the world with unprecedented speed. By 2020, more than 4.5 billion people had internet connections and 3.5 billion people had their own smartphones (while only 2.5 billion had access to a decent toilet). Fierce competition between tech companies, the availability of open-source software and the activities of the maker movement, which battles the big players by distributing open-source designs for new products, have combined to make today's most powerful tools of production more affordable and accessible than ever. And as this book will explore, the rate of change is not slowing down, even if the economy does. While it took 75 years for the traditional telephone to reach 100 million users from its invention, and the mobile phone 16 years, it took only three years for the popular chat app WhatsApp to hit that milestone. Artificial Intelligence (AI) tools are being adopted by users at an even faster rate, with ChatGPT, a popular chatbot, getting to 100 million users in a matter of months since its launch in late 2022.

The resources required to start a business are also declining. Only a few decades ago, British entrepreneur James Dyson had to risk his mortgage to build a prototype and launch his first cyclone vacuum cleaner. Today, as this book documents, you can have an AI service generate a decent virtual model of a vacuum cleaner, and get a physical, 3D print of that design made for pennies. While television companies still charge millions to market consumer products, new media empires are being built on Instagram and TikTok by creatives who can make content on £30 cameras and distribute it to the world for nothing.

This is the optimistic view of abundant opportunity that has been promised by the technological progress we have seen since the end of the twentieth century. But the reality in many parts of the economy, and in many people's personal experience, doesn't fit this sunny narrative.

While the cost of sequencing a genome has fallen from $1 million in 2001, to just $100 today, health outcomes in many wealthy democracies have stayed the same or worsened in the last five years as the cost of new drugs to treat some of the world's most abundant diseases has risen.

Venture capital investment into new technology start-ups recently hit all-time highs – more than $250 billion was raised in 2021, enabling a generation of entrepreneurs to build new products – but only a tiny fraction of this funding, 2.8 per cent in 2020, went to companies with female founding teams, severely limiting many people's entrepreneurial opportunities.

Thanks to streaming services like YouTube and the Khan Academy, 93 per cent of children in wealthy nations have access to completely free online educational resources. At the same time, during the pandemic an estimated 1.5 billion children couldn't access online learning, while the cost of obtaining a recognized degree in higher education has rocketed. The average student in the United Kingdom leaves university with debts of £36,000, having spent 1,800 per cent more than the same degree would have cost in 2000.

New software can do in seconds what would previously have taken many hours of human work. But there has been little time to help people reskill, robbing those displaced by machines of both their income and pride in their professions.

Despite the rapid fall in the cost of new tools, and the expanding access to them, only certain groups in society and particular parts of the economy have benefited. The future is, indeed, not distributed evenly.

FINDING SYNERGIES

That the spread of new technology causes inequality and disruption is hardly a new concept. But it's becoming an increasingly urgent problem. In the technological frenzy of the last few decades, it was obvious that there would be differences in the way people and industries adapted. It is naturally easier to change the way a company works in less regulated industries and in smaller businesses like those in retail, than in more complex and regulated sectors like healthcare and education. Different parts of society, and different demographics will adopt and apply new technologies at different rates. Young families, people with limited disposable incomes and older people living with chronic diseases are less likely to have the physical, emotional and financial resources to take advantage of new tools and learn new skills, even when the other barriers to adoption are lowered. This needs to change.

Some argue this is the inevitable way of things. In her influential book *Technological Revolutions and Financial Capital*, the economist Carlota Perez suggests that technological revolutions generally have four phases, which she labels as *irruption*, *frenzy*, *synergy* and *maturity*. These have been present in every major period of innovation, from the original Industrial Revolution to the ages of steel, telecoms and now, this Fourth Industrial Revolution. In the first two phases of change, *irruption* and *frenzy*, new technologies emerge and create clusters of inventions, encompassing everything from canals to the telegraph, and from email to the smartphone. These typically fuel bouts of financial frenzy – in the form of boom, bust and a few more booms along the way. As the new inventions and products spread, however, the inequality and disruption they have caused catches up with them, and regulations and new institutions are introduced to more equitably share the benefits of these new tools, known as the *synergy* and *maturity* phase.

The social and political consequences of the latest explosion of tools are now becoming evident. The social contract in place in many economies since the end of the Second World War – a contract that supported free enterprise but, in return, expected businesses to provide stable, well-paid jobs, fair working conditions and significant contributions to worker's welfare through national insurance, healthcare provisions and pensions – is under strain. Old industries are collapsing, job security is vanishing, and global companies are ruthlessly exploiting new technologies and legal loopholes to sidestep regulation and tax liabilities.

Views are divided on how a new settlement is reached in the modern age. Some political and business leaders are convinced that the process of *creative destruction* is inevitable but that the financial and labour markets will ultimately find ways to adapt to these new technologies. We will eventually settle into a new normal with a refreshed group of key industries and companies, all sorted out by the market. Walmart once provided plenty of jobs, now it'll be Amazon, and the existing system of trade-offs between the state and big corporations can continue. But many emerging technologies are undermining the very reason large companies were able to exist in the first place, such as high capital requirements and centralized processes. As a result, the economies of scale that accrued from being a global entity in the twentieth century are starting to crumble.

Others look to alternative political systems and welfare models and argue that the big technology companies are simply too powerful. They should be broken up, more heavily regulated or even taken into state control, like the unaccountable monopolies that dominated telephones, railways and oil in the early 1900s. It's been done before: Standard Oil was split into 34 companies in 1911, giving birth to Exxon, Mobil and Chevron, and AT&T was broken up into eight separate entities in 1984. In the UK, the first post-war Labour Government nationalized 1,062 privately owned and municipal gas companies to create the state-run Gas Council. In the face of egregious profits and rising energy prices in 2023, talk of nationalization of such companies has begun again. Instead of being exploited by a large corporation, they argue, the state will rein in the private sector, or a nationalized industry will support you.

A NEW SETTLEMENT

The point of this book is to argue for another way. Instead of looking to companies or nationalized industries to establish a new settlement for the twenty-first century, we can build on the increasing desire of millions of people to start their own businesses. With the right support, we can help people find self-directed work and seize on innovations in artificial intelligence (AI) and sustainable energy, biotech and robotics, becoming entrepreneurs in a new, innovation-led economy.

This would be no mean feat. In the latter half of the twentieth century, entrepreneurship in higher and lower income countries alike struggled. For many decades, new business creation flatlined and in some countries declined. Our educational and financial systems were built on the idea of having a steady career, predictable income and a lifelong profession, not the instability and challenges of being self-employed. From mortgages to pensions, the US healthcare system or French employment law, the deck is stacked in favour of people being employees, not entrepreneurs. Culturally, we have lionized the successes, and often overlooked the excesses, of Silicon Valley CEOs who scale global businesses, while often taking for granted the immense contributions the sole proprietor businesses, the gig workers and skilled tradespeople make to our economy. As larger companies let people go, and the state struggles to cover its growing costs, supporting the entrepreneurial movement and closing the digital divide is the best route we can take.

Despite its recent growth, entrepreneurship is still too often overlooked. This was made particularly clear during the COVID crises where targeted help for large businesses and employees on payroll arrived much sooner than support for the self-employed. While the reason for this most likely comes down to the bureaucratic challenge of supporting smaller and younger organizations like start-ups, the impact has been long lasting. A study by King's Business School of over 5,000 entrepreneurs across 23 countries revealed that the pandemic had a much more significant impact on the mental health and working hours of entrepreneurs than salaried employees, revealing how unready the world is for a more entrepreneur-led economy.

Change is possible, though. While much of this book documents why and how more of us will become entrepreneurs in the coming decades, it is also a request for a new *entrepreneurs' settlement*, a kind of Bill of Rights for the self-employed, which will help more people take that first step towards self-directed work and support them on that journey. An attempt to find a balance between private work and our collective welfare just as we did in the twentieth century.

And it is urgent. Almost exactly 50 years ago, in the third quarter of 1973, the West's productivity growth plunged. It was the first of five consecutive quarters of declining productivity, and the beginning of the end of an almost unparalleled run of economic growth following the Second World War. This was the beginning of what the economist Tyler Cowen describes as the Great Stagnation. Despite all our progress in bringing more people into the workforce, the globalization of the economy, the advent of the internet and increasingly powerful smartphones – Western economies are still growing more slowly than they did in that previous golden age.

The reasons for the slowdown are debated, but the cure is in my opinion self-evident. In the decades to come, millions, perhaps billions of more entrepreneurs, properly supported, will be able to seize on a new generation of empowering technologies to drive human productivity upwards again, benefiting themselves and the societies of which they are a part.

As Michael S. Malone wrote in his 1985 book *The Big Score*: 'In the race for the world's technological leadership, it is increasingly coming down – as it should – to the solitary individual and his or her own imagination'. I hope this book encourages you to become one of those individuals.

James Wise
Cheshire, England
2023

Building something new

Jessica was going to quit her job long before the pandemic. The first in her family to go to university, she'd done well in her law conversion exams and joined a respected legal practice in Manchester, England in 2012. 'I didn't know any lawyers growing up,' she said, 'but I knew it was an industry where smart people got paid well.' Teachers at school and university encouraged her to investigate it. 'You were never out of work if you were a lawyer; people respect you.'

The reality, however, turned out rather differently.

She spent six years working in family law, and her frustration with the industry grew. It was slow, hierarchical and lacking passion, and she didn't feel like there were many opportunities to progress. So, in early 2021, Jessica quit.

'It felt like the biggest decision in the world,' she recalled. 'I didn't sleep properly for months. I was changing my mind all the time, I needed a clean start and a new challenge, but then I got this fear I was making a huge mistake: Who quits a job like that?'

Jessica wasn't leaving to do nothing. On the side of her day job, she had been toying with new digital tools and testing out ideas. She started by reselling clothes online. She worked on designs for a sustainable furniture store. She had even drawn up plans to launch a salad bar. Eventually she settled on doing something closer to her professional experience – developing a new way of doing wills and testaments online.

'I'd see people come into our office and spend hours and a small fortune on their wills when most of them could be written in 15 minutes,' she told me. 'Sometimes you need a lawyer to guide you through more complex situations, but mostly it's a tick-box exercise.'

Outside her regular office hours, Jessica built a website and workflow and designed the branding – all without writing a single line of code, by using new website builders that required little technical knowledge. Within a few weeks she had a first version of her product working, all built for a little under £1,000.

Her new site got up and running and served its first customer in January 2022. Today she provides online wills and inheritance documents in 15 minutes for £60 – one quarter of the cost of seeing a solicitor in person. By the end of 2022, her business was earning more processing wills online than she had when she started as a solicitor in an established law firm.

THE START OF A MOVEMENT

Working in venture capital, I've met thousands of entrepreneurs embarking on journeys just like Jessica's – from aspiring restaurateurs developing new cuisines to theoretical physicists building quantum computers. In the many business pitches I've sat through, I've heard about the myriad problems people see in the world today, and the new and innovative solutions they are finding to solve them.

For the last few decades, this idea of entrepreneurship, of working for oneself and setting up a company, has been closely linked to Silicon Valley, and the explosion of start-ups and technology companies that are now a large part of our personal and professional lives. This first phase of this entrepreneurial movement has been revolutionary, with new products built at a speed and scale unlike anything humanity has seen before. It has undoubtedly also created new challenges and made a small group of people exceptionally wealthy and influential in the process.

We are now entering phase two of this entrepreneurial movement, with the opportunities, tools and mindset which underpinned Silicon Valley's incredible success building software companies proliferating across the world and into new industries. In fields as diverse as space travel and renewable energy, healthcare and politics, individuals, and small, entrepreneurially minded groups – with comparatively minimal resources will usurp the large companies and institutions that determined much of the course of the twentieth century. The most successful and most valuable businesses in the coming decades will be able to achieve much more, with far fewer employees, than ever before.

This second phase won't just see the launch of more globally disruptive start-ups in new industries, although that will certainly happen. It will also usher in a huge shift in the way we choose to work. As new digital tools become ever more abundant, traditional careers become less stable and cultures change, we will see many more people choose to become self-employed or join small, entrepreneurial endeavours, rejecting big corporates in favour of more creative, self-directed, and perhaps volatile working lives – by building companies themselves.

This second phase is already underway, with the number of people leaving well-established careers and professions to start their own business at record levels. Terms such as *the Great Resignation*, coined during the pandemic, have already entered the popular lexicon, as millions of people have rethought what they want to do professionally. Some have left the workforce; others have become carers as the costs of health and social care rise. A large proportion, however, have chosen to start something new. In fact, given that so many of these people are now forming companies, the venture capitalist and prolific blogger Fred Wilson suggests that, rather than defining this movement as a resignation, we should call it *the Great Formation*; a new era of work where individuals look to solve problems through founding companies and forming communities, rather than take the more trodden path.

Of course, millions of people across the world have worked this way forever, but the modern idea of an entrepreneur has been captured by technologists building highly scalable products, and global businesses. This book is an effort to wrestle that term back, to what it means for most people. An entrepreneur is an individual who creates a new product or offers a superior service while bearing most of the risks and enjoying most of the rewards. From plumbers to masons, travelling salespeople to writers, biotechnicians and barristers, entrepreneurs can come in many shapes and sizes.

In the last few decades of the twentieth century, this group of microbusinesses, the self-employed and independent workers had a hard time, with the percentage of the workforce who worked this way in high-income countries falling to single digits. Between the 1980s and the early 2010s, there was a global decline in entrepreneurial work, with fewer new businesses being started each year. In fact, in low income countries there was a correlation between countries becoming richer and people leaving the informal economy of trading or farming (entrepreneurial work, but rarely paid well or above board) for more stable employment in large companies. In a situation where you live hand to mouth, there's an understandable appeal to stable incomes and employees' rights, even if it comes with a loss of autonomy and the dignity of ownership. As GDP grew globally, so went the argument, the world would shift away from self-employment and microbusinesses to more stable forms of work, and only the rich would seek more speculative, entrepreneurial opportunities.

Despite those decades of decline in new business formation, things have now started to turnaround, with self-employment, microbusinesses and start-ups on a growth trajectory that could see them become the major form of employment in just a few decades time, upending almost 150 years of the status quo. More of us than ever are destined to be entrepreneurs.

FREE SOLO

The number of people already experimenting with new ways of working is growing fast. In the United States, a 2019 survey by the accounting software firm QuickBooks estimated that 28 per cent of the working population had made money selling online with a side business or had a hustle outside their day job. In 2023 this is estimated to be an astonishing 45 per cent, with 46 per cent of Gen Zs (people born between the mid-1990s and mid-2010s) in the USA and 39 per cent in the UK estimated to be supplementing their existing job or studies this way. These side hustles are rarely enough to live off, with a median income of $200 a month, but it shows the increasing willingness of people to think creatively about their careers, try new things and take an important first step towards self-employment.

Many people are also cutting their entrepreneurial teeth for the first time in the gig economy. In the 2022 iteration of the consultancy McKinsey & Company's 'American Opportunity Survey', an astonishing 36 per cent of respondents – equivalent to 58 million Americans – identified as independent workers, up from 27 per cent in 2016, as new services like Uber, Deliveroo and Amazon Mechanical Turk made it easier than ever for people to find short-term employment in anything from delivering pizza to writing website copy.

Over the last few decades the number of fully self-employed people – i.e. people who register themselves as the sole employee of the company in which they work – has also grown significantly. This is especially true in the UK, with double the number of people working as self-employed today than in the early 1980s. According to the UK Parliament's statistics, the number of people who define themselves as self-employed in Britain has grown from a low of just 3.2 million in December 2000, to a peak of over 5 million at the start of 2020, a 60 per cent increase in less than a generation, before the pandemic boosted these numbers even further.

America has also seen a significant increase in new business formation in recent years, with a record 5.4 million new applications filed in 2021, surpassing the record set in 2020 of 4.4 million, which itself was over 20 per cent higher than the number a year before. President Biden proudly announced in 2023 that more than 10 million new business applications had been filed under his administration, more than any other president on record. In the Netherlands, a country with much stronger labour laws supporting traditional employment than either the UK or USA, the number of freelancers and self-employed also grew, from over 630,000 in 2003 to 1.1 million in 2019, according to their National Statistics body. This is a truly global movement.

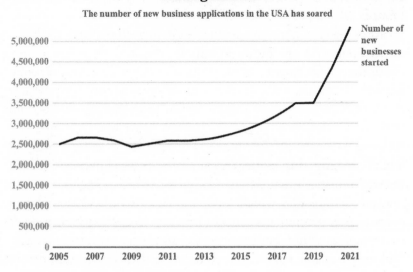

Getting Started

The number of new business applications in the USA has soared

(Source: U.S. Census Bureau, Wired)

This groundswell of interest in going it alone is particularly strong among the younger generation. Even before the pandemic accelerated the number of new businesses being started, the Centre for Entrepreneurs claimed in 2016: 'Young people are more entrepreneurial than ever, starting twice as many businesses as the baby boomer generation.' Multiple reports refer awkwardly to this group as Millenipreneurs or Gen-HustlerZ.

While the specific politics, regulations, and wealth of a country all have an impact on the ability of someone to start a business, the international trend towards more entrepreneurial work is undeniable. In their 2022 survey, the Global Entrepreneurship

Monitor found that over 50 per cent of people of working age in countries as diverse as Brazil, Qatar and Kazakhstan intended to start a business themselves in the next three years (all countries with extremely different social and economic structures). In China, the number of small private companies and sole proprietorships, known as *getihu*, has also rocketed, and while some people dispute that the statistics are entirely accurate, even sceptics estimate that almost 30 per cent of the population are now employed in this way, in a country where such work was all but outlawed in living memory.

Almost everywhere you look, people are choosing new ways of working that are more self-directed and independent and where they have greater ownership and responsibility for what they earn.

THE POWER IN YOUR HANDS

What's causing this shift? One of the major catalysts for the renewed interest in entrepreneurship, is the increasingly powerful array of technologies which are being developed and distributed at an unprecedented pace. Over the last decade, the arrival of smartphones, cloud computing, social media and e-commerce platforms has given millions of people the ability to open stores online, pitch their services via video conferencing, or work collaboratively on design software, all without needing to learn a single line of code or hire an experienced co-worker.

If you had set out to run a high-street store in the UK for a year in the 1990s, it would have cost upwards of £30,000 before you'd paid for a single piece of stock or hired any staff. By 2000, the advent of the web made it possible to set up a website and run a store online – albeit, with very basic functionality – for around £10,000 a year, but without the virality offered by social media you had to spend much more than that on marketing to raise awareness. Today, services like Canada-born Shopify and China-based Taobao have given billions of users the ability to set up sophisticated shops and sales experiences online for free.

Or look at the manufacturing industry. Creating a unique metal part, such as a lamp stand, cost thousands of pounds and days of work in the 1990s. Today, thanks to free 3D design tools and 3D printers, it can be done with loose change, and in under an hour.

Even in white-collar professions, like the legal industry, tasks which used to take hours or even days can now be done in minutes, as Jessica found out, thanks to advances in software. Where previously a tradesperson had to advertise in the Yellow Pages or shop windows to gain attention, you can now be discovered instantly online with the click of a button. This combination of new tools, and a global focus on regulatory improvements, has meant the cost and time associated with registering and starting a business almost anywhere in the world has fallen drastically.

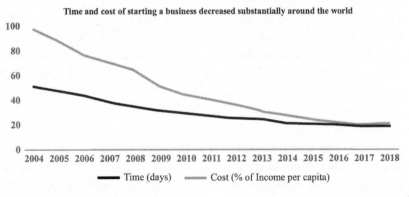

Time and cost of starting a business decreased substantially around the world

(Source: Worldbank.org, December 2018)

We are still in the foothills of this change. In the coming decade we will see similar exponential improvements in the output, and fall in cost, of many more fundamental technologies that will broaden the *entrepreneurial frontier* – the breadth of opportunities where individuals or small teams will be able to build new and desirable products. As each generation of these new technologies – from genomic sequencing to additive manufacturing, robotics to AI, – becomes cheaper, more powerful and, most importantly, more accessible, large corporations will shrink or collapse, and more and more people will be emboldened to build superior solutions and services themselves.

The cumulative effect of all these breakthroughs has created what the futurist and commentator Azeem Azhar calls the Exponential Age. That such a fall in costs and increase in power happens in the world of software is expected. After all, software, once coded, is very cheap to replicate and run. We're now seeing exponential improvement in the cost and power of more fundamental technologies, such as drug development and material sciences – which, as this book will explain, is accelerating the overall pace of change as each technology improves individually.

Whether it's honing a craft, manufacturing new materials, providing healthcare or designing new therapeutics, this book will show how an individual with the right creative approach and support can start a business at a fraction of the cost and time required only a few decades ago. And further ahead, as new AI models become available and robotics get cheaper, it's clear such opportunities will only expand.

CHANGING OF THE GUARD

As more people decide to use these tools to strike out on their own, the twenty-first century is set to see a radical change in how we work, and who we work for. Many stable, corporate careers will be displaced by entrepreneurial start-ups. Mega-corporations will continue to be dismantled, making way for small and even single-person companies and community-led projects. Even publicly run services will be disrupted, placed under pressure to keep up with this revolution and hopefully able to deliver more responsive and personalized services by empowering front-line staff. On an individual level this change is both concerning and exhilarating. At a societal level it marks a reversal of a trend that has been underway for over 200 years.

The twentieth century saw great shifts in the location of power for most countries. Democratic economies were caught in a great pincer movement – a capturing of our working lives on one side by medium sized and large corporations, and on the other side by a centralized state. Remarkably, for many countries this gradual transfer of power – from a handful of industrialists and landed aristocracy at the beginning of the 1900s to state-run institutions and big businesses by the end of it – was mostly peaceful and successful. In the UK for instance, government control over the economy, and the number of people working for the state, grew from 13 per cent of GDP in 1900 to 35 per cent by 2000. At the same time, more people than ever started working for fewer but larger corporations. Some of these were heavily regulated monopolies, built in the aftermath of the world wars, and others were large private enterprises, riding high on the waves of globalization and new technologies.

In the process, many countries lost a critical part of their economy and culture: the self-employed and small business owners. Self-employment in particular dropped sharply in this period. In 1860, according to historian Steven Gillon, as much as 80 per cent of the workforce in the USA was self-employed or worked only for their family. In many cases, this was in back-breaking, informal work in the field, generally replaced by better regulated and more dependable work in manufacturing and construction jobs. However, this squeeze on the self-employed continued at pace until the end of the century. By 1970, that number had fallen to under 10 per cent of the workforce, in a country that was supposedly renowned for its entrepreneurial zeal. The Bank of England estimates that the proportion of self-employed people in the British economy also almost halved between 1900 and 1950, reaching a low point of just 7 per cent. Only in the 1980s did that number slowly start to rise again. And in communist and socialist countries the numbers were even lower, with China making self-employment and private enterprise incredibly difficult during the 1960s and 1970s; only a tiny proportion of the working population could legally operate this way.

The rise of the public sector and the mega-corporation brought plenty of benefits. They provided millions of permanent jobs, granting many people their first experience of economic stability.

The expansion of the state provided much needed and critical services, such as universally accessible education and healthcare, through institutions like the NHS in the UK. The rise of mega-corporations like Walmart and H&M led to cheaper food, clothing and home appliances. They were able to do all of this because they had found economies of scale that made being large and centrally controlled an efficient way to provide services and products, and to a great extent these two forms of organization drove huge productivity gains and economic growth throughout much of the century.

This economic settlement, split between the public sector and private companies, shaped not just employment but our entire financial and psychological well-being. The pension and mortgage industries leveraged the more predictable incomes these organizations provided to offer workers unprecedented access to debt and with it the ability to buy homes and save for retirement. Income and national insurance taxes were able to be raised to fund much needed state services, taken from the more stable monthly pay packets of workers and the profits of their companies. Even our sense of self-worth and identity was increasingly derived from our profession and our status in a firm, where you were expected to progress up the corporate ladder over time. In the 1800s, most people's lives were defined by the family, religion or region into which they were born. By the end of the twentieth century, the corporation had become so integral to our way of life that your profession, and the company you worked for, was one of the first things you mentioned when meeting someone new. For many people, this remains the case today.

Whether squeezed out by big business, a large state or the financial institutions that favoured stability of income, the self-employed were put through the wringer in the twentieth century. By the 1960s, the American Dream was less about being a risk-taking, self-sufficient innovator – a modern-day cowboy, as it were – and more about advancing your work title and pay packet. Ambitious employees were fighting for the corner office, not freedom from the office. Surveys of parents in the 1960s found that they wanted their children to be lawyers and pilots, not self-employed tradespeople or travelling sales representatives.

Today businesses are hiring fewer people, and automation is replacing both white- and blue-collar jobs, leaving many to either choose or have to become self-employed. But some of the institutions and cultural prejudices of the previous era are holding back a new generation of individual innovators and self-directed workers. Adapting to this new way of working will undoubtedly bring disruption but this huge shift in the way many people work will also provide, with the right support, a potential remedy to the three great challenges of modern work: fairness, automation and dignity.

FAIR WORK

Over the last 250 years, as many nations industrialized, their economic structures gradually shifted from aristocracy to meritocracy – from a world where wealth and influence were determined by family connections, to one in which the more skilled you are, the more likely you are to be rewarded.

This change was often slow and uneven. For those at the bottom of the economic ladder during the Industrial Revolution, it made little difference whether they were working in servitude to someone who had inherited their status as a Lord, or in the 'dark, satanic mills' of a self-made industrialist. Both were awful experiences. But over time, the rise of meritocracy has undoubtedly meant that more people have a greater chance of improving their lot, through hard work and skill, than ever before. And even if meritocracy is imperfect and remains out of reach for many, the concept that we should all start on a level playing field in life, and that effort and output should be rewarded, is amongst the most popular and widely held political beliefs in the world today.

However, in many ways the benefits of meritocracy seem to be fading. Despite much lip service being paid to the concept that hard work determines your future, the great institutions that are supposed to uphold that principle – from universities to free markets and democratic bodies – are no longer the bastions of social mobility they once promised to be.

While a majority of people in democracies still believe that a life of hard work and skill *ought* to be the basis for reward, fewer and fewer people believe that it actually is. A 2021 study in the UK, by King's College London, showed that a majority of people still thought that hard work and ambition were the major drivers of success at work, but a significant percentage felt that good contacts (44 per cent) and a wealthy family (29 per cent) were either essential or very important factors in getting ahead.

In the corporate world, meanwhile, progress up the career ladder can appear more like a Ponzi scheme than a free market for talent. While the average employee's wage has increased by 18 per cent over the last four decades, pay for the CEOs of the largest firms has risen an astronomical 1,322 per cent, according to the research group the Economic Policy Institute, despite little evidence that CEOs have become 13 times more effective in this time.

Instead, an economy which nurtures entrepreneurship can renew and refresh the promise of meritocracy by removing the power of those gatekeepers and institutions that skew the playing field. Entrepreneurs don't need an Ivy League university on their CVs to start a business. The software tools that are rapidly disrupting traditional industries do not care if your parents were members of the right tennis club or place of worship. Self-directed workers do not have bosses, so cannot be impacted by management's bias to promote people like them, rather than the best employees.

Of course, those starting their own businesses are not entirely free from the hangovers of the twentieth century. As I will explore, finance for entrepreneurs is more abundant than ever, but it still skews heavily towards people who have maintained some of the social signifiers of success of the last few decades, even if their underlying business doesn't always justify it.

But this is changing, and the emergent world of self-directed, self-reliant and more entrepreneurial work is certainly one remedy for the feeling that traditional career opportunities are stacked against you. While entrepreneurship may be riskier for some people than climbing the corporate ladder, it also opens the door to rewarding work for many people who were never given the key to that door in the first place.

FINDING WORK

The spectre of mass unemployment has always loomed large during periods of technological change. After all, the definition of success for most technologies is that they provide an output that is cheaper or superior to existing labour. And such concern is not unwarranted. It's estimated that over the course of the previous century, technological progress, in everything from farm machinery to factory robotics, made a mind-blowing 90 per cent of jobs in the USA redundant.

This was acutely true in agriculture. In the last 30 years, the number of people working in farming-related industries globally has fallen by one billion, from 44 per cent of the global workforce in 1991 to under 28 per cent today, mostly due to huge improvements in farming machinery. However, at the same time total employment rates and global GDP have grown significantly, in part thanks to cheaper food and better agricultural output, nullifying the idea that technological progress necessarily creates structural unemployment.

And in modern manufacturing – once the great employer of the West and, more recently, the East – it is increasingly true that factories are getting more productive without human labour. Amazon's warehouses already use one robot for every three humans they employ today, up from eight to one in 2014. It won't be long until robots outnumber humans on the roads, warehouses and factory floor as well as in the farmer's fields. Despite this most countries across the world are still experiencing record levels of employment.

While new technologies have replaced tasks performed by humans, and undoubtedly caused disruption in the process, historically and still today it has resulted in the creation of more and better-paying jobs elsewhere. In the last few decades, only a handful of job titles have completely disappeared from annual surveys, and while the loss of roles like elevator operator will be mourned by some, many new tasks, jobs and professions have been created.

Some argue that we are now entering a new paradigm. Advances in automation, robotics and AI may replace tasks and jobs at a speed and scale that we haven't experienced before, turning this gradual shift in work underpinned by technological progress into a highly disruptive process that will create mass unemployment. Undeniably farms, factories and firms adopting these technologies are doing more with less, leaving many people out of employment in the process.

The potential impact of AI in particular has generated plenty of column inches. This branch of computer science uses huge statistical models to give software the ability to solve increasingly complex problems, appearing to match or surpass human intelligence in a growing number of domains. AI has been described as 'enough to make one believe in God' by Google's former head of AI, and as something that 'could spell the end of the human race' by Professor Stephen Hawking. Concern about the breadth and potency of some new AI services led to over 1,000 leading academics and technologists to call for a pause to the development of certain types of models in early 2023.

The speed of change in the adoption of AI has felt particularly relevant recently, with the launch of several new large language models (LLMs) from organizations like Google, China's Baidu and Microsoft-backed OpenAI giving anyone the ability to generate images, code, answers to exam questions or holiday itineraries from a simple text prompt. While it's just the most recent development in what will be a decade of new AI tools giving people what feel like superpowers, it is already causing anxiety about future employment. From writers who worry publicly about it replacing their copy, to lawsuits from artists who say these models have been built on top of their hard work. The future relationship between AI and many professions is only going to become more complex.

However, as with the rise of the microchip and the internet, the most entrepreneurial and creative people, properly equipped, are far more likely to benefit from new, artificially intelligent tools, than larger and less innovative companies. Joseph Schumpeter, arguably the most important economic thinker on entrepreneurship in the last 150 years, argued that creativity is part of the very definition of entrepreneurial endeavour. Entrepreneurs mix action with innovation to create something new. While AI is getting increasingly good at mimicking many human skills, from generating art to having deep conversations, it is just as quickly being adapted by innovative entrepreneurs to build something new, creating more products, jobs, and wealth in the process, as we shall see multiple times over in the chapters to come.

Assuming the ability to access artificially intelligent services expands in the same open and accessible way that most software applications have, then AI is far more likely to be co-opted by entrepreneurs in the twenty-first century, while undermining the advantages of scale and resources currently held by larger organizations. As the MIT economist Daron Acemoglu argues in his extensive work on AI's impact on employment to date, and its possible role in the future, 'AI can be a powerful tool for deploying the creativity, judgement, and flexibility of humans rather than simply automating their jobs.'

In one of the more comprehensive reports on the future of work, the World Economic Forum (WEF) agrees, saying that while AI is likely to make up to 85 million jobs redundant between 2020 and 2025, applications of AI will ultimately create 97 million new jobs. What specific roles these new tools will create is beyond the imagination of even the most powerful computer, or for that matter human intelligence, but the WEF rightly states that 'there will be a stream of new business opportunities empowering a culture of entrepreneurship and innovation.'

AI applications will certainly disrupt many existing sectors and upend many traditional careers with it. But far from threatening the end of employment, it should inspire a new generation of innovators to seize on these tools, enabling a fundamental shift to a more self-directed way of working.

FULFILLING WORK

While the threat of automation and the relative absence of meritocracy may feel like abstract issues for most people in their daily working lives, a far more tangible experience for us all is a sense of dignity in what we do. The foundations upon which people build their sense of self-worth are complex, but undeniably what we do for a living, and how we're treated while doing it, matters immensely. Studies show that having pride in what we do matters more to people than compensation, once it is beyond a basic income level, and many people say they would happily take a lower salary for a greater sense of purpose in their work.

However, in today's world of work, both dignity and a sense of purpose are under threat from multiple directions. The rise of algorithmic decision-making and software platforms has undermined human relationships in the workplace. When your boss is a piece of software and your customers interact with you through a mobile app, it's easy to feel like a cog in a machine rather than a human with value. This doesn't just apply to gig-work. Professions which used to command high levels of trust and respect, such as teaching and caring, have seen a deterioration in pay, and an increasing lack of autonomy, as centralized bureaucracies overreach to control more of what front-line carers can do.

At the same time, an anti-work movement has cynically started to dismiss many new professions as unnecessary – undermining and belittling those striving in them today. Popular books and articles, such as anthropologist David Graeber's *Bullshit Jobs*, define whole categories of work as 'a form of paid employment that is so completely pointless, unnecessary, or pernicious that even the employee cannot justify its existence'. It's hard to have a sense of dignity in your work if cultural gatekeepers keep telling you it is worthless.

The anti-work narrative is always present, even Aristotle wrote that a 'mechanical or commercial life' was 'not noble, and [against] virtue'. There will always be someone or a small group that is unnerved by anyone trying to better themselves through working hard, or attempting to do something different to the norm. While a vast majority of people say that their work is 'very or somewhat important to them personally', the cultural hangover from previous decades that treats many forms of work, especially practical and sales roles such as front-line social carers and builders, salespeople and gig workers as less worthy, is still very present.

Finding dignity in work, and in the workplace, has been a centuries-long battle. Great CEOs always stress the importance of giving employees a sense of pride in what they do, and the trade union movement has been as much about ensuring workers are treated with respect for their labour, as guaranteeing safety and financial settlements.

I believe the way people find dignity in work is to be self-directed in what they do, care about the goal they are working towards, and to own the fruits of their own labour. In short, being an entrepreneur. In fact, the primary reason people give for starting their own business today is not for the financial reward, but rather to be in control of their own destiny – to be their own boss.

Shifting to a world of work where a majority of people are in self-directed employment or have greater ownership of and power in their jobs, could be one of the great emancipatory movements of the twenty-first century.

And while most of this book will focus on self-directed entrepreneurship, this also applies to people who still work in large organizations and as public servants. In his seminal book, *Dignity at Work*, the sociologist Randy Hodson argued that showing trust, granting responsibility and autonomy, and giving people ownership of their work, results in a sense of pride, as well as better productivity. This doesn't only apply to start-ups, but large companies and public institutions as well.

Allowing people to take ownership of their work, whether by encouraging entrepreneurs to take the leap and try something new, or by granting employees greater autonomy and responsibility, is a proven way to give people a sense of dignity. This should be a priority for both corporations and the public sector as they seek to retain and inspire their staff in the face of the coming entrepreneurial exodus.

THE DIGITAL DIVIDEND

While there are many advantages to more entrepreneurial work, the fallout from shrinking corporations and less steady employment will no doubt be immense. The challenge for us individually is to navigate these changes, and work out how our passions, creativity, skills and resources can best be used to build something people want. The challenge facing society and our political institutions is how to make this transition to a more innovative economy effective and equitable.

This will not be easy. The cost of software tools and their increasing accessibility has collapsed, but for a vast number of people the promise of economic freedom, self-management, and the ability to choose what to work on remains an empty one. The economic, cultural and educational barriers to entrepreneurship, which were put up over the last century, remain significant.

At a global scale, over half the world still doesn't have access to broadband internet. In Low-Income Countries (LICs), a monthly broadband subscription costs 12 per cent of average national income, while the cost of a basic smartphone, which hovers at $150, represents more than 1.2 months' wages.

Even in wealthy countries, the digital divide is pernicious. In the UK, high-tech and advanced manufacturing jobs are among the most productive roles in the economy, making up 34 per cent of exports. But this highly valuable and impactful sector represents only 2.9 per cent of all employment. In fact, across the developed world, rather than seeing a rapid increase in both productivity and wages, the median wage has barely moved at all because few people receive the tools or training or have the resources required to seize on new opportunities.

Simply having an internet connection does not stop someone being digitally excluded. In 2018, 10 per cent of the adult population of the UK were estimated to be 'internet non-users' – i.e. having access to broadband internet but unable to use basic services. The same survey suggested that over 11.7 million people lacked the digital skills for everyday life in the UK. And even if you can navigate daily digital challenges, there is still a big gulf between that and building a digital-first business.

Demographics matter too. A person managing a chronic disease, or a family with tight resources and young children, is far less likely to have the emotional energy to learn new skills, even if the other barriers to doing so are low. Countries with populations who skew older have additional challenges in adjusting to this change.

In spite of there being seemingly endless new opportunities, for many people the challenges above can make the very idea of starting a business feel as distant a reality as Silicon Valley itself.

Even if the digital divide and demographic challenge are overcome, some people argue that the economic benefits from most start-ups and entrepreneurship are minimal, with only a tiny number of founders building truly impactful companies. As the economist Robert Solow wrote back in 1987, 'You can see the computer age everywhere but in the productivity statistics.' The *Solow paradox* – that technological adoption has yet to have a meaningful impact on productivity – is still a challenge to the often self-congratulatory technology sector today.

The first phase of the entrepreneurial revolution may have brought disruption and increasing inequity, but closing this digital divide, and providing entrepreneurs with a new set of rights and supports – what I will describe later as *digital scaffolds* – can ensure that this second phase provides a dividend instead. And in the second phase, as entrepreneurs tackle the even bigger challenges we face in healthcare, housing, energy and transportation, we will undoubtedly see the productivity and economic gains that the world desperately needs as well.

To achieve all of this will require an effort on the same scale as the industrial revolutions of previous centuries, where trade unions, progressive politicians and business leaders, philanthropists and social activists changed laws and built new social institutions to balance the transformational power of new technologies with the welfare of workers. While there were many failures and missteps along the way, those Herculean efforts did much to ensure the previous shifts in the way we work eventually led to the greatest period of progress in human wealth, health and happiness in the history of civilization.

The first step on that journey is to understand who this generation of entrepreneurs are, and how millions more people will work in this way in the years to come. 'I never thought I'd be an entrepreneur growing up,' Jessica told me when we discussed her experience of leaving the law and starting a company. 'It's wild.'

2

The makings of an entrepreneur

Ask people to name an entrepreneur, and they'll most likely mention a business magnate like Elon Musk, the co-founder of PayPal, Tesla and SpaceX; or Jeff Bezos, the founder of Amazon, who utterly transformed global retail. A hundred years ago, people might have named rich and successful industrialists such as Thomas Edison, the founder of General Electric, or Henry Ford, who brought mobility to the masses.

As well as wielding huge influence over popular culture (with Elon Musk seemingly determined to be a part of every news cycle), this type of hyper-successful founder has come to dominate much of our discussion of entrepreneurship – the cliché entrepreneur is now an individual who comes from a modest (if rarely poor) background, drops out of an elite institution and goes on to build a global business empire and huge fortune in just a few years.

It's undeniable that the power and prominence of this type of entrepreneur has grown over the past half-century or so. The Fortune Rich List of 1957, one of the first of its type, claimed that just one of the ten wealthiest people in America at that time was a self-made entrepreneur – the oil tycoon Haroldson Lafayette Hunt Jr. By 2020, according to Forbes, nine of the top 10 were self-made entrepreneurs, with Alice Walton, the heir to the Walmart fortune, being the only inheritor on the list.

The same story is true in Britain. When the *Sunday Times Rich List* was published in 1989, just 43 per cent of the entries had made their own money. As was said at the time, the surest way to a fortune in Britain was to be a landowner – preferably with a title. Today, almost all of the 100 richest people in the UK are entrepreneurs, who built their own businesses.

The increased interest in super-successful founders is not just due to their wealth and influence, but also because of the undeniably important role they play in the economy. Scott Shane, a Professor of Entrepreneurial Studies, goes as far as to argue they are far more important than the average founder of a business. 'We need to recognize,' he says, 'that only a select few entrepreneurs will create businesses that . . . create jobs, reduce unemployment, make markets more competitive, and enhance economic growth.' He goes on to argue that public policy should focus mostly on these 'unicorn' founders, and not on encouraging more people to become founders of small companies.

These multibillionaire success stories are a tiny and skewed sample of what an entrepreneur actually is, and the focus of this book is instead the role of the everyday entrepreneurs who form the backbone of our economies. Small- and medium-sized enterprises (SMEs) account for over 90 per cent of businesses and 50 per cent of employment of the worldwide population. In the most populous countries in the world, such as India, over 90 per cent of the working-age population are employed in the informal sector, sharing many of the precarious risks and volatility in earnings as entrepreneurs do. In China it is estimated that almost 30 per cent of people work in sole proprietorships. The long tail of entrepreneurial work already makes up huge swathes of the economy in high- and low-income countries, in blue-collar and white-collar roles – and it's growing. So, to give this vast workforce its due, and to understand the policies required to make such work more rewarding, we must reclaim the concept of being an entrepreneur and champion the individual strivers, skilled tradespeople, microbusiness, freelancers and creatives who make up a vast majority of the entrepreneurial class today.

What does this group of people really look like? A government statistician would have a very different idea of who a modern-day entrepreneur is compared to typical media coverage. Rather than high-tech innovators like Steve Jobs or self-made celebrities like Kim Kardashian, the most common profession for the self-employed or sole business owners – almost 20 per cent in fact – are the construction and trades sectors.

Rather than being young college dropouts, like much technology-industry folklore, entrepreneurs are far more likely to be middle-aged. A 2019 FreshBooks survey showed that the average age of someone setting up their own company, is 42.

And they rarely scale to be huge, global empires. In fact, more than 60 per cent of business owners in the USA never go on to hire more than one other person. A large number of the self-employed class toil away on their own.

By discussing an entrepreneurial revolution, am I simply saying we should prepare for a future economy dominated by middle-aged, self-employed builders? Not quite. While these statistics do challenge the popular narrative of entrepreneurship, they also present a rather narrow view of what this new approach to work is and how this demographic will change.

A better insight into what the future of self-employment looks like is from a 2021 survey of editors of economic journals called *Entrepreneurship in the Future*. Many of these editors believe the future of work is more self-driven, blurs the lines of work and personal passions, and uses the term *everyday-everyone* entrepreneurship, to describe the future of work. They describe a future of entrepreneurship where more of the populace, supported by social media, online learning platforms and crowdfunding can launch businesses overnight. A tighter definition of this *everyday-everyone* entrepreneur in my view is someone who:

- has meaningful ownership of what they produce;
- earns in a proportional way to their, or their products', success;

- can be self-directed for most of their time; *and*
- can choose how to solve a problem – and who to work with to solve it.

To understand the future of entrepreneurship and to define the roles that I believe will become more important in the years to come we need to dig deeper into each of these ideas.

OWNING IT

One of the biggest differences between being an entrepreneur and being employed by someone else is, of course, that you own more of what you make. Ownership of a business is not always an easy thing to establish, although setting up an entity that you can own is, thankfully, becoming easier in most parts of the world over time. It does, however, have a huge impact on the financial and psychological aspects of working at a company. On the positive side, it means that you are mostly responsible for your success, you get to keep what you earn, and you are able to build wealth over time from the assets the company owns and what they produce, not just your labour.

This latter point is particularly important in a more innovation-led economy. As new technologies become available which allow entrepreneurially minded people to build products, rather than just provide services, sole proprietorships and microbusinesses will be able to sell much more than just their time. Take, for instance, the traditional employment model of a plumber.

Today, many plumbers are self-employed and/or run microbusinesses, made up of a handful of apprentices. It's hard for plumbers to scale their businesses; after all, there are only so many hours in the day. Perhaps you can service three or four homes, depending on the nature of the problem and the distance between the customers. Owning a company as a plumber today has some value: it means you're responsible for the hours you work, the types of job you do and the profits after parts and other fees. If you wanted to sell the business later in life, it would have a little value, perhaps in the brand you've built as a trusted provider of services and the employees that you have trained up. But a lot of the value in owning the business is not commercial; it lies in being in control of your own time and resources rather than being an employee for someone else.

However, new technologies and ways of working are making it easier than ever for self-employed people like plumbers to 'productize' their services – and capture more value from the products they own rather than just selling their labour.

Imagine, for instance, the smart home of the future where every tap is connected to your home Wi-Fi, your pipes have smart valves to control pressure and your smart thermostat talks to your heat pump to control your internal house temperature (this is not too far away . . . plenty of homes like this exist already). Such automation may appear to threaten the role of the plumber, but complications always happen. When they do, you may not need to call your plumber, but could first message them using an AI-powered chatbot. This bot, enabled by services like OpenAI, but owned and trained by your plumber, can give you 24/7 advice on how to get the hot tap working in the bathroom whether your actual plumber is awake or asleep. If the issue persists, it can raise an alert to your human plumber, who can then decide whether they need to order you a new part (which they will be able to do seamlessly), jump on a video call, or, as a last resort, attend in person. Once the new part turns up, your plumber can recommend you use one of their pre-recorded augmented reality guides, which show you how to put the new tap in place in a way that is completely personalized to your home. You get a better, around-the-clock service, and your plumber can now support many more homes, selling their digital product, not just their labour.

Does this sound fanciful? Not according to StrictlyPlumbers.com, a 'plumber marketing company' that is already selling Plumber Bot for $99 a month. There are hundreds of similar companies, providing tools to plumbers to help them productize their service. And as later chapters will discuss, the speed at which such services are improving is only accelerating.

As we move to a world where parts of our labour, both white-collar and blue-collar, can be replicated by robotics, software and smart devices, ownership of the services you produce becomes even more important. As an employee at a large services firm, you are at risk of that company replacing part of your labour with automated solutions. By owning the solutions, and making them superior through innovation and personalization, you get a greater share of the rewards.

Of course, ownership of a business entails much more than just receiving the company's profits or dealing with its losses. You become responsible for every aspect of its operations, even if you have employees to help you manage some of the day-to-day. This can be a hugely stressful experience. According to a 2015 study by insurance provider Simply Business, almost half of the 2,000 self-employed individuals surveyed cancel social plans at least once a week, a quarter take less than 10 days' annual leave and 25 per cent have fallen ill due to stress and overwork. A survey by the same organization in 2022 found things had only got worse, with 'new research show[ing] the mental health of small business owners has worsened with a fifth reporting battling depression.' Being the boss has its challenges, and individuals and the state need to prepare people for this psychological burden as more people start-up companies themselves.

Ownership also matters for more than just sole proprietorships; it's increasingly important for organizations of all sizes. For the thousands of start-ups that I review every year in my job, employee ownership through being granted shares in the company is the norm. The early hires at a start-up almost always own a meaningful share of the company, which they keep even if they leave the business, and a majority of the businesses I work with continue to distribute shares in the company to all new employees as they grow, in some cases even when the business employs hundreds or thousands of employees and after it goes public.

This makes a huge amount of sense. After all, joining a business with just one or two other employees is a huge risk, and you are unlikely to be compensated for it with a plump salary given that these small businesses won't be generating much revenue early on. In some sense this ownership is a form of reward for making an entrepreneurial leap. Early employees are also likely to play an important role in the biggest decisions the company makes, such as how a product is built, or sales are made. As such they can be just as much a part of the creative, problem-solving process that is required in any successful entrepreneurial pursuit and deserving of equity in the business as a result.

This is one Silicon Valley trait I strongly recommend, even for small outfits with a handful of employees. Whatever someone's salary, offering them equity in a company is a sign that they are considered an integral part of its success, and not just a gun for hire. It's also proven to be highly effective in improving overall performance. In a 2021 survey by Morgan Stanley, 93 per cent of executives and 75 per cent of employees said that owning part of the company they worked for, such as via stock options, was the most effective way to motivate employees.

In their 2022 book *Ownership: Reinventing Companies, Capitalism, and Who Owns What,* authors Corey Rosen and John Case argue that employee ownership creates stronger companies, helps workers build wealth and fosters a fairer, more stable society. By giving more people a stake in what they're building, they argue, we'll be able to tackle economic inequality as more people will share in the gains of capitalist success, while improving productivity with more motivated teams. What's not to like?! While I don't believe it is a solution to all the world's problems, it certainly has its merits, and it is likely to be a practice that more people adopt as we move into a more entrepreneurial economy.

Given the importance of ownership, and the likelihood that it becomes more prevalent, it makes sense to consider both those businesses with a sole founder and those started by small, highly effective teams who have significant ownership, as part of the everyday entrepreneurship I believe we will see more of in the years to come.

THE POWER IS YOURS

The definition of entrepreneurship must go beyond people who simply have ownership in a company, but also to people who have control over when they work and who they work with. Entrepreneurial work differs from traditional careers in that entrepreneurs theoretically have control over their time – subject to their economic needs – and so I include tradespeople, freelancers, and gig workers in this movement too. This additional freedom can come with significant downsides: if you don't work, or your product doesn't sell, then you don't get paid. For most of the people in the world who are self-employed, this is not always a realistic option. Many must find work to survive, and the psychological burden of doing this at the end of every day or week, rather than finding a new job every two or three years as an employed person might have to do, is significant. Even for those people living in economies with stronger social safety nets, not working, or losing work means they must take on the additional work of investing in themselves, building new skills, a brand and a network and buying their own tools. Working in this more flexible manner also comes with its own bureaucratic challenges, such as filing your own taxes, in ways that people working in large corporations don't have to do.

For many people though, the trade-off between working as a freelancer rather than an employee is worth the risk, and in my view that's a very entrepreneurial stance to take.

There are still some significant differences between solo business owners and freelancers. The value created by a freelancer or gig worker is almost entirely determined by the hours they work. They trade their skills for a service, but beyond the improvement of their skills, and perhaps a future reference for other work, the main way they benefit from each transaction is the price they charge per hour. Historically, at least, this has meant that, whether they are carpenters or copywriters, the business without the entrepreneur themselves is worth nothing – with the possible exception of their client list.

But despite the close identification of the person with the business in the freelance world, it is undeniable that their work can be just as entrepreneurial as starting and running a company. In some ways being a freelancer is even more entrepreneurial in terms of the risk profile of working this way – given the singular risk to the business of losing its only employee and owner and the need to compete in a more open marketplace.

Freelancing as a way of working is increasing rapidly as corporations recognize more of the advantages of working with contracted third parties, rather than building a large internal workforce. *The Economist* noted in January 2023 that 'A survey of nearly 500 American firms found that 18 per cent were using more independent contractors than in previous years; 2 per cent said they used fewer.' And its big business: by one estimate, skilled freelance workers in America earned $247 billion in 2021, up from about $135 billion in 2018.

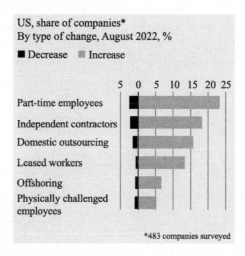

(Source: *The Economist* 2023, Atlanta Fed Survey)

According to Pieter Levels, an entrepreneur, blogger and creator of *Nomad List* – a popular site for finding digital work as a travelling freelancer – such contract work will be the fastest growing form of employment by 2035. By then he argues, there are going to be 9 billion people on earth, and 6 billion of those will be in the labour force. Based on current trends, he says, '50 per cent of those will be freelancers. That's 3 billion people, and 1 in 3 is going to be a remote worker, or digital nomad . . . that's 1 billion digital nomads.'

As discussed above, the line between being a freelancer and building a product is becoming increasingly blurred as people find more and more innovative ways to productize themselves; to use software to quickly replicate their workflows, build unique approaches to their client's needs and eventually build automated replicas of their own styles or techniques using AI. Whether or not such people are *incorporated* in a legal sense will vary by the laws of each country, but I certainly think they should be included in any definition of entrepreneur going forward.

TOUGH GIGS

Similarly, but even more contentiously given current legal debates, I consider people working in the gig economy to be part of the new entrepreneurial culture as well. A gig worker is generally defined as someone whose contract with an employer is based on flexible, temporary and very short-term work – often involving connection with clients or customers through an online platform. Whether it's delivering food, driving a taxi or performing at a music venue, this way of working is exploding. A CNBC report in February 2020, before the COVID pandemic, stated that the number of gig economy workers in the USA had grown by 15 per cent, or to six million people, since 2010. A combination of the impact of COVID, the crash in technology company funding and the ongoing legal challenges in different countries have slowed this rapid expansion in gig work, but it is still going to be an important part of our workforce for the foreseeable future.

Gig work is entrepreneurial in many ways. People working in this sector generally have a choice over which platforms they engage with and for how many hours they work, and they can work on multiple projects – gig and non-gig – at the same time. In fact, a 2021 study in the UK found that for 71.5 per cent of such workers, gig work made up less than half of their income – it was a side hustle, a way of supplementing their main income.

And like all entrepreneurs, people working in this sector take most of the risks and – in theory at least – earn most of the rewards. A part-time assistant on Upwork, or a driver on Uber, make most of the money from the gig, and earn proportionally to the success of their effort. While the platforms themselves take a fee (which ranges from 5 per cent to 30 per cent) it is usually far less than half.

However, even though companies like Uber define the suppliers of services via their platforms as entrepreneurs and contractors, some organizations put in place restrictions which limit the person's ability to choose when they can work, for how long, and with whom – drastically reducing the entrepreneurial aspects of this type of employment. In 2021, judges in the UK's highest court unanimously upheld a 2016 Employment Tribunal decision that Uber drivers were in a 'position of subordination and dependency to Uber'. If a platform can determine the hours you work, the customers you work with, and punish you for using other platforms, you look far more like an employee than an entrepreneur.

Whether a job in the gig economy can be considered a part of the entrepreneurial revolution therefore depends in part on the platform. For many, gig economy platforms are a blessing which have lowered the barriers to finding work. A UK Government survey in 2018 found that a majority of gig workers were at least satisfied if not happy with the additional independence and flexibility this way of working offered. For others, these platforms are another form of traditional employment; you just have an algorithm for a boss.

A more positive aspect to gig work is the increasing body of evidence that shows it's an important first step on a longer entrepreneurial journey; working in the gig economy, it seems, increases the likelihood of someone starting a start-up themselves. Researchers from Rice University and Washington University studied the impact of the entry of ride-hailing services, such as Uber and Lyft, in nearly 1,200 US cities and towns through 2016.

In these areas, new business registrations and start-up loans given to newly incorporated businesses each rose about 5 per cent after ride-hailing became available. And interest in entrepreneurship, as measured by online searches for phrases such as 'how to start a business' or 'how to incorporate' rose by 7 per cent, well above the national average.

Whether a sole trader, a shareholding employee in a start-up, a freelancer or someone working in the gig economy, the common entrepreneurial aspect to all these roles is that the individual, or small team, is responsible more than anyone else for their work. They bear most of the risks and enjoy most of the rewards. They have choice when to work and what to work on. This is the backbone of the *everyday-everyone* entrepreneurship that will define much of the way we work in the decades to come.

It is important to note, as we round off our definition, that entrepreneurialism is different from invention – a point that is often overlooked. Inventors may come up with new ideas, but it is entrepreneurial endeavour that puts these ideas into action. Inventors are mostly motivated to create something new, whereas entrepreneurs want to disseminate something new into the world. Of course, some inventors are also entrepreneurs, but plenty aren't. Many great inventions have languished in a laboratory drawer until a more entrepreneurial mind discovered them and brought them to market. History is peppered with examples of entrepreneurs making fortunes from other people's inventions. For a long time, Italian physicist Guglielmo Marconi was credited with the existence of the radio. However, it was the German physicist Heinrich Rudolf Hertz who first proved the existence of electromagnetic waves, and it was Nikola Tesla who showed how they could be used for long-distance communication – just one of the Serbian–American's incredible inventions. Through a combination of entrepreneurial zeal, Patent Office shenanigans and pure luck, Marconi initially won the patent for the radio – and with it, riches and global recognition. While entrepreneurs do need to apply their efforts innovatively, to fill a niche in the market, they do not need to be inventors.

MIND OVER MATTER

Perhaps the most important trait of all for an entrepreneur, though, is mindset. The fundamental and defining nature of the entrepreneur is not the legal definition of their work agreed on in court, but rather an attitude. It is their decision to see a problem, to reject rather than accept the status quo, and then to act to initiate change that defines this way of working.

Joseph Schumpeter went to great lengths to stress that entrepreneurs had a fundamentally different psychology when it came to work. They had, he argued, *an institutional capacity to see what stood in their way, an energy of will and mind to overcome static habits, desires and emotions, and the capacity to withstand social opposition.* In my experience it is these mental attributes that are the necessary foundation for anyone wanting to set something up themselves, a business or otherwise.

The good news is that the human mind is always looking for improvements, for innovation, for better, cheaper or faster solutions. This applies equally to the software engineer and the plumber, the nurse and the civil servant. On a day-to-day level, this mindset might be employed countless times. You may look at the utensils drawer in your kitchen and think that it needs a child lock. You may be filling out a form at your work's reception desk and think, *We don't need those additional boxes.* Perhaps, on your way to pick up the children from school, you think of new ways you can car share to save on costs; or you're doing the weekly shopping and hunting for deals on bulk-buys. These are all micro examples of what we do every day that help us challenge ingrained habits, and the starting point for the *everyday-everyone* entrepreneurship of the years to come.

The critical question is, if the mental attributes required for entrepreneurship are so abundant, why did so few people take this life path in the twentieth century? And why is this changing now?

A first, obvious reflection is that the ability to identify an improvement or an innovation is an integral part of the entrepreneurial mindset, but is not sufficient on its own. Change requires action too – the word *entrepreneur* derives from the French for 'one who undertakes'. And making change happen is hard and can be expensive. It's one thing being able to tweet about how you'd like to see a difference in the world, or even to write a book about it. It's fundamentally more difficult to act on that view and effect real change. But it is this action, irrespective of success or failure, as well as the desire for change, that really defines an entrepreneur. As Peter Thiel writes, in his bestseller *Zero to One*, 'brilliant thinking is rare, but courage is in even shorter supply than genius.'

And courage is the right word.

The likelihood of failure is one of the great challenges of entrepreneurship. In the United States, the Bureau of Labor Statistics found that, of the small businesses that were started in 2018, 79 per cent made it to their second year (2019), and 68 per cent made it to the third year (2020). So, one in three businesses that started in 2018 didn't make it to year three – and that was before we felt the full impact of COVID.

And if failure is a likely outcome, rejection is almost certain. One of the hardest parts of working in venture capital is that, in 99 per cent of cases, we have to say no to so many budding entrepreneurs. Although my fund, Balderton, has invested $5 billion in the last 20 years into almost 250 companies, they represent under 1 per cent of the total number of businesses that have pitched to us. Raising capital, it is said, is a process of 'exhausting all the "No"s'.

This is the way venture capital is designed. Our focus is on a tiny proportion of new businesses, the outliers with the potential to create astronomical returns. Overall, this is a hugely positive thing for entrepreneurs. The venture model means that founders and employees can invest much more capital in R&D, and successes in the few companies that make it underwrite the failures of the many that don't, allowing for more innovation and risk-taking endeavours. But that academic point is surely cold comfort to the many thousands of entrepreneurs we turn down for funding every year.

And, of course, these rejected businesses are just the tip of the iceberg. Behind each of those were many millions of new projects, personal causes efforts, in the public and civic sector, which never got off the ground, or came quickly back down to earth on hitting the intransigent and deeply entrenched set of behaviours and processes that make up the status quo they were trying to change. Indeed, avoiding change and preserving the status quo is often baked into our educational and financial institutions, the very institutions that are supposed to nurture creativity.

SCHOOL OF HARD KNOCKS

Education, certainly in the Western world, has had a very mixed impact on entrepreneurship. In his 2021 book *Super Founders*, the venture capitalist Ali Tamaseb points out that, while it is true that 35 per cent of the founders of multibillion technology enterprises went to a top 10 global university, 65 per cent went to one not considered to be in the top tier or didn't go to a university at all. In fact, his study found that there was almost no, or at best a very weak, correlation between education level and business success (and similarly no correlation between age and former industry experience, despite the broader narrative of technology founders being young and often inexperienced wunderkinds).

These figures are based on the founders of multibillion-dollar businesses, not the usual entrepreneurs. But further education, in almost any academic field, can put people off starting businesses, rather than encourage it. While there is little academic agreement on a correlation to date, there have been plenty of research projects over the years that suggest tertiary education is at best neutral in the decision to become an entrepreneur or not. Indeed, there's growing evidence that while many educational systems focus on enabling people to develop skills for the modern corporate world, they simultaneously limit rather than foster the qualities that are key to successful entrepreneurship – traits like creativity, salesmanship and independent thinking.

In the seminal 2011 paper 'The Creativity Crisis', Professor Kyung Hee Kim used the Torrance Tests of Creative Thinking (TTCT) to study creativity in American children over three decades. The drop in scores over time, she argued, was statistically highly significant. In Kim's words, the data indicates that 'children have become less emotionally expressive, less energetic, less talkative and verbally expressive, less humorous, less imaginative, less unconventional, less lively and passionate, less perceptive, less apt to connect seemingly irrelevant things, less synthesizing, and less likely to see things from a different angle.'

If, as Schumpeter argued a century ago, creativity and the capacity to withstand social opposition is fundamental to the entrepreneurial mindset, there is little evidence to suggest our formal education systems do much to embed it, and some evidence to suggest they suppress the passionate and unconventional character traits that entrepreneurs need.

Current models of education are built on the idea that, for a vast majority of people, education stops between the ages of 16 and 21. At some point in that bracket, most people in the developed world go from full-time student to full-time worker, and beyond on-the-job training, never look back. People may say that the education system provides students with the building blocks for the world of work, but the world it was designed for is not one of constant career shifts, new skills development, the highs of success and the lows of failure. After all, if that were the case, there would be a much greater acknowledgment that education must be lifelong – to meet the need for different skills as opportunities develop and old careers fade over one's working life. Unsurprisingly then, in a survey of entrepreneurs only 6 per cent of them stated that their experience of university and college education was a major influence on them starting a business.

The good news is that, as we will explore later, new educational services are increasingly popping up to provide necessary, lifelong support for budding entrepreneurs. Venture capital investment in postgraduate education services hit a record $16 billion globally in 2020, reflecting the growing demand for such services. But this investment is mostly going into new platforms and institutions, highlighting the limits of the current educational system to support new ways of working – and learning.

IT TAKES A VILLAGE

The lack of support for entrepreneurs goes much deeper in our culture than just how we are educated. It permeates our places of work as well. The reason that big firms often fail to keep up with innovators, and are thus disrupted by new start-ups, can be as much a cultural issue as an economic or technological one. In his award-winning book *The Innovator's Dilemma*, the American academic Clayton Christensen argues that large businesses are often hardwired against innovation, which takes time and resources and is often incremental. Successful firms already have many customers who are well served by their products and services. As a result, it is often difficult to get management buy-in for the resources required to try something new – especially if it is unlikely to have a positive impact on the upcoming quarterly or annual results.

Replication, rather than innovation, is stitched into the culture of large firms. Strict hierarchies, with levels of management keen to show they are towing the boss's line rather than upsetting the ship, naturally create rewarding environments for those working to the same paradigm.

Going deeper still, the challenge or resistance to entrepreneurship often goes beyond our educational and corporate institutions. It can be found in the very fabric of our society. The social status of entrepreneurship – in educational institutions, corporations and media coverage – remains one of the biggest barriers for people to start a business themselves.

For most of the twentieth century, working as a skilled tradesperson, as a sole trader or owning a business, wasn't seen as particularly prestigious. As mentioned in the previous chapter, parents wanted their children to become doctors, lawyers or pilots in the 1960s, not builders or makers. The disdain in certain countries for the entrepreneurial path continues to have an impact today. Humans are naturally social beings. But being sociable has a cost, which includes a tendency to punish those who are at odds with the norm. Thinking differently, speaking out, risk-taking and carrying the consequent responsibility are all behaviours that can result in social chastisement – irrespective of success or failure.

It's clear that the media culture of a country has an impact on this too. The public perception of entrepreneurship, informed by media representations, has proven to have a strong influence on people's desire to become entrepreneurs.

Fortunately, the public perception of entrepreneurship is shifting. Just look at long-running hit TV shows like *The Apprentice* and *Dragons' Den* – imperfect representations of reality as they are, they do have a positive impact on the number of people who want to start a business. In countries where entrepreneurship is held in high regard, the overall rates of entrepreneurship are correspondingly higher too. In a 2020 survey, new parents in the UK said 'business owner' was now one of the career paths they would be most happy with their children taking, a significant change over the last few decades. It ranked above lawyer and engineer, and only just behind doctor – which itself can be a very entrepreneurial career especially for those choosing to be a General Practitioner. We're not all the way there yet though. The future jobs that parents least desired for their children were sales roles, possibly the most essential part of building any business and the core skill of many entrepreneurs, but one not widely embraced despite its importance.

NURTURE AND NATURE

Given all of these hurdles, what drives people to become entrepreneurs? Many people have argued that there is an entrepreneurial gene, a genetic trait that makes some people take more risks and avoid the trodden path, while some people look for the support of a more stable career. Simply put, they believe some people are born to be entrepreneurs or not. As the eighteenth-century political commentator and agriculturalist Arthur Young saw it, 'humans are not born innovative, instead their natural state is, sleepy, and indifferent . . . enchain[ed] men in the exact paths of their forefathers . . . without thought'.

Like most eighteenth-century projections of genetic heritage, this is evidently rubbish. But while it may not be in your genes, there is evidence that your upbringing and early life – and in particular the people you grow up around – certainly can impact the likelihood of you starting up your own business. Dr Anton Howes, an economic historian and head of innovation research at The Entrepreneurs Network, a think tank, argues a key factor is the availability, or otherwise, of role models. 'People innovate because they are inspired to do so – it is an idea that is transmitted,' he said. 'Incentives matter too, of course. But a person needs to at least have the idea of innovation – an improving mentality – before they can choose to innovate, before they can even take the costs and benefits of innovation into account.' He goes on to suggest that it is seeing or hearing about other people who have found new solutions to challenges that can change your mindset.

Dr Howes is certainly right in this regard. It seems evident that entrepreneurs inspire more entrepreneurship – they create a virtuous circle around them. Entrepreneurs are often found in social clusters – if people have worked with entrepreneurs, lived near them, even shared office space with them, they are more likely to go on to become entrepreneurs themselves.

In 2020 the econometricians Vera Rocha and Mirjam van Praag looked at the employees of start-ups in Denmark. They found that everyone who worked in these start-ups was naturally 'exposed to the idea' of entrepreneurship purely by their working proximity to the founders. But Rocha and van Praag also focused on how other shared characteristics influenced the decision-making of employees. For instance, they found that female employees of start-ups were more likely to go on and found a business of their own if the founder of the start-up was also a woman – a very clear and important impact of positive role modelling. They also discovered that the more similarities there were between founder and employees, the more pronounced was the founder's influence. So, the effect was stronger if the employee and founder were both women, and were also both mothers (or also both *not* mothers). It was stronger if they were both women, and of similar ages; or if they were both women with similar educational backgrounds; or even if the women shared the same place of birth.

An even bigger influence on the likelihood of someone becoming an entrepreneur than the person you work with is, it seems, the person who raises you. A study of the careers of Swedish people born before 1970, to parents born after 1920, found that the children of entrepreneurs were about 12 per cent more likely to be entrepreneurs themselves, at some point in their life, than the children of non-entrepreneurs. In fact, adopted children were found to be 45 per cent more likely to be entrepreneurs if their adopted parents were also entrepreneurs – a huge statistical correlation.

But role models also need to be matched with resources. While it's becoming much easier and affordable to start a business, having access to actual capital, not just cultural capital, still matters. One study of more than a million inventors, published in 2018 in *The Quarterly Journal of Economics*, found that children from America's high-income families (the top 1 per cent) were ten times as likely to become inventors as those from families with below-average incomes. And this vast imbalance doesn't just apply to blue-sky inventions. Success in downstream product innovation is also hugely weighted in favour of the sons and daughters of higher-income households.

It may be true that people can to some extent be born with the entrepreneurial mindset, a familial inheritance – and that the entrepreneurial mindset can be learned from those around you as well. From my own experience, having met thousands of entrepreneurs from every possible background, in the private, public and charitable sector, the desire to make change, to improve the world, to take on responsibility and seek reward and success even in the face of failure is universal. But what differentiates those willing to make the leap from those who don't, for whatever reason, is a combination of the cultural experiences and community support available to them, as well as the resources of time, energy and finances. And it is this last reason that is cited across most studies to explain why people don't follow through on starting a new project. Who has the time and resources available?

With all the other financial demands on your life – from housing to heating, food and travel costs, especially in the current cost of living crisis – it is clearly a huge privilege to have the time or the money to take a risk and try a new endeavour, whatever your background.

The good news is that we are in the midst of a technological revolution which is changing an individual's ability to find solutions to problems, and distribute those products, like never before, and it's already having an effect.

In a survey of the editors who coined the term *everyday-everyone* entrepreneurship, most on the panel agreed that by 2030, entrepreneurship will be 'integrated in everything we do, not just in work but also in domains such as parenting, leisure, or community service' and even more ambitiously, this form of entrepreneurship will 'attract more media and research attention than high-growth entrepreneurship'. The story of the next decade will be less about Elon Musk's latest escapades and more about the proliferation of projects and businesses set up by you, your friends, family and community. Given the importance of role modelling, this is a prerequisite for the great shift in the way people work giving them the confidence, permission, support *and* resources to look at the problems around us and say, *I can fix that*.

The other critical prerequisite is that we have access to the technologies to help us do it – which is the focus of the next chapter.

3

Growth curves

A big part of a venture capitalist's job is to ask the right questions. In a short period of time, often under an hour, you must understand the motivations of the company's founders, the product, the market and the competitive advantages that will enable their business to become a global leader. Getting the information you need out of a founder's pitch requires a lot of skill, but the most important question I like to ask is a pretty simple one: Why now?

Why now? is a critical question to ask when making any prediction about the future. The reason for the great shift in entrepreneurialism that is happening today, the *Why now?* is easy to answer: because technology is getting better, faster.

Technological advances in your own lifetime are easy to identify. As a child of the late 1980s, I still think of smartphones, wireless internet and streaming as recent inventions, even though they've been with us for decades. History ends abruptly the day you are born. From then on, it's the present.

For my parents' generation, colour TV and computers still stand out as the great leaps forward. The crowning achievement of the twentieth century, landing a man on the moon, is still remembered by older people as a triumph of modern technology, even though it's now closer in time to the First World War than to the present day. Going back further still, people born in the first decade of the 1900s lived to see the invention and adoption of radio, cars,

aircraft, indoor toilets and electricity in the home; a string of life –
changing products that improved billions of lives.

At the turn of the century, these technologies took about a
generation to move from breakthrough to mainstream. It took 30
years for electricity and 25 years for telephones to reach 10 per
cent adoption in the USA. Even then it was an uphill struggle for
these new tools to spread widely. Hampered by cost, legislation and
conservative attitudes to change, the telephone took a further 50
years to go from 10 per cent adoption to ubiquity. Recent inventions
such as the mobile phone, the internet and streaming services were
able to spread successively quicker, thanks to a combination of
compounding improvements in the power of new technologies,
the telecoms infrastructure already in place and broader cultural
willingness to try new things.

To get a sense of just how much quicker such breakthroughs can
now spread, and the impact they can have on the way we live and
work, let's look at a few examples of technological innovation and
entrepreneurialism that had global reach.

CONSUMPTION SPREADS FASTER TODAY

(Source: Nicholas Felton, *The New York Times*, HBR.org)

HEALTHY DISCOVERIES

Not all new technologies take off like proverbial rockets. Many
major technological advances went unnoticed for hundreds of

years. Vaccination, an innovation that has transformed human life, seems to have been used and forgotten about again and again over the centuries – in China, in India and in Turkey – until the eighteenth century, when the English doctor Edward Jenner noticed that milkmaids who had contracted cowpox seemed immune to smallpox, and then developed a methodology for replicating vaccines which led to them eventually becoming widespread.

While invention is important, it is the widespread adoption of a new technology that matters. It often takes widespread adoption of a new product to create entrepreneurial opportunities. It's worth pausing briefly to describe how this works out in practice. And, as always, a good place to start is with clean underwear.

One of the main causes of death in the eighteenth century was the lack of washable underwear. Back then, clothes were generally made of wool. If you've ever worn a knitted woollen sweater, you'll know they are both extremely itchy and hard to wash. Hands were dirty. People itched and scratched, and they didn't wash before eating. Microbes passed from waste to hands to food to stomach, causing infections and disease that, in the absence of proper medical support, would often prove fatal.

Fortunately, among the many breakthroughs of the Industrial Revolution was cheap, washable and mass-produced cotton.

Cotton clothing was hardly a new invention. It had been used in India and China since about 5,000 BCE. Herodotus, the ancient Greek historian, mentions Indian cotton in the fifth century BCE as 'a wool exceeding in beauty and goodness that of sheep'. Alexander the Great's battle-hardened troops started wearing it when they arrived in India, impressed by cotton's comfort and durability. But cotton clothing was rare and expensive, and it remained the preserve of the elite for millennia.

The turning point came centuries later, when this comfortable, washable material became available and affordable in the countries of Europe. Innovations in shipping, regulatory changes (including the easing of restrictions on imports of Indian cotton in the eighteenth century), inventions like the flying shuttle and Hargreaves' spinning jenny and the introduction of first water-powered and then steam-powered mills all served to lower prices – as did the ruthless exploitation of slave labour on plantations.

As a result of these changes, the cost of cotton cloth fell by a third between 1770 and 1801 and halved again by 1815. Suddenly a set of cotton undergarments cost less than a day's wages. For the first time, ordinary people could afford washable cotton underwear. The itch/scratch cycle of transmission was broken; countless lives were saved.

As David S. Landes points out in the introduction to *The Wealth and Poverty of Nations*, 'Commoners of the late nineteenth and early twentieth century often lived cleaner than the kings and queens of a century earlier.' Cotton had been around forever, so it wasn't the invention of cotton clothing that made the difference, but its mass production and widespread affordability. Its adoption added decades to life expectancy – not just for the aristocracy, but for everyone, including the adults and children who laboured barefoot in the heat and dust of Lancashire's mills that helped produce a lot of it.

Just as important as the invention and then the mass production of new products, like cotton, is the adoption of new practices and behaviours that put these products into action. One of the greatest entrepreneurs in the history of human health, Florence Nightingale invented few new products but managed to completely change global health outcomes for the better by revolutionizing the way healthcare was practised.

In the mid-1850s she saw the conditions in which wounded soldiers were treated during the Crimean War, and was appalled. The two British military hospitals serving the wounded had just two thermometers between them. Scurvy and infectious diseases were killing ten times as many soldiers per year as were dying on the battlefield. By improving hygiene and nutrition, insisting on good practices such as handwashing, agitating for better sewers and ventilation, and introducing proper training and a disciplined, caring approach to nursing, she was able to cut the death rate among the wounded soldiers from 42 per cent to just 2 per cent. When she saw the urgent need for more hospitals near the war zone, she stung the government into action with an impassioned letter to *The Times* and worked with another great Victorian innovator, Isambard Kingdom Brunel, to create a new kind of hospital, made up of prefabricated ward units that could be made in Britain and shipped out to the Dardanelles. The now famous Renkioi Hospital was erected in a matter of weeks and had a dramatic effect on mortality rates.

Her success in putting ideas into action, coupled with her own irrepressible energy, gave her significant leverage in the corridors of power, which she combined with an unusual commitment to backing up her arguments for reform with hard data, properly researched. Her efforts led to the establishment of the Nightingale Training School at London's St Thomas' Hospital. She wrote the first modern training manual for the profession, *Notes on Nursing*, in 1859, and her ideas were taken up throughout Britain and then in America, Australia, India and Japan, eventually changing the face of front-line healthcare around the world.

Not only did Florence Nightingale overcome establishment resistance, but she also lived in a period when women weren't expected to do such things. She broke the rules, embarrassed the politicians when necessary and embodied the true entrepreneur's dynamism and resilience. 'I see the difference now between me and other men,' she wrote. 'When a disaster happens, I act and they make excuses.' Her story is a fantastic example of how change happens when invention, mass replication and entrepreneurial drive are combined.

BRIGHT IDEAS

Health is so important that it is naturally an area where innovation is keenly felt. But many of the other necessities of life we take for granted are available and affordable for ordinary people today only because of continuous innovation over many decades, or even several centuries.

The fact that we have easy, instant and universal access to light – to illuminate our homes, our workplaces and our streets, and to lengthen our days – is the result of often piecemeal progression from rush lights and torches to tallow and wax candles, to oil lamps, to gas mantles and finally to increasingly powerful and economical electric lights. Each new technology made lighting cheaper, as well as more efficient. The cost of an hour's light in 1800 – in terms of the time you would have to work to pay for it – was roughly 600 times higher than today. In mediaeval England, the cost of a single candle, burning for two or three hours, was so high that most people's lives were ruled by the sun. When the light went, the day ended. Productive winter evenings were only for the rich.

Travel, too, was often a luxury. For the man and woman in the street, the two great liberating technologies of the nineteenth century were the railway, from about 1830, and the safety bicycle, from the late 1880s.

These inventions, and others like them, have transformed people's lives and welfare beyond measure. But the pace of change is exponentially faster today than before, as the fundamental tools of rapid innovation are becoming more widely available.

Communication tools are perhaps the best modern example. For 98 per cent of human history, the speed with which most detailed pieces of information could be carried was generally limited by the speed of a despatch rider on horseback, though Julius Caesar's legions also used messenger pigeons (as did Paul Julius Reuter, when he launched his original stock exchange news service in 1850). Smoke signals and beacons had carried simple messages since ancient times, but it was Napoleon who authorized the first line-of-sight telegraph network. This used semaphore to spell out military reports along chains of hilltop towers that could transmit his orders from Paris to Calais, Lyons or Strasbourg in 10 minutes or less.

Several competing electric telegraph systems were developed in early Victorian times, and the world's first undersea cable, linking Britain and France, was laid in 1850. When the first successful transatlantic cable was completed, in 1866, it could handle just eight words a minute. A ten-word message cost $100, the equivalent of ten weeks' salary for a skilled man at the time. But the rate of change was accelerating, and the acceleration has continued. Multiplex cables, telephones, radio, telex, fax, communications satellites and now the internet and smartphones have made it possible to send almost unlimited amounts of written, audio and visual information, instantaneously, to anyone, virtually anywhere in the world.

As usual, our technical abilities have advanced more quickly than our ability to use them. It takes time to adapt to new tools and realize what we've got, let alone for it then to permeate daily life. The truly revolutionary impact of many recent advancements in communication technologies came into focus in the first months of the COVID-19 pandemic, when billions of people found themselves needing to work together while they were locked out of their offices and shut in their homes. Without today's instant and cheap communication, the economic effects of lockdown would have been many, many times worse. But where remote working was possible, the reaction to this overnight lockdown was astounding.

A survey of businesses run by the consulting firm McKinsey & Company in 2020 revealed that most companies they interviewed were almost fully operational again *in just 11 days* after working from home was enforced, thanks to our readiness to adopt digital tools. This compares with official company estimates that had said it would take an average of 454 days for their company to operate remotely – a damning indictment of how little some executives had understood the digital skills already available within the workforce. The same survey claimed the pandemic had caused businesses to bring forward their adoption of digital technologies by three to four years.

The public reacted equally quickly to this imposed lockdown. Within just a few months of the start of the pandemic, according to another study from McKinsey & Company, three out of four Americans had tried a new platform for buying something online. This wasn't just young people, either: the polling firm Mobiquity found a 47 per cent increase in the number of baby boomers reporting that they had ordered food delivery online; a 193 per cent increase in the number ordering groceries online; and a 469 per cent increase in the number who used telemedicine.

Telemedicine was particularly important, of course, and a huge credit to the governments across the world who accelerated their plans to adopt new technologies during the pandemic. While success was varied, the speed at which solutions like videoconferencing for healthcare appointments was rolled out, showed just how quickly change can happen and how new technologies and practices can be developed when the pressure is on. Dr Sam Wessely, a general practitioner in London, said at the beginning of the pandemic in April 2022: 'We're basically witnessing 10 years of change in one week.' A change in healthcare practices that Florence Nightingale would have greatly admired.

VIRTUOUS CIRCLES

This was, of course, the result of an almost unimaginable external shock, forcing the hand of companies and governments who previously didn't have the resources, will or capabilities to change. Even before the pandemic, though, we were adapting to, and adopting, novel technologies faster than ever before. To explain why this is happening, many people turn to Moore's Law: the observation that the number of transistors in an integrated circuit doubles about every two years, and with it the speed and capabilities of computers. But a lesser-known and increasingly important economic principle is Wright's Law. In 1936, economist T.P. Wright observed that the cost of producing aircraft engines decreased as the number of engines produced increased. His studies suggested that it isn't time which is the key determinant of improved productivity, as Moore's Law suggests, but rather the scale of production.

Imagine that a company produces a new type of smartphone. The company incurs a certain cost to produce each smartphone, which includes the cost of materials, labour and other expenses. At the beginning of production, the company might produce only a small number of smartphones, and the cost per unit will be relatively high. As the company increases production and begins to manufacture more smartphones, the cost per unit will decrease. This is because the company can take advantage of economies of scale, negotiating better deals with suppliers and finding improvements in their logistics and manufacturing process. All of this reduces the cost of production and eventually the price to the consumer.

Wright's Law has been a useful tool for predicting the future cost of a product or service based on production volume, and it's been a remarkably accurate predictor in the fall of costs of production for things like lithium-ion batteries and electronic devices. It's also important because it explains why we're seeing more and more *exponential technologies* becoming available. Exponential technologies are technologies which see faster improvement in their productivity over time, through falling cost or increased output or both. Wright's Law suggests that products will become cheaper to produce as production is scaled, and when those same products become part of the supply chain – as a smartphone is for the development of mobile apps, or a battery is for an electric vehicle – then Wright's Law compounds, resulting in a virtuous circle and exponential improvement. Evidence suggests we are hitting this inflection point for new technologies ranging from AI to biotech, renewable energy and robotics, which are explored in later chapters. It also explains to a huge degree why the entrepreneurial revolution of the twenty-first century is happening now as these tools which have such wide applicability, often referred to as *general purpose technologies*, become more powerful and affordable.

CONTAGIOUS THINKING

As Nightingale's story shows though, change isn't driven only by invention and production. It also requires an entrepreneurial catalyst and a willingness to change deep-set behaviours. Alongside Wright's Law, and the rise of multiple exponential technologies, an even more important shift in mindset has been happening across the globe. In a more interconnected world, the spread of good ideas, best practices and a curiosity for the novel is increasing the speed at which new tools are being adopted. This trend was evident in the increasingly fast adoption curves of the last century, shown by comparing the uptake of the telephone and the smartphone above. For some new technologies the time from invention to mass production to mass adoption can now be measured in days, not decades, in part because of this cultural shift.

Product	Time to 1 million users
Netflix	3.5 years
Facebook	10 months
Spotify	5 months
Instagram	2.5 months
ChatGPT	5 days

(Source: Catherine Buchholz of *Statista.com*)

A great example of the blistering pace at which new tools are being adopted is ChatGPT, a chatbot powered by an increasingly powerful form of AI called a large language model (LLM). There are many companies developing such models, but one of the early leaders in the space is San Francisco-based OpenAI, who created ChatGPT. Hundreds of millions of people have already used chatbots or virtual assistants, like Apple's Siri or Amazon's Alexa, for tasks as simple as setting an alarm, changing an airline ticket or buying groceries online, by using a text or voice prompt rather than some other user interface like a mouse. What is radically different about ChatGPT, and tools like it, is that rather than retrieve information, such as finding the weather in Paris, it generates answers based on the huge amounts of information used for training the LLM. As a result, ChatGPT can provide responses to questions as simple as calculating the time difference between two countries, or as complex as summarizing long phone calls, writing *de novo* code for web applications and even creating new songs and poetry. To get a sense of just how powerful this tool is, the paragraph explaining Wright's Law on smartphone production above (see page 63) was entirely written by ChatGPT, using it's GPT-4 (Generative Pre-Trained Transformer 4) model, provided in response to the prompt: 'Give an example of Wright's Law in 300 words.' Let's hope it doesn't work out how to ask for royalties as well.

The ways entrepreneurs are already using the transformative power of tools like ChatGPT, and other AI models, will be explored later in this book. In my view, the truly remarkable thing is not so much its ability to generate answers in line with human ability, and sometimes beyond, but the speed at which it was adopted. Launched publicly in November 2022 with no marketing budget, the tool reached 1 million users in just five days and 100 million users in three months. It spread like wildfire across social media platforms, online communities and within large enterprises as early adopters shared examples of what it could achieve. This was of course aided by the fact that it was made freely available, for a limited number of uses, and could be used for entertainment, such as writing Christmas carols, as much as productivity. But the fact that such rapid adoption is now possible, aided by a highly connected online community and an increased willingness and excitement to try new tools, is a clear signal that we are crossing the chasm not only in terms of the power of exponential technologies but also in terms of our desire to utilize them in entrepreneurial ways.

But will these new tools result in more entrepreneurship, or cement the dominance of the handful of companies that know how to use them? At the beginning of the twentieth century there was a similar explosion of new technologies, from electricity to the telephone, the automobile and mass-production line, all of which brought significant improvements in what came before them, and fairly quick mass adoption. It resulted in an uptick in new businesses being started, but saw a far greater increase in manufacturing and services roles and the mega-corporations that provided them. So why will things be so different this time around? Aren't we all just destined to become employees of an AI model, rather than users of it? A critical part of the answer is that these new technologies are changing the economics that justified the existence of large farms, factories and service companies in the first place. In fact, they are pathing the way for the *everyday-everyone* entrepreneurialism of the twenty-first century by placing power in the hands of individuals.

4

Of farms and factories

In Berlin, they are squeezing a fair-sized lettuce-farm down into a glass and steel cabinet no bigger than a Coca-Cola machine. In Massachusetts, they are making self-contained 3D printing units that can turn powdered metal into drill bits, watch parts and power steering components at a scale and price to rival standard methods of mass production.

Whether it's through miniaturization, automation or just improving processes, the farm and the factory are shrinking. A clutch of exciting new technologies – from AI and machine learning, remote sensing and cloud computing, gene splicing, nanotechnology, advanced robotics and additive manufacturing (the engineer's name for 3D printing) – are set to change the way we make, grow and consume the things we need, giving entrepreneurs new tools with which to build their businesses. People have been talking about the Fourth Industrial Revolution for years now. Suddenly, it's happening all around us.

Infarm, the German company that's pioneering the development of vertical farms, already has over 1,000 units installed in supermarkets and distribution hubs in Europe, Japan and North America. When you wander along the fresh produce aisle in one of these stores, you are confronted with a row of tall, brightly lit, glass-fronted cabinets, filled with lettuce, spinach, strawberries, herbs and dozens of other crops, all growing without soil in an environment where water, light, temperature, fertilizer, CO_2 levels and other key inputs are dynamically controlled in real time by tubes and ultraviolet lamps.

But these retailers, including Whole Foods, Metro, Marks & Spencer, Aldi and Crisp, haven't had to become farmers overnight. Every individual mini farm is managed remotely by Infarm's operators, plant biologists and data scientists back in Berlin. Using robotics, cloud computing and an array of sensors to monitor growth, the farms can all be controlled centrally, allowing Infarm to adjust and constantly improve the virtual farming process. If it's discovered that a specific combination of hours of light and nutrients will improve the yield of a particular crop, new control algorithms can be applied and updated in a matter of seconds to improve the performance of these mini-farms, meaning the push of a button can improve the yield of in-store farms from Berlin to New York.

Infarm was launched in 2013 and is based in Gartenfeld, a rundown industrial area that used to be dominated by a Siemens cable factory. The three Israeli founders are not just aiming to 'shrink the farm', using their computer-controlled hydroponic methods to grow crops 400 times more sustainably than land-based agriculture. They also want to eliminate pesticides and cut back on farming's carbon footprint by reducing the unnecessary transport of food crops. 'Many of the items on supermarket shelves are imported from Africa, Israel or Spain,' says Infarm founder Erez Galonska. 'They travel an average of 2,500km [1,550 miles] and pass through more than 20 pairs of hands to get here. We can produce nutritious vegetables and fruit with amazing flavour, fresher than crops flown in from overseas, grown right on the spot, in front of the customer's eyes.'

Because the crops mature almost three times as fast as they normally would, these vertical farms can be astonishingly productive. Larger modular units are being developed, some the size of a double-decker bus, each capable of producing up to 680,000 plants per year. If they work, these new units will be able to grow 300 different crops at a time, using just 5 litres of water per kilo of crops, instead of 320 litres used for the average kilo of crops, and producing as much fresh food as 10,000 square metres of conventionally farmed land.

Customers love the flavours and variety. Supermarkets love being able to offer real-time freshness and having real security of supply. Investors are hoping that the company will be able to continue on its path of global expansion. Imitators are watching with interest to see if they can pull it off. Eventually we may see Europe's largest fresh produce farm run by a small team of entrepreneurs in Infarm's HQ, a former washing machine factory in Berlin. These hundred or so plant biologists, robotics experts and software engineers wouldn't need to go near a muddy field either.

While Infarm is shrinking and rethinking agriculture, Massachusetts-based Desktop Metal is busy shrinking the factory.

Most people are familiar with the idea of additive manufacturing, or 3D printing, as a tool for prototyping or the one-off creation of solid objects, usually using plastics or other polymers. What they don't know yet is that advanced versions of this technology can now be used to mass produce strong, dense and durable metal components on an industrial scale.

The dream of printing materials like you might a newspaper article goes back decades. In 1950 a far-fetched science fiction story called *Tools of the Trade*, by Raymond Fisher Jones, talked about making spaceship parts using 'the molecular spray technique'. That's not quite how it works today, but it's the right general idea. A specialized printer is used to build up powdered metals such as steel, copper or many different alloys, in microscopic layers, to form the desired shape, which can involve complex 3D geometry that would be impossible to cast or machine. The newly formed object is then placed in a furnace and heated to near its melting point, in a process known as sintering, which compacts the metal particles and fuses them together to create a solid object as dense and strong as a conventionally produced component.

Desktop Metal is making waves, attracting substantial investment backing from Ford, BMW, GE and GV (formerly known as Google Ventures) and secured a high-profile listing on the New

York Stock Exchange in 2020. Its smallest systems consist of a printing unit the size of a three-drawer filing cabinet that can safely be sited in the corner of an office. They are used for making fully functioning prototypes and for producing short-run or one-off unique items (such as a single replacement thermostat housing for a vintage Mercedes) without the need for special tooling. At the other extreme, the company's mass production system, which can produce more than a million parts a year, is much larger – 5 metres long and 2 metres wide, roughly the size of a family car. That may seem big to fit in an office, but it's very small indeed for a self-contained factory.

By giving designers and engineers the chance to make their own parts in a matter of hours or making it possible for large-scale production runs to take place in a space no bigger than the average corner office, 3D printers are starting to reshape our idea of what a metal-working factory is. It no longer has to be big, dirty, polluting and staffed by underpaid engineers. Just as Infarm is challenging our assumptions about the nature, size and location of farms, Desktop Metal and its immediate competitors are rewriting the rules for factories.

I've been involved with and invested in companies improving farming and factories for over a decade, so I am aware of the challenges they face. While some will fail, the few that succeed will likely have a major impact on our climate, health and way of working, and in the process they are opening up a world of opportunities for entrepreneurs who know how to seize them. Today, thanks to smartphones and cloud computing anyone can launch a website with a few cents and a laptop. What will happen when you're able to create designer food, or personalized furniture, with the same speed and ease?

For centuries, our improving quality of life has been defined by the rise of farms and factories, the principal organizing mechanisms for productive employment. But what role will entities like this have in our future, in a world where a few hundred people can build machines that can replace the entire output of farms, and an automated factory can be condensed into a single room? And what does this mean for wider society? One obvious change will be the reversal of the centralization of work under large employers, which has been underway since the start of the Industrial Revolution. To get a sense of where we are going, it is worth looking back at how we got here.

There are many contenders for the title, but one of the first recognizable examples of the factory, as we've come to know it, can still be seen at Cromford, in Derbyshire. Cromford Mill, opened in 1772 and now the centrepiece of England's Derwent Valley Mills UNESCO World Heritage Site, was the world's first water-powered cotton mill. It was designed and built by Richard Arkwright, a late developer who worked as a barber until he was 28 before going on to become one of Britain's richest and most successful entrepreneurs. Arkwright got his first break when he stumbled upon a new kind of dye for fashionable men's periwigs, but he went on to use the money he made to develop a machine that could spin threads of cotton using metal and wooden cylinders instead of human fingers.

Arkwright and his backers designed Cromford Mill to use water draining from nearby lead mines to drive a large waterwheel and power the Water Frame, the machine that automated the spinning process for the first time. Cromford Mill became the most efficient cotton factory in the world, eventually employing 1,150 people and making Arkwright extremely rich. He died in 1792, leaving a fortune worth roughly £250 million in today's money.

Cromford Mill is a fine example of how a new technology, in the hands of a ruthless and ambitious innovator like Arkwright, can lead to vastly improved productivity. Spinning had previously been done at home, mostly by women, using the traditional spinning wheel featured in fairy tales like *Sleeping Beauty* and *Rumpelstiltskin*. Then, in the 1760s, came the spinning jenny, a simple machine that nonetheless boosted output by a factor of eight. When this was combined with Arkwright's Water Frame, each worker at Cromford Mill could produce 500 times as much spun cotton as a traditional hand spinner working in a cottage or workshop. The regime at the mill was harsh, with two 12-hour shifts, starting at 6 a.m. and 6 p.m. But mechanization meant most of the tasks required little skill, and the workforce at Cromford Mill was largely made up of women and children, some as young as seven years old. Outsiders were attracted to move to Cromford by the promise of a steady income, and terraced houses were built for the mill workers, with a pub, a shop and a chapel, in what became the first iteration of the 'company town'.

As Arkwright and his competitors expanded their operations across the north of England, demand for people to operate the new factories exploded, creating a new phenomenon, the industrial working class. Britain's population was growing fast, from 6.4 million in 1770 to almost 12 million in 1820, and a huge shift was taking place, from agricultural labour to factory work. One recent study estimates that, by 1817, 60 per cent of males across the northern counties of England were employed in these new manufactories.

The factory system – combining innovative new machinery with the division of production into small, specialized tasks – fundamentally changed what a given set of workers could produce. But that didn't translate into individual empowerment and an explosion of entrepreneurship; in many cases, the reverse was true.

What the invention of the factory did do was spark an uneasy 250-year relationship between organized labour and the capital owners and entrepreneurs who built, financed and operated the factories.

Before the beginnings of industrialization in the northwest of England, economic activity was hampered by a rigid social hierarchy, with the idea of free trade and fair employment mostly restricted to the fringes of society. Right up until the seventeenth century, 85 per cent of the working population in the UK could be classed as peasants – individuals who worked in agricultural roles for a single employer, who was almost always the landlord and the local magistrate, too.

For most people living in rural communities, work was not separated from other aspects of their lives. The idea of a job, based on a purely economic relationship between one party and another, was completely alien – and sometimes even prohibited by law. Power lay wholly in the hands of those who wielded the sword or owned the land, not those who toiled in the fields.

This social pyramid, often claimed to be ordained by God and firmly enforced by the king and the aristocracy, remained broadly unchanged for hundreds of years. Yet even in the shadow of the feudal power structure, some entrepreneurs and independent craftsmen still managed to find their own way. Throughout the Middle Ages, 15 per cent of the working population of Europe was made up of artisans, such as goldsmiths and carpenters, stonemasons, wheelwrights and glassmakers, who depended for their living on their specialist skills.

The breakthroughs of the Industrial Revolution, and the rise of factory work, where power began to shift to those who owned the means of mechanical production rather than just land or skill, upended traditional economic roles. The local blacksmith had always been a sole trader; the cooper would use his own tools and could easily get the wood and metal he needed to make barrels. Their livelihoods were as secure as could be expected in those volatile times. But the cotton spinners, in their cottages, could no longer match the speed and productivity of the new water-powered mills. They had no chance of purchasing the equipment needed to compete with Cromford Mill, with its mechanized water frame and Arkwright's highly organized labour force. They could no longer own the best means of production, so were forced to work for those who did. Taking a job in one of the new factories became the only way to earn a living.

The rise of the factory and organized labour split society then, as it still does in many parts of the world today, causing enormous disruption, reshaping our personal and professional lives and sometimes leading to rioting, machine-breaking and attacks on employers and property. It was widely believed that a machine similar to the spinning jenny had been invented some years earlier by Thomas Earnshaw, an English watchmaker, and that he had destroyed his own machine when he realized how many jobs it would endanger. This turned out to be a myth, but it reflected a common and justified fear that mechanization was going to take the bread from the mouths of the poorest.

For the workers inside Cromford Mill and the 20 other cotton factories that sprang up across the north over the next decade, however, the picture looked rather different.

Exploited as they were, they had the security of an income. If Cromford was threatened by machine-wreckers, the *Derby Mercury* newspaper reported in 1779, 'Five or six thousand men can be at any time assembled in less than an hour by signals agreed upon, who are determined to defend, to the very last extremity, the works, by which many hundreds of their wives and children get a decent and comfortable livelihood.'

TURNING ON A PIN

To get a sense of why the factory so quickly became the beating heart of economic activity, we need only look at the most famous factory of the age, the pin factory described on the very first page of Adam Smith's 1776 classic, *The Wealth of Nations*:

> One man draws out the wire; another straightens it; a third cuts it; a fourth points it; a fifth grinds it at the tip for receiving the head; to make the head requires two or three distinct operations; to put it on is a peculiar business; to whiten the pins is another; it is even a trade by itself to put them into the paper; and the important business of making a pin is, in this manner, divided into about 18 operations.

Adam Smith's detailed, memorable and highly influential description was, to say the least, stylized. Smith had never been anywhere near a pin factory. The industry, at that time, was concentrated around Laigle, in Normandy, and his facts were derived, apparently at third hand, from a description originally written by Jean-Rodolphe Perronet, who had observed pins being made and had listed a sequence of 12 operations, performed by nine workers.

In *The Wealth of Nations*, Smith's account, embellished by a little white lie ('I have seen a small manufacturer of this kind . . .'), was intended to demonstrate the advantages to be gained by the division of labour into specialized tasks. By adopting this approach, he said, ten workers could produce 48,000 pins per day, 4,800 per worker. Without the division of labour, he claimed, a single worker would be lucky to turn out 20 and might be able to produce only one good pin a day. (Other contemporary French sources put this figure much higher, however – although that may have been driven by national pride).

Smith's idealized notion of the factory was certainly different from the reality of the life of late-eighteenth century factory workers, although he did recognize that this new way of working had some unpleasant outcomes. The uneven power relationship between the owners of the factories and those they employed could leave the latter exploited, until they could find other employment. And working in such repetitive ways could lead to the worker losing their desire to 'exercise his invention in finding out expedients for removing difficulties'. In short, repetitive factory work might make people less inventive or entrepreneurial. These were trade-offs that Smith saw as justified given the alternatives.

As the productivity of factories was determined more by specialized machines and less by the skills of the workers operating them, the machinery and the ability to invest capital in it became the most valuable element of the production process. Unskilled and semi-skilled people were essential, but easily replaceable, leading to widespread abuses of power in the factories and appalling working conditions. The human element was treated like generic machinery, and the workers did not share the benefits of the huge increases in productivity brought about by mechanization.

In 1771, just as Cromford Mill was being built, Robert Owen was born. As he grew up, he trained as a draper but then moved into the cotton business, buying and selling spinning machines, setting up his own textile factory in Chorlton, Manchester, and eventually buying and running the New Lanark Mill, on the River Clyde, which had originally been owned by Richard Arkwright.

Owen had become increasingly alarmed by the low wages, cruel treatment and poor living conditions of the workers. He began changing the way his mills operated, providing schooling and early years childcare, and calling for legislation that would put into law basic protections around pay, working hours and holidays.

Owen's principled views came at a cost, and he eventually had to sell most of his shareholding in the New Lanark mill to other investors. But his enlightened innovations brought him worldwide fame and attracted many eminent visitors, including the future Tsar of Russia, Nicholas I.

As a result, when the British parliament began considering reforms to improve the conditions of the poor, in the depression that followed the Napoleonic Wars, Robert Owen was asked to give evidence to a special committee set up by the Duke of York. At the hearings, in 1816, Owen claimed that at New Lanark 'the quantity of work done by two thousand persons, young and old, with the aid of machinery, is as much as was formerly accomplished by the whole labouring population of Scotland.' But productivity wasn't everything. One of the underlying causes of human misery, he told the committee, was the direct competition between human labour and machinery.

The testimony he gave has stood the test of time, both as an incredible insight into the sheer power new technologies can have in transforming productivity, and the plight of those who are exploited by them. Within a single generation, the productivity of the entire nation had exploded. Before the Industrial Revolution, Britain had processed £2 million worth of cotton annually. By the end of the century this business was worth £600 million a year. But the nature of work, the power imbalance between workers and their employers, the opportunities for entrepreneurs and the role of the state had all been changed beyond recognition.

While Robert Owen wasn't the first, he quickly became one of the most prominent people to recognize the way workers suffered in increasingly mechanized and inhumane environments. He fired some of the first shots in the long struggle that continues to this day, involving owners, employees, customers and the state, to improve working conditions while maintaining ever-improving outcomes.

Owen's activism led to a number of reform initiatives concerned with defending workers' rights, attempting to establish an eight-hour working day and raising the minimum age for factory work. Owenism also involved many more ambitious attempts to bring about social change, such as his efforts to establish new utopian settlements, few of which lasted more than a year or two. But it is mainly remembered today as an early example of a social movement that recognized the way new technologies can shift the balance of power so completely that new institutions, laws and cultural norms are needed to create a new equilibrium.

It is easy now to think of grimy factory floors, long hours, poor pay and dangerous, unguarded machinery as things of the past. The work involved in modern manufacturing has become far less physical and repetitive than it used to be, but despite the progress brought about by political leaders and organized labour seeking to improve the lives of factory workers, the situation of many individuals has only gradually improved to this day. The plight of Charlie Chaplin's character in *Modern Times*, in which the protagonist is so used to the repetitive, mind-numbing task of tightening nuts on the production line that he cannot stop when his shift ends, is all too close to home for many millions around the world.

Tragedies like the Rana Plaza disaster in Dhaka, Bangladesh, in 2013, which killed more than 1,100 workers when an overcrowded garment factory collapsed in a heap of rubble, show that there is still a need for economic and legislative support for such workers around the globe. Fortunately, changes to improve the working conditions of garment workers at least have been put in place, but to avoid further exploitation and tragedies, we need to get ahead of the next wave of robotics, AI and new materials which will define much of the work done in the factories of the future. As we will come to, we will need a Robert Owen for the start-up century too.

PEOPLE POWER

The Victorian idea of the dignity of hard labour was always a slightly suspect concept, usually promoted by those who did not have to spend their lives working in unfulfilling jobs in unpleasant conditions at the beck and call of uncaring employers. The digital revolution will not remove the necessity for hard work, but it does at least hold out the promise of new kinds of factories and farms in which people will not be used simply as cheap substitutes for machines.

Many of today's dull, repetitive, low-paid, unskilled chores are and will continue to be passed over to machines, as we move towards a world in which, ultimately, only the tasks that need human judgement, initiative, social nous and creativity will be done by people. Existing manufacturers are already adapting to these new solutions. General Electric uses 3D printing to produce fuel nozzles for jet engines, and Nike uses 3D printing to produce prototypes for shoe designs, both examples of hard and often low-paid labour being replaced by smart technology. Although there is a long way to go before robots can match the dexterity of human movement, exoskeletons – machines which can be worn to make lifting and carrying easier – are already making the historically back-breaking work of moving heavy loads around in warehouses, well, less back-breaking.

At a 2022 investor event Donald Allan Jr, CEO of leading American tools producer Stanley Black and Decker, praised advances in automation and the highly skilled technicians on his assembly line. 'You've gone from a situation where if you did a power tool assembly in China or Mexico, you might have 50 to 75 people on a line...' he said. 'The automated solution that we've created in North Carolina, current version, has about 10 to 12 people on that line because of the high level of automation.' To get a sense of where we are heading, he went on to say 'the 2.0 version looks like it's going to get down to two to three people on the line.'

But why will this result in a Cambrian explosion of entrepreneurship, and not just replicate the mass centralization of power as happened under the previous industrial revolutions, replacing factory owners with technology overlords and algorithms? The first difference is, with advances in automation and AI, these factories will simply not need the same number of human workers as they did before. The other key difference is that the accessibility of new technologies like 3D printing, is making the means of production itself more available for anyone to rent or own. The economic power that factory owners, from Arkwright to Boeing, wielded in the past through their control of capital, machines and labour is now being challenged by tools like Desktop Metal which millions of people can have in their garages. Skill and ingenuity will instead become the battleground for successful production.

Open Bionics, a British-born business, is a fine example of this. They develop medical devices that enhance the human body. Their first product is the Hero Arm, a prosthetic which has been developed and is available for people living with a below-elbow limb difference. Prosthetics are life changing for their patients, but they are also incredibly expensive. Prosthetics can range from £1,500 ($1,875) for a finger to well over £40,000 ($50,000) for a more complex limb. For children, though, these rarely fit for long because they grow out of them, and an ill-fitting prosthetic isn't just useless but can be dangerous to the user's health as well. Open Bionics uses computer-vision, additive manufacturing and a host of smart software solutions which mean they can make highly advanced prosthetic arms on demand. The patient can even scan their own arm to get a perfect fit, and especially appealing to kids is the ability to choose a design based on superheroes like Black Panther or Iron Man, albeit without the jet boosters.

The ability to make unique, one-off pieces like a prosthetic arm designed precisely for one person, and to then have that piece inspired by designs from your favourite Disney character, at a fraction of the cost of a traditional prosthetic, is possible only thanks to several inventions. It requires additive manufacturing and advances in computer vision, with the compounding power of Wright's Law making each piece more affordable. It also requires brilliant and determined founders who could access these technologies. Even a decade ago, it is almost certain that the founders Joel Gibbard and Samantha Payne could have only pursued their mission to make prosthetics more accessible by joining a large medical devices company, with access to huge factories, expensive manufacturing equipment and integrated global supply chains. Even then they would have found it hard to undermine the existing, expensive solutions in the market given internal pressures. Today, they have managed to build a product that helps thousands and is now approved by Medicare in the USA and the NHS in England.

As Infarm above shows, a similar transformation is happening in the other great employer of recent times, agriculture. Farms are perhaps the most obvious example of how new technology has changed the way people worked over the last few centuries. The number of people employed in agriculture has decreased significantly across the globe as farm practices have become mechanized and more efficient. In the United States, for example, the number of people employed in agriculture as a percentage of the total labour force has declined from around 50 per cent in the early 1900s to less than 2 per cent today. In the place of millions of small farmsteads, and mostly self-reliant farmers, arose huge, global businesses which centralized processes and leveraged machinery to mass-produce goods. Cargill, among the largest agricultural companies in the world, was founded in 1865 by William W. Cargill, as a grain storage facility in Conover, Iowa and now employs over 150,000 people in 70 countries.

Even these leviathans are under threat from new, hyperlocal and hyper-targeted technologies which are enabling a new wave of entrepreneurship. One example of this is HigherSteaks – a Cambridge, UK based agritech business, founded by Benjamina Bollag, which creates cultivated meat products, aka 'lab-grown' meats. Their unique approach to cultivating a specific type of cell called induced pluripotent stem cells (iPSCs) means they can grow meat in a lab far more efficiently, ethically and with a much lower carbon cost than traditional meat producers. The fact that a small group of determined scientists, armed with the latest breakthroughs in technologies like iPSCs and lab equipment, can create products like lab-grown bacon is just one of a myriad of examples of how new technologies and founders are outpacing even the largest companies in the world, like the farming giants.

Just as happened in the 1900s, these new opportunities will emerge as other tasks and jobs are made redundant by the advance of technology, just as vacancies for chauffeurs, mechanics, car salesmen and, eventually, traffic wardens arose to replace the jobs of the ostlers, farriers, dung collectors and saddle makers made redundant by the advent of the motor car. The cost of automation is falling all the time, and the logic of business economics is inexorable. 'With automation, you invest once and the price goes down over time,' said Orie Sofer, the head of Infarm's hardware lab. 'With human labour, the price should go up over time as they get better.'

If this is the future of farming and factories, what then for the other great institution that dominated the way we worked in the twentieth century, the firm?

5

The fall of the firm

Like many other successful businesses, Chloe's start-up was fuelled by personal frustration. 'I had a bunch of festivals lined up for the summer, after my first year at university,' she said. 'And I wanted some outfits that looked great but that I wouldn't mind getting covered in mud and beer.'

Chloe spent some time swiping through styles on fast-fashion sites. But she felt uncomfortable buying wear-once clothing that she would then throw away. As a student of textile design, she was also aware of the sweatshop conditions in many of the clothing factories in Bangladesh and China's Xinjiang region.

So, she decided to rework pieces of clothing and design new styles herself. Not knowing where to start, a friend recommended Depop for inspiration. Depop is a UK-based marketplace for second-hand clothing that's used every month by three million Gen Zs – people born between 1997 and 2012. Users buy and sell clothing and lifestyle pieces, ranging from unique Nike Jordan sneakers for £1,000 or more, to pre-loved T-shirts and personalized socks at pocket money prices.

Chloe began by snapping up any pieces off the app that were under £10 and which she thought she could use. 'Once I'd tried out a few different design ideas in Photoshop, I printed off some iron-on designs and added them to the various pieces I bought off

Depop. I shared them on Instagram and Snap, too,' she recalled. 'I was blown away by how supportive my friends were about the idea. I started selling bandeau tops initially, as they were really popular at the time, but added more styles and fabrics as people sent me feedback.'

'It was supposed to be a summer project, but I ended up making £11,000 in the first six months and I felt I had to keep going.'

OPEN ALL HOURS

Depop, a service now owned by the marketplace company Etsy, is one of many new online services that are transforming modern work. It allows anyone to set up a shop, take payments, build a community and promote their products for free, taking a small percentage share of each sale. Like the original internet marketplace, eBay, and newer platforms like Canada's Shopify, it provides easy-to-use tools and technologies that are radically changing the way new e-commerce businesses are started and run.

The UK, where Depop is most popular, has long been known for its commercial zeal. Napoleon's famous slight about Britain being 'a nation of shopkeepers' (more likely taken from Adam Smith's *The Wealth of Nations* written in 1776, when Bonaparte was seven) should have been welcomed. The most successful nations of the last hundred years or so have been those that have managed the transition from agriculture and manufacturing to a mastery of commerce, services, trade and design. Being a shopkeeper wasn't a bad place to start.

But over the past few decades, it became increasingly difficult to start a new retail store in Britain, the ancestral home of the shopkeeper. Clothes retailing is a sector that doesn't require much in the way of machinery and space, but you needed a lot of resources and capital behind you just to get going. One recent estimate put the basic cost of setting up a new shop outside the London area – in Manchester, for example – at £172,000, or five-and-a-half times the average yearly household income. Much of this initial investment will be earmarked for rent, staff costs and stock. But the burden of regulations and rates (local business property taxes), licences and insurance premiums has increased in recent years, driving up the cost. The start-up shopkeeper will also need a system for taking payments, with services like Visa and MasterCard always keen to take a cut on each transaction, not to mention inventory services, accounting and payroll tools. In 2003, according to the World Bank, it cost on average an entire year's wages to set up an offline business almost anywhere in the developed world – a prohibitive sum for most people.

THE PEOPLE OF WALMART

The expense and complexities of opening a physical store meant that becoming an independent shopkeeper was a pipedream for many people in the late twentieth century. While some entrepreneurial newcomers did manage to break through, the logistics and the capital requirements meant it was increasingly easy for a large business to buy out smaller operators and run a chain of stores under a single organizational umbrella. Companies like Best Buy for electronics, Walgreens (and its UK subsidiary, Boots) for beauty and pharmaceuticals, and The Home Depot for home supplies, became dominant players. Throughout the twentieth century, megastores and multinational organizations captured a much greater share of most retail markets than standalone companies. And the greatest example of the success of these megastores is, of course, Walmart.

Walmart's first Discount City Store was launched in 1962 in Rogers, Arkansas. It began life as a modest cut-price store, looking to beat the competition by offering lower prices and concentrating on volume. Walmart's spectacular growth has taken it from being a one-man start-up to (arguably) the biggest private sector employer in the world, with 2.2 million staff in 26 countries. Right from the start, however, the apparently straightforward Walmart was quick to take advantage of the latest breakthroughs. The company was an early adopter of each new generation of retailing technology, from barcodes to electronic point of sale. And its astronomical ambitions didn't stop there. In the mid-1980s, when the company needed a better way to keep track of its logistics network and real-time sales, it built its own satellite communication system, which became the world's largest privately owned satellite network for many years. All of that to sell fresh produce at the lowest possible price.

One of the main reasons for the rise of such big organizations, and a driver of Walmart's success, is what's known as the theory of the firm, an idea first set out in 1937 by the Nobel Prize-winning British economist Ronald Coase in his paper 'The Nature of the Firm'. Coase argued that there are two competing forces at the heart of every organization: on one side is the cost of overheads and bureaucracy, which limits the size of a company, and on the other the benefit of savings gained by completing transactions within the firm rather than having to outsource them to third parties.

For Walmart, it was clear that it was easier to keep most of its operations in-house. It was simply more efficient to handle services like payroll, accountancy, logistics and delivery, even communications infrastructure like its private satellite network, within the organization than to rely on third parties to provide them. Even if outside suppliers could potentially provide each of these services more cheaply, the problem of finding and managing these external resources and keeping their performance up to scratch made the apparent savings a false economy.

For Walmart's employees, from shop-floor workers and van drivers to accountants and lawyers, it made more sense to work for the ever-expanding retail giant than to take jobs in smaller organizations that were struggling to compete. Setting up a retail store themselves was a non-starter: it was going to be prohibitively expensive, and they would have to depend on third-party support services to help them compete with Walmart's huge internal operations.

The theory of the firm holds true for many other sectors of the economy beyond retail. The rise of financial services giants like AIG in insurance and HSBC in banking, industrial leviathans like

Dow Chemical and BAE and even creative industry leaders like Walt Disney and News Corp reflect the competitive advantages enjoyed by large, multinational firms. With their economies of scale, and the agglomeration effects of having many groups of highly-skilled employees under one roof, they could usually beat smaller competitors and start-ups on brand, price and service. In the corporate world, big was beautiful.

The overwhelming dominance of these large organizations shaped society and people's careers and aspirations in many ways throughout the last century. As large, well-established organizations were generally resilient to economic boom and bust, an individual could spend their working life with a single company. An accountant would work in the accounting department, and while the specific techniques you needed in your role might vary over time, the organization itself had layers of management and training and support to help you develop the skills required over the course of a long career.

With a safe, steady job and a fairly predictable future income stream, you were a good prospect for many other services. When you wanted a mortgage, banks were ready to lend you many times your current salary, confident that you could pay it back on time and with interest, as they had seen people with similar career trajectories do before. Professionals in large organizations could borrow easily, get better insurance rates, enjoy benefits like healthcare cover, company cars and access to many different forms of financial support that weren't available to people who had less predictable incomes, like the self-employed.

The idea of the stable, lifelong career in a single organization was so pervasive that much of the social safety net established by governments after the Second World War was based on the notion of a profession for life. Whether you were a lawyer or a toolmaker, you paid taxes and saved for your pension, all on the assumption that you would receive a regular and predictable monthly salary. If you were unfortunate enough to be out of work, you were provided with a modest level of support to cover life's basics while you got back on track. When you retired, you would get a small pension from the state and a larger one from your organization, which enjoyed significant tax incentives in making its contributions to your pension plan.

WINNING THE RAT RACE

The aspiration of working for a well-known company and having a career for life is now a deep-rooted part of global culture. As early as 1955, bestselling novels like Sloan Wilson's *The Man in the Gray Flannel Suit* captured the joys, challenges and anxieties people faced in their desire to get ahead in the corporate world. By 1975, the film *Rollerball*, set in the 'not-too-distant future' of 2018, imagined a world where a handful of international corporations had become so powerful they had replaced governments and controlled all the globe's resources; everyone was an employee, rather than a citizen, with disputes settled through deadly gladiatorial sport.

In his seminal work on management, *The Organization Man*, the American sociologist William H. Whyte argued that the concept of the organization had made its way into the very soul of a generation. He described how the members of this new generation were keenly aware of how much more deeply beholden they were to the organization than their elders had been.

'They are wry about it, to be sure,' he wrote. 'They talk of the "treadmill", the "rat race", of the inability to control one's direction. But they have no great sense of plight. Between themselves and the organization they believe they see an ultimate harmony . . .'

'The pressures of the group, the frustrations of individual creativity, the anonymity of achievement: are these defects to struggle against – or are they virtues in disguise?' he asked his fellow countrymen.

By the early 1990s however, just as the concept of the firm was reaching its pinnacle, the reasons for the success of large firms, as posited by Coase in his paper 60 years previously, were beginning to falter. Coase had argued that firms made sense for as long as the cost of the extra bureaucracy of building services internally was less than the cost and resource spent finding and managing third parties to provide them externally. When multinationals began to realize that, as global markets opened, there were countries such as India and China with workforces to whom they could outsource parts of their business, hiring expensive, local talent became less attractive. If outsourcing to companies like Infosys and Tata Consultancy Services meant services like software engineering and call centres could be provided equally well at a much lower cost, it no longer made sense to take on the burden of running those departments internally. It had been difficult, in the past, to find, coordinate, manage and work with people remotely. But greatly improved telecoms systems suddenly made it both possible and affordable.

The second big shift came in the 2000s, with the rise of the internet and the gig economy. Where managing and allocating tasks to large numbers of people, especially in logistical work such as food delivery or taxi services, had previously taken a lot of staff and resources, new technologies provided easy solutions. Together, the internet, cloud computing and smartphones changed the rules of the game for take-aways and taxi agencies just as globalization had for multinationals the decades before.

Within just a few years, start-ups like Uber and Airbnb appeared from nowhere and captured far greater market shares than any previous taxi companies or hotel chains had ever dreamt of, while formally employing only a tiny fraction of the staff that had been needed previously. They did this by using platform business models and outsourcing the labour element to local contractors, and by setting up collaborative arrangements that gave them access – without the burdens and obligations of ownership – to other people's assets, vehicles and accommodation. This gave them the ability to grow at lightning speed, with very few employees.

In 2014, Brian Chesky, Airbnb's founder and CEO, responded briskly to a boast by Marriott Hotels, the world's largest hotel chain, that it would add 30,000 new rooms in the next 12 months.

'We will add that in the next two weeks', Chesky tweeted.

These platforms haven't just changed the cost and speed at which work can be done, it's also changed the quality of working life. Many of the laborious and tiresome tasks that used to occupy office workers' and managers' time have been drastically simplified in recent years.

At the same time, the equation for talented individuals in project-based roles, such as graphic designers or software developers changed, as they no longer had to rely on working for just one specific organization to be in gainful employment. The internet made finding work significantly easier, lowering the transaction costs and time to find customers for goods and services, and so changing the way people could work. Working freelance gave them the option to balance other commitments in their life, without worrying that taking a month off was going to leave them in the doghouse with their now non-existent manager. The market for their work suddenly grew massively, as did the competition, with the ability to bid for work at any company with an internet connection. And they were able to scale their professional network much quicker, with other platforms such as LinkedIn, Upwork or Facebook becoming free or cheap ways to advertise what they were doing.

Suddenly the glue that Coase argued kept employees and firms together was starting to dissolve.

THERE'S A BOT FOR THAT

What may be the final nail in the coffin for the firm is the increasing ability of entrepreneurs to replace entire swathes of a company's productive activity with automated, software-driven processes. As the power of new software tools has grown, so has the ability of individuals and small groups of innovators to access and make use of these tools, without the need to build big organizations employing large numbers of staff.

One of the best examples of this is that essential task for virtually any modern company, building and operating a website. Twenty years ago, if you'd wanted to build and host a commercial web application, one that could run a basic service, for a few hundred thousand users, with transaction abilities and stock management, it would have cost you around $100,000 per month.

You'd have needed a physical server in your office, where your website would be hosted, with system administrators to keep the server secure and running smoothly. You'd have needed a team of web designers, engineers and graphic artists to keep your site up to date – and you'd still have been keeping your fingers crossed that the whole thing wouldn't collapse whenever there was a surge of web traffic. When Elon Musk was building his first web company, Zip2, in the late 1990s, he had to turn his website off every evening because he couldn't afford the extra servers and developers to keep it running around the clock.

At that time, in 2000, there were around 360 million people in the world with internet connections. Today, more than 4 billion people access the web every day and the cost of running even highly sophisticated web applications has come down to earth with a bang.

E-commerce platforms like Shopify enable users to build entire online stores, complete with checkout facilities and logistics tracking, without knowing a single line of code. You can then choose to outsource the hosting of this service with a single click, choosing between cloud providers like Amazon Web Services, Microsoft Azure, Google Cloud, Alibaba Cloud and many others, all competing to offer extraordinarily low prices.

What's needed to set up and run a decent-looking website with some basic functionality today? In round figures, one hours' work and £10 a month. No software engineering experience required. Like Chloe mentioned above (see page 83), with her fast-growing Depop clothing site, you don't even need to know much about how web design or cloud computing works. You can learn as you build with thousands of hours of free content online.

And it's not just websites. More and more of the business support functions that used to work best as part of a larger organizational framework are now available as software-driven online services.

The key to this is the use of APIs – application programming interfaces – which allow applications to talk to each other, and interact seamlessly and reliably. APIs make it possible to combine several software services to provide a complete organizational workflow, pulling together, collating and acting on information from many different sources, without the need for any human intervention.

What does this mean in practice? Well let's take the example of a single manufacturing workflow – the design, production and distribution of a new kind of reusable packaging.

Tetra Pak is one of Europe's great entrepreneurial success stories. It was founded by the Swedish entrepreneur Ruben Rausing in 1951, initially as a subsidiary of his food packaging company. Ruben and his wife Elisabeth wanted to find a more efficient, affordable and hygienic way to package and ship liquids like milk and soups. After a lot of research, they came up with the idea of constructing a tetrahedron-shaped package out of a tube of paper, which could be heat-sealed. The Rausings and associates bought a factory and machinery, and started to roll out their sales teams first across Europe, then globally, building a business that now generates $13 billion annually, has saved billions of tonnes in wasted paper packaging and employs 25,000 people.

But what if you were to set out to design, manufacture and distribute a new reusable package today? Computer-aided design (CAD) tools, have been in use for over 40 years and are now the design tool of choice for most engineers. They are so widely available that Tinkercad, a browser-based tool owned by Google, is available for free for anyone with an internet connection. With Tinkercad you can use your mouse to design any 3D shape you can imagine. Of course, doing this without a background in engineering can be intimidating, but helpfully there are over 17,000 videos on how to use Tinkercad, available free on Google-owned YouTube, with guides on everything from creating a simple mug to designing an entire house.

Once you have your design, how on earth do you make it? Hubs.com, a global platform which connects engineers with over

3,000 digital printers, has an application programming interface (API) which allows you to send your Tinkercad design to any of their independent manufacturers across the world with a single click. The design will be checked by the Hubs algorithm to ensure it has a feasible print structure, and through an automated auction process will provide you with hundreds of combinations of prices, locations, lead times and materials for manufacturing your design.

Now you've made your choice of manufacturer, your file will be processed in the cloud and sent to a 3D printer or CNC-machine, to be produced automatically in plastic, wood or metal. You then need to distribute your new reusable package. But API-first solutions have you covered here too. Distribution services like Flexport and Shiply offer instant prices and delivery times to ship any product from almost any place on earth to another, over air, land and sea.

And what about getting customers? Procter & Gamble have 99,000 employees across the world and spend over $10 billion a year on advertising and marketing. How can a single person compete with them? Well, even marketing operations are being replaced with software. Services like Copy.ai use the latest developments in artificial intelligence to create copy writing for any product using just a couple of keywords.

For instance, given *only* the words 'Wise reusable packaging', Copy.ai's algorithms automatically produced the statement below:

> 'With intelligent features and an environmentally friendly design, this package works perfectly for all your needs. Upgrade your packaging with reusable, water resistant, and fibrous paper. You'll be the talk of the office when you bring lunch in Wise Reusable Packaging.'

Impressive, but why stop at text for your marketing campaign? You can now feed this marketing spiel into an AI service to read it out using a posh English or broad Midwestern accent for radio or podcast commercials with a service called ElevenLabs (at ElevenLabs.io).

If you feel that process wasn't simple enough, there are now several companies able to turn text prompts into viable 3D models, so we will soon be able to simply write 'design a 3D-printable reusable package' and it will produce hundreds of possible designs on demand.

This is just the beginning of a new AI-driven maker movement. Now the APIs connecting these services can be stitched together by AI 'agents', software services that can navigate the code base of a product like Shopify or Flexport and connect to the API or frontend interface for you with a simple written request. Even the most technophobic of us should be able to manage that.

So a single person, with a laptop, internet access and a budget of less than £100 can design, produce, ship and market a product like Tetra Pak's in the space of an afternoon – with no other human directly involved in the process. It's hard to imagine Coase would have much faith in the future of the firm in the face of such rapid change.

DOWNSIZING

If today's technologies can work such miracles, why is our economy, and so much economic policy, still so doggedly focused on supporting people to find jobs and build careers in mega-organizations in agriculture, manufacturing and services? The world is changing fast. But such a huge rewriting of the rules takes time and sometimes you have to look back decades, not just a few years, to appreciate how much has already changed.

In 1990, the ten most valuable companies on the S&P 500 – which included firms like Coca-Cola, AT&T, General Electric and cigarette manufacturer Philip Morris – employed over three million staff between them. Just 30 years later, the ten largest companies on the S&P 500 now including Apple, Microsoft, Amazon, and

Google – are worth almost ten times as much, in dollar terms, but employ less than half the number of people.

Indeed the number of workers required to generate $1 million in revenue for the average S&P500 company has fallen significantly as well, as more value is created by fewer workers using steadily improving technologies and processes.

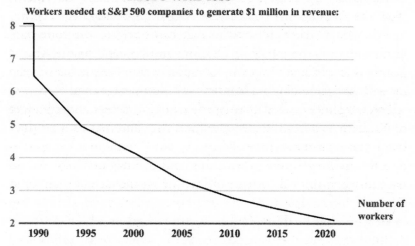

More with less

Workers needed at S&P 500 companies to generate $1 million in revenue:

(Source: Bradley Saacks / Semafor, Bank of America NB.

Successful firms are also zealously outsourcing more work to contractors and third-party services than ever before. *The Economist* estimated that the intensity with which large American firms are outsourcing has doubled from 11 per cent in 2005 to 22 per cent in 2022. This growth is especially pronounced among tech titans such as Apple and Microsoft. *The Economist* notes, 'As firms grow larger and adopt more technologies, thus becoming more complex and unwieldy, they outsource more operations—precisely as Coase would have predicted.' As technology evolves further, so too will the way firms operate. *The Economist* continues: 'businesses around the world . . . are getting better at measuring workers' performance based on their actual output rather than time spent producing it', making it easier to contract too and manage freelancers as one might have done an employee a few years ago.

While the largest firms are shrinking in terms of relative headcount, they are growing in terms of revenue share. The top 1% of US firms by sales earned a staggering 80% of all sales in 2018. As the writer Matt Clancy puts it, when it comes to earnings the economy is populated by a few 'superfirms' and a multitude of small- to medium-size businesses struggling for what's left.

Whether it's through better management practices, automation, or outsourcing, the top firms are hiring fewer people and this trend is only going in one direction. Companies that have failed to keep up with the technological frontier, like Xerox, Sears and Roebuck, which were once looked up to by the aspiring managers interviewed in William Whyte's *The Organization Man*, are shadows of their former selves if not defunct.

The challenge now is working out exactly *which* roles in traditional firms will be outsourced or replaced by advances in AI, and over what time period. Forecasting such change has been notoriously difficult due to the speed at which different technologies have advanced. In 2017, when Tesla announced fully self-driving vehicles were a couple of years away, you would have been forgiven for thinking that trucking and logistics firms might be the first to downsize their human staff. Many years later, progress on self-driving vehicles has been piecemeal, while advances in other areas of AI, such as the LLMs described above, suggest that it is knowledge workers who may be more at risk from automation than truck drivers. As Daniel Susskind observed in his 2020 book *A World Without Work*, the type of education or training required by a human to perform a task has never been a reliable guide as to whether a machine will find that task easy or difficult to perform. In the long run, almost all tasks will be replaced and our jobs will involve new ones.

What I believe we can predict is that fewer of us will have either the opportunity or desire to work in medium or large firms, leaving more of us then ever having to start-up businesses ourselves.

Entrepreneurs will also have to utilize new tools, offer unique skills, build scalable or personalized products and rely on partnerships with other entrepreneurs to thrive. They will be able to remain small in terms of employees, or even work alone as they scale their revenues and profits, continuing the trend we see today.

As firms shrink or disappear, more of us will have to hone our entrepreneurial instincts, rather than the corporate skills much of our education system has focused on to date. Before turning to education however, we need to get a sense of what this type of work may look like in the future. To do that we need only look at what the generation of creatives, freelancers and solopreneurs are already doing today.

6

A creator's economy

Like many millennials, Teri Ijeoma already had a number of careers behind her by her early thirties. After graduating from MIT, the Texan spent time in a bank, as a management consultant, and at a non-profit before going into teaching. 'I was assistant principal of the elementary school, my salary was about $60,000 a year, and I was exhausted,' Teri revealed in a podcast in 2021.'I used to do real estate as a side hustle. And then I started doing investing as a side hustle, I thought maybe one day I would be able to sell enough homes to get to that million-dollar level.'

After a tough few months with colleagues at her school, and the death of a close friend, Teri decided to strike out on her own, and turn what she had learned through her career in finance, education and real estate into a training course to provide financial literacy and advice to others in her community.

'I never in my life would have imagined that this would be me. And especially not that it would happen this fast. I had no idea that investing would turn into what it is for me today.'

Becoming an independent advisor is not a new profession, especially in finance. From personal tax advisory to get-rich-quick seminars, many people have set up their own training and education companies in the last few decades. However, what was different for Teri – other than her experiences and personable, communicative style – was the way she did it. Rather than set up an office in her local town, she travelled the globe, and taught the world, from her laptop.

Teri did this by sharing her learnings and monetizing the content in videos, on YouTube and elsewhere online. The content was so good at helping people understand how to manage their finances that it spread fast, and by 2020 Teri became the single highest paid teacher on teachable.com, a platform that provides access to tens of thousands of teachers online, covering topics from automotive repairs to Aristotle, machine learning to sixth-grade arithmetic.

Founded in 2013, teachable was originally a side project itself, designed as a way for existing teachers to share lesson plans with students directly. Over time it became clear the platform could do more than that. Its software makes the process of becoming a teacher and building a student following so easy that many people, who had never considered teaching before, started using it, and for a range of subjects beyond the usual school curriculum. At the end of 2019, the company had over 22,000 teachers using it, and at its peak 7 million students. The average course makes around $8,000 a year on the platform, enough to supplement, but not replace, a full-time teaching role. Teri is one of just two people who earned over $10 million in 2020. And it appears she's just getting started.

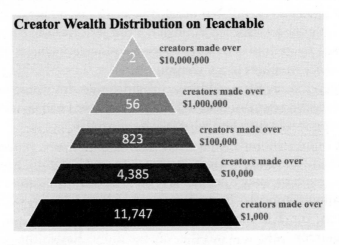

Creator Wealth Distribution on Teachable

2 — creators made over $10,000,000

56 — creators made over $1,000,000

823 — creators made over $100,000

4,385 — creators made over $10,000

11,747 — creators made over $1,000

(Source: Bloggingguide.com)

ARMY OF ONE

The ability of a single, driven individual to make over $10 million a year – 300× the median income – with no employees and minimal overheads is extremely unusual. To make that kind of wealth in previous generations would have necessitated legions of staff, soldiers, religious followers or a lot of capital for speculating. Thanks to global online platforms, the creator economy has completely changed that.

In 2022 the online creator economy was estimated to be worth $100 billion and more than 50 million people worldwide consider themselves creators, although only 2 million of these people earn enough from the profession to declare this as a main source of income in their tax returns. Teri is not alone in conquering the new entrepreneurial opportunities this online economy has created. According to a 2019 report by *Business Insider*, Ryan Kaji, a nine-year-old YouTuber from Texas, has earned an estimated $26 million from his YouTube channel *Ryan's World* where he reviews and unboxes toys. Senegalese-born Italian social media personality Khabane Lame worked as a machine operator at a factory near Turin before turning to TikTok in 2020, putting up satirical posts of overly complicated 'life hacks'. Two years later he'd built the largest following on the platform, with hundreds of millions of views and earning a rumoured $100,000 per post.

These people, of course, are an extreme exception to the rule. Despite one in four Gen Z-ers saying that becoming an influencer like Ryan Kaji is their dream job, in reality a vast majority of people in the creator economy who produce educational or entertaining content for a living – don't earn a fraction of that amount.

Of the 2 million people who do make money as creators, nearly half of them earn their money on YouTube. To make $60,000 a year, you need on average 1 million followers, and to produce video content on average twice a week – this is no mean feat. With their 2 billion monthly active viewers and growing, YouTube remains one of the most powerful platforms for creators on the planet. However, similar to the Teachable pyramid above, a vast majority of people who put up content on YouTube hoping to become stars cannot make a living, and many people believe that generating an income this way is only getting harder.

Li Jin, founder of the investment firm Atelier Ventures, goes as far as to say that creators who rely on platforms like YouTube and TikTok are being exploited. Despite contributing to the value of these platforms through their content, creators lack the benefits and protections of traditional employees, and get a very slim share of the revenues they create. She argues that at the very least they deserve some form of ownership in the companies for which they are producing content, allowing them to benefit from the success of the platforms who ultimately control their incomes. She goes as far as to say the current dynamics are like 'taxation without representation' or 'twenty-first-century serfdom'. The power imbalance between creators and the platforms they use has led to some creators attempting to form a digital union – and threaten to remove content en masse. However this battle between creators and the platforms pans out, it's likely that only a small fraction of people who dream of working this way full-time will be able to make a living from it alone.

OLD CRAFTS NEW TRICKS

The entrepreneurs seizing on these new ways of working are not all using cutting-edge technologies or producing digital content. Many of the world's oldest crafts and trades are also finding opportunities to flourish outside of the decaying organizational structures of the twentieth century.

The British shoemaking industry, a profession which has been around for thousands of years, is often thought to have had its golden era in the mid-to-late nineteenth century. The first shoe machine (strictly speaking it was a boot machine) entered production in the early 1800s to serve the British Army. But bespoke shoemakers were in high demand throughout the century, with an estimated 28,574 different shoemakers working in London in the 1840s. However, agglomeration by large firms such as John Lobb and Henry Maxwell and international competition meant that by the end of the century, that number had fallen to 3,000. By the late twentieth century the industry had dwindled to a few hundred artisans, if that, leaving the profession facing extinction with fewer apprentices looking to join while experienced craftsmen retired.

Indeed, finding work as a skilled, independent craftsman such as a shoemaker has become much more difficult in the last few decades. The globalization of manufacturing meant that international labour could produce shoes at a lower cost, while the advent of new machinery meant they could be produced at greater speeds and quantities, a deadly combination for a patient and hardworking craftsman. The journalist and menswear expert Derek Guy believes that this has resulted in poorer products. He writes about how new ways of sharing quality work online, through sites like Instagram, are helping these old, skilled professions fight back.

Now apprentices from the few remaining hubs of traditional bespoke shoemaking are building avid fan-followings – and finding clients – by advertising their passion and particular techniques on social media sites like Instagram. These individuals, Derek argues, can produce superior quality shoes, in part because they have a direct relationship with the customer, who follow every part of the production process through posts and live videos. This puts pressure on the shoemaker to deliver high-quality products, but because of this direct relationship they don't need the auspices of an extravagantly expensive Mayfair store, or internationally renowned brand-name as they may have done to garner such attention in the pre-social media era. Their work speaks for itself.

Shoemakers are far from alone. From wood-carved tables to wicker chairs, niche crafts are finding a new lease of life online as traditional middle-parties get cut out by digital platforms, and consumers seek more personalized products and relationships with the creators.

ONLINE ALL HOURS

Now that you don't need a physical storefront to find customers and advertise your wares, more and more people are becoming digital shopkeepers to earn a living as a solopreneur.

Setting up a store online, like Chloe's Depop shop described above, has never been easier, nor more popular. Shopify, just one of the many popular services used to launch e-commerce stores online, now has over 1 million businesses that use their platform, making a combined $41 billion in total sales in 2021.

While platforms like Shopify, BigCommerce and WooCommerce make it simple for individuals to create an online store with no technical know-how, sellers still need to bring their own digital footfall to their sites, which can require large marketing budgets. However, online marketplaces like Amazon, eBay and Etsy solve this problem for retailers as well, integrating products into their search and recommendation engines – for a cut, of course – dramatically reducing the resources required to get a product noticed and those first sales going.

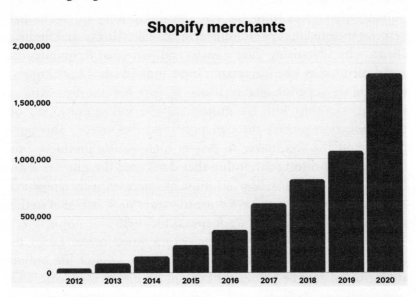

(Source: Shopify.com)

The income from running an online store can vary widely, as it does for content creators. According to a survey by Shopify, the average active store earns around $7,500 per year. It isn't enough to live off, but running multiple stores at the same time, or combining it with other online revenue streams, is easily done as well.

Launching your own online store is a global phenomenon. Taobao, a Chinese software business, has created more wealth for online tradespeople than possibly any other internet business in the world. It was founded in 2003 as a part of the AliBaba Group's response to eBay's expansion into China, and its initial launch was heavily affected by the SARS epidemic that swept much of Asia that year, forcing many shops online for the first time. Providing tools for Chinese entrepreneurs to start online stores, run as direct sales or auctions, Taobao's broad product suite allows people to sell high volume goods – or more luxury wares through its Tmall spin-off – using mobile or web payments. They also provide a range of tools to give sellers everything they need to create, market, and sell their products. At the end of 2020, Taobao and Tmall made up a staggering 29 per cent of global e-commerce, more than double Amazon's market share. Like other such platforms in the West, Taobao saw a spike in new entrepreneurs using the platform over the course of the pandemic. An average of 30,000 new stores were opened each day in 2020, when much of the world was in lockdown, a trend that continued well into 2022 as China continued rolling restrictions on citizens freedoms.

Much like online content creation, e-commerce comes with its own challenges and can result in highly volatile income streams. Starting a store can leave you holding unwanted stock given the rapid turnover in interest in certain products, while changes to search algorithms on platforms like Taobao or popular US shopping site Etsy are often complained about by the many millions of people who rely on them for their living. Add in all the additional effort involved in shipping and marketing online, and you'll quickly find you can earn less than the minimum wage even if your store's turnover is fairly healthy. Nonetheless, as a way to get going as an entrepreneur in the digital age, starting an online store is a popular and affordable route.

TAKING A PUNT

The rise of digital shopkeepers, Instagram crafters or online teachers, are just a few examples of how many of us are taking on entrepreneurial work and spurning traditional careers. While this has been happening in retail and crafts for a while, the revolution is now having major repercussions on some of the world's most regulated industries, and none more so than the highly lucrative and seemingly staid world of high finance – an industry being upended as the result of mass decentralization and new technology.

In the riotous 2013 film *The Wolf of Wall Street*, Leonardo Di Caprio, playing the eponymous Jordan Belfort, swings open his office doors to reveal a packed office floor of (mostly male) traders in various states of frantic anarchy. Some are screaming into desk phones, pumping penny stocks to gullible clients. Others are analyzing reams of paper and staring, cigar in mouth, at black and red flashing screens. It is a heaving mass of seemingly uncoordinated madness, and Leonardo smiles approvingly.

The film captures some of the absurdities of the stockbroking profession at its peak in the 1980s, when a loosening of regulations and the advent of new telecommunication and information systems allowed stock traders to run riot. Jordan Belfort's firm, Stratton Oakmont, was already seen as a highly lean but risk-taking outfit, and he was subsequently sentenced to jail for crimes related to stock market manipulation. But the profession of being a stockbroker in the 1980s still required a significant amount of infrastructure: salespeople, accountants, technicians, fundraisers, office support and lots more. By the time it was closed for fraud in 1996, Stratton Oakmont employed just under 1,400 people, which was considered a small number for a stock brokerage.

Today an even wilder trading floor exists. Its members individually make and lose anywhere between a few bucks and millions of dollars every day, and it has been blamed for manipulating some of the biggest stocks on the Nasdaq. But this new financial force has no employees, no offices and no shared capital pool. In fact, the only thing it has in common with Belfort's trading floor is that it appears to consist primarily of men – although we don't even know that for sure.

WallStreetBets is a Reddit forum, a discussion board on one of the most popular websites in the world, focused on sharing ideas and strategies for trading equities and cryptocurrencies. By the end of 2021, the forum had over 12 million members, many times more people than have access to a Bloomberg terminal – the technology of choice for professional traders for the last few decades. This community shares tens of thousands of messages daily discussing individual stocks and trades and making crude jokes, mostly about Elon Musk. The forum has grown steadily since it was founded in 2012, but in January 2021 it exploded, gaining international attention. Users on the forum, armed with nothing but a smartphone, a 'free' trading app named Robinhood and anywhere from a hundred bucks to a million dollars in their individual accounts, began to target public stock prices of ailing companies such as Nokia, Blackberry and GameStop. These companies were targeted partly for their nostalgic branding; GameStop was a particular favourite place for teenagers to buy and sell physical cartridges for computer games a decade ago, before the advent of online gaming marketplaces. But the major reason the community focused on these shares was that they were being shorted by global hedge funds, including some multibillion-dollar institutions, who were hoping the stocks would collapse in value as the underlying businesses failed to perform.

By coordinating the buying of these stocks on the WallStreetBets forum, thousands of individual retail traders – traders not associated with a professional institution and trading their own money – made the share price rocket. And because of the way the financial institutions looking for GameStop's demise had structured their financing, what was a small move started by WallStreetBets' users quickly spiked into a 3,000 per cent rise in GameStop's share price.

The move was so significant that some funds such as Melvin Capital had to temporarily close trading and find emergency support, while one Reddit user, Keith Gill, who operated on YouTube and Twitter under the username 'Roaring Kitty', saw his $53,000 investment in GameStop stock reach a value of $48 million by the end of January.

Inevitably the GameStop stock has plummeted back down to earth since, undoubtedly with more people losing money than making it, and the almost 40-year-old business is working on how to reinvent itself. But the shock rise of an ailing stock, driven not by a single firm but by many sole traders working from home, and the subsequent losses suffered by major hedge funds, has already changed financial markets across the world, and been the subject of books and films. It is another example of how individuals who once needed the resources and networks of huge firms now have the ability to make a living working alone, even if it means taking risks with their own capital and dealing with the roller coaster of the stock market.

THE LONE CODER

Creating content, selling goods online and even financial trading are all increasingly popular ways to make a living online. However, one of the best-paid ways to sustain a comfortable living working for yourself today requires rather more experience to get started, and that's being a software engineer.

Many of the companies I work with will claim that the best products require full-time engineering teams working closely together, and that is often true. But as software has become critical to more industries and demand for software engineers has outstripped supply, many companies have had to hire freelancers, giving people with coding expertise the leverage and ability to fly solo if they wish.

The popular developer website Stack Overflow estimates that two million people around the world work this way today, and it's certainly lucrative for those who have chosen to do so. The annual salary of most software contractors is well above the average income, earning an average $61 per hour across the globe. According to Glassdoor, the average salary for a software contractor in the USA is around $100,000 per year, and that's before you adjust for more in-demand skills. While the very best developers won't match Teri or RoaringKitty's income in a year, they can make a very comfortable living, setting their own hours and income targets.

But the most successful self-employed developers are not people who sell their services per hour, but rather people who build code, applications, or products themselves, which they can then ship digitally to customers across the world. Selling products rather than just selling your time is infinitely more scalable and much more profitable when it works.

The best example of how a single software developer built a product that scaled globally and still serves billions of people today is the founder of Linux, the world's most prevalent operating software.

While many of us are aware of Windows, the operating system that made Bill Gates the richest man on earth, far fewer are aware of Linux and its creator, Linus Torvalds. Linus never seemed interested in building a big business. The Finnish computer scientist has been criticized for his direct style over the years. As he once said, 'I'd like to be a nice person and curse less and encourage people to grow rather than telling them they are idiots. I'm sorry – I tried, it's just not in me.'

Perhaps because of this blunt style, Linus has few and sometimes no direct employees, but has managed to work directly with over 15,000 individual collaborators at over 1,000 different organizations as the main developer of the Linux kernel, one of the single most important libraries of code on the planet today. In fact, with NASA using a version of Linux software in multiple missions, including a recent flight of an autonomous helicopter on the surface of Mars, it's the most important code off the planet as well.

While Linus hasn't contributed code to the Linux kernel for a while, and his original work is estimated to make up just 2 per cent of the total code base of modern versions of Linux, he does still have authority over what code is or isn't in the master version of Linux. To look at it another way, the person who controls arguably the most important code base on the internet, doesn't have any employees working on the product. And he achieved most of this work from his home office – often working from a treadmill – starting the remote work movement over 30 years before coronavirus forced many of us to join him.

BE THE PRODUCT YOU WANT TO SEE IN THE WORLD

What Linus Torvalds has achieved from his home study and walking desk, often without a single employee, was almost inconceivable a generation ago. Today, millions more people work this way, whether it be in content production or skilled crafts, as bedroom traders or software developers. As farms, factories and firms all begin to shrink, and employ fewer people, more of us will have to go solo. This will not be easy, both for financial and cultural reasons, but thankfully new technologies are giving us the ability to create products and services in industries well beyond those mentioned above.

I say it won't be easy as despite the extraordinary success of people like Teri, Linus or the shoemakers of Instagram above, a vast majority of people working in the creator-industry or gig-sector today struggle to make ends meet. As we will discuss in later chapters, the ability to supplement and smooth our income from online projects or part-time work may be a big part of our future way of working, but for many people it will never be enough to live off, despite the number of us who dream of being YouTube stars.

At the same time, as AI tools become more powerful, many of the goods produced by the creators mentioned above are becoming easier to replicate, with increasingly little skill. While the very best content creators will always command a decent fee, just as the best singers and footballers do, it is already hard enough to make money producing content, and that's before the arrival of generative AI models that specialize in making art, music and even short videos using simple text prompts.

Content producers aren't the only ones facing this new challenge – AI tools are lowering the barriers to entry, and so increasing competition, for many traditional white-collar jobs as well.

One company that pitched to me in early 2023 had taken the concept of using AI models to replace human-hires to an extreme. The two founders were the company's only human employees, but they showed me how they had built an entire team to help them run their business, composed of AI assistants. Customers could email issues to, and get a useful response from, their AI customer services assistant. They had an AI marketing assistant that could generate step-by-step guides to promote products on social media on demand. Their AI design assistant could create 100s of ad campaigns, with some simple text prompts, for the founders of the company to choose from. They even had an AI lawyer to answer questions about their terms and conditions.

(Example of an AI-generated ad – the shoe, design and tag line were all generated from a model trained on Nike advertisements with no human involvement. Source: thenextweb.com)

They are not alone in using AI agents to provide a service at a fraction of the cost it would usually take to hire such talent. Digital marketing company Codeword announced in January 2023 that they had created two AI 'interns', Aiden and Aiko, who were already assisting in editorial and engineering processes. In early 2023 Joshua Browder, the founder of the consumer-support company DoNotPay, announced that his company would be launching a host of 'robot lawyers' – powered by AI, who 'will be able to help a defendant fight off a traffic ticket in court.'

Scott Belsky, the American entrepreneur and Chief Product Officer at the software company Adobe, describes the change these innovations are bringing about as the *Death of Creativity's Learning Curve*. 'Welcome to an era,' he writes, 'in which the friction between an idea, and creatively expressing that idea, is removed. Whether it is as an image, an essay, an animated story or even a video, you can simply talk (or write) about what you see in your mind's eye and get immediate output.'

As the learning curve becomes shorter, founders will be able to achieve a lot more without needing to build a team or raise huge sums of funding, but the competition looking for creative ways to use these tools will become even more intense.

A HUMAN TOUCH

While these models are getting much better at replicating some types of human work and speeding up repetitive processes, they still cannot match human levels of ingenuity, creativity, or empathy.

Forecasting the impact of AI has been notoriously difficult to do, but there's good reason to believe that many skilled trades and health care roles, jobs which require multiple disciplines, dexterity and a personal touch, will still need to be provided by humans even in light of recent jumps in AI capabilities. A Goldman Sachs report produced in early 2023 forecasts that an astonishing two-thirds of *all roles* will be at least partially automated by AI, with the roles most exposed to replacement from AI likely to be in the legal and administrative space.

They also forecast that roles in construction, grounds maintenance, personal care and healthcare services will remain relatively untouched. This will almost certainly accelerate the trend of skilled trades like construction and health care commanding increasingly well-paid salaries, even for the self-employed. Research by the Federation of Master Builders in the UK found that while the average wage for a humanities university graduate in England was £32,000 a year, the average self-employed roofer was earning £42,000 a year across the UK once fully trained. When you focus in on regions, things look even rosier for tradespeople. In London, a bricklayer can earn wages of up to £90,000 a year. As more of us go solo in our careers, learning a skilled trade or working in healthcare seems like one of the best ways to navigate the challenge of AI. As we will come to later, this must come with an improvement in the way society values such important, human roles as well.

FINDING YOUR CO-PILOT

How can those of us in other careers stay ahead in such a seemingly fast changing world?

As the rise of creators like the content-producers, digital shopkeepers, and solo software engineers above show, in every instance where technology has made production of an asset more accessible it has created more entrepreneurial opportunities, rather than constrained them. There is no reason, yet, to expect that these new AI tools will be fundamentally different. So how will people seize them?

One concept I find useful, described by the CEO of Microsoft, Satya Nadella, is to think of this new generation of tools as co-pilots. They are there to help you reach a destination, but can only provide assistance; it's you, as the creative mind and entrepreneur, who chooses the destination and the route to get there. An even more optimistic term for this generation of tools is jetpacks – we could do the same thing without them, but with AI assistance we can get to our destination much quicker!

The entrepreneur and founder of the AI software company Qatalog, Tariq Rauf, suggests people looking to build their own product with these tools can use a simple framework he refers to as the 5Cs. First, you must *contain the problem*: this means you have to identify a niche where many people are really struggling and define their issues as tightly as possible. This will help you with your business proposition, but also in choosing what type of AI model you may need to help you, should the challenge be operational (such as ordering healthy food from local restaurants), content-based (such as writing reports about a new climate-changing technology), or data-driven (such as compiling data from different medical trials to help physicians).

Secondly, you must *construct the user-experience*. While new tools, like Google's BARD or Microsoft's AI-powered Bing, can help you to build a product, even if you have never coded before, only you can define what your potential customers need to navigate the service, whether it be a mobile app, a simple presentation or a complicated piece of hardware. This unique customer insight – an understanding of the pain that the people you are building for feel, and an idea of how to help them solve it – cannot be replicated by AI. Nor, if you work hard enough to understand it, can it be replicated by your competitors.

Thirdly, you need to *compose the product stack*. The stack is a term used to define the different pieces of technology you want to put together to build your product, and once again this is where only a creative and innovative mind can find a solution. For example, perhaps you want to automate the creation of unique parts for someone's home bookshelf – as the builder of the service, you need to pull together the tools which capture photos from a mobile app, automatically create 3D shelf models from online tools, and connect the output to a 3D-printing and shipping service to make sure the product is manufactured and delivered. Connecting unique solutions like this sounds easy but is often a key part of the defensibility of any small business.

Fourthly, you will have to *correct the errors*. Even the most advanced software services, and AI models, are full of bugs and make mistakes, sometimes rather creepily referred to as 'hallucinations' when it comes to services like ChatGPT. Human input is still required to get a product from 80 per cent correct to perfect, which is where a lot of potential customers still need support.

Finally, you must *capture value*. This seems obvious, but once you have defined your problem, built the interface and solution, and corrected the errors, you need to make sure your service does something faster, cheaper or more impactful than anything else out there to the point where customers are willing to pay for it. The *5Cs* are just one way to think about building a new business, but it certainly highlights many of the key issues aspirational entrepreneurs need to consider.

Looking back at the ways many hundreds of millions of people have gone solo in the last decade, from content creators to online retailers, will hopefully inspire many more people to try this way of working. The spread of new tools, such as generative AI, will empower entrepreneurs to build countless new products, but will mean those in the creator economy will have to change the way they work as well. As we look at the decade to come, there are many industries, from healthcare to space travel, which are being disrupted by technological advances and opening up even more ways for entrepreneurial minds to apply their creative thinking. Exploring some of these areas is the focus of the next chapter.

7

New frontiers

In my day job, I'm surrounded by optimists. The enormity of the challenge of building a start-up demands that those who take it on are both hugely optimistic, and perhaps a little in denial. Outside of the office, however, the prevailing mood can be very different. I often meet people who haven't started a business yet and who feel all the best ideas are taken, that the low-hanging fruits driven by the advent of personal computers and the internet have been eaten, and the barriers to getting started on something new are just too high. Some worry we are in for a period of significant economic challenge, of international instability, a rising cost of living, and high interest rates, making it harder to start a business. Even technology analysts are warning that the speed of development – in microprocessors and use of the internet – has begun to diminish.

These arguments have some merit. A handful of software companies, such as Google, Apple and Microsoft, seem to have consolidated their positions as the owners of many key pieces of our digital lives: search engines, smartphones, e-commerce and cloud computing have been run as near oligopolies for the last decade. Meanwhile, governments across the world are in a race to regulate technology companies, but seem to end up with legislation that cements the strength of incumbents. Large multinationals have the resources needed to adapt to new rules around content moderation or data protection, while start-ups struggle to keep up. On top of all of that, new AI models are being released at a rapid pace, meeting and exceeding the capabilities of many forms of human work from marketing content to coding. In this environment, you can be forgiven for thinking that we will all end up working for one of a handful of digital leviathans, rather than as creatives, freelancers and entrepreneurs starting up our own businesses. You might be tempted to heed the call from the pessimists, the talking heads fearful of change or jealous of the ambition of others, to simply stop trying because it's just not fair.

The rest of this chapter is my attempt to strongly reject this view. Warren Buffet, one of the most successful investors in history, likes to say: *Never bet against America.* But given the recent growth in entrepreneurship globally, it may be more accurate to say, *Never bet against humanity.* More than ever before, now is the time to start up; more than ever before the power is yours.

Even in industries which have seen the number of new businesses multiply in the last few decades, opportunities still abound. Despite the recent explosion of new financial services start-ups, which raised $100 billion in funding in 2021 alone, only 1 per cent of the total value of the financial services industry is currently run by technology businesses. In retail, a sector filled with millions of online stores – and hundreds of thousands of start-ups, alongside goliaths like Amazon and Alibaba – only 12 per cent of global commerce is done online today. Even in sectors that appeared to be dominated by 'big tech', such as social media and AI, disruptors like TikTok and OpenAI have arisen in the last couple of years, challenging the idea that these sectors were ever owned by unbeatable monopolies.

To get a sense of where new entrepreneurial opportunities lie ahead, let's look at what's changing in the fields of health, AI, energy, housing and the final frontier – space.

HEALTH

Health is our most important asset, underappreciated when we have good health but unavoidable when it is compromised. Improving human health is one of the most impactful, and hopefully rewarding, things any entrepreneur can attempt. Fortunately, a range of new innovations and treatments are now becoming available to spur innovation, driven by three big technological advancements – device miniaturization, personalized health data and greater data processing power.

To get a sense of the scale of improvement, take the advances we have made in understanding the building blocks of human life, DNA. The cost of sequencing a genome, a set of DNA instructions, has fallen by 99.9 per cent in the last 20 years, helping us decipher the heritage of our oldest ancestors, or spot a single cancerous cell in a sample of millions of healthy blood cells. But genomics is just the start. To get an accurate view of a human body, you need to capture the whole picture of what's happening inside it at any one time.

Not so long ago, devices which could accurately capture such information didn't exist, meaning that the vast majority of health care was based on analyzing the symptoms, rather than causes, of an illness and applying pattern recognition across patients.

Biomarkers – molecules in your body that could indicate a pathological process or a disease – could at one time be identified only by using hugely expensive and slow laboratories. The miniaturization of devices has meant that these can now be captured and recorded by home tests of your saliva, blood or urine. This means a doctor anywhere in the world, or a small team of physicians with a limited budget, can quickly get to cell-level accuracy in their diagnosis of a patient using a device small and cheap enough to be kept in your bathroom.

I mean bathroom quite literally. Withings, a French start-up, announced in 2023 the launch of its U-Scan product, a device placed in the toilet which can analyze urine. With more than 3000 metabolites, urine contains a huge amount of health data, and their product can capture and share this data with doctors or nutritionists at the click of a button.

While some people may find the idea of tiny devices monitoring them unnerving, this has huge implications for healthcare. In most modern health systems, you live in a bifurcated world. You are either healthy, in which case you are mostly left alone except for a few reminders to get some exercise and eat well. Or you are ill, in which case only a handful of large health providers have access to the tools that can help you. As demographics have changed, and with many health systems left underfunded, this traditional model is under strain globally.

Instead, technologies like those mentioned above can monitor your health continuously and accurately, unlocking new ways to spot diseases and treat patients, saving money and lives in the process. This next generation healthcare system will require a new infrastructure layer to connect systems and many new entrepreneurial healthcare providers to provide personalized insights and suggestions for you utilizing this wealth of information. New operating models for care delivery – like virtual and home-based care, asynchronous engagement and remote monitoring – are already having an impact.

I've seen this change first hand, sitting on the board of Sophia Genetics, a public software company that enables doctors to identify cancers and rare diseases from genomic data. This is, of course, helpful to the doctor's own patients but, because of the company's unique algorithms, the work of one doctor can be used to improve the accuracy of Sophia Genetics' software anywhere in the world. So, the accurate diagnosis of a certain cancer in a patient in Lyon, France, will increase the chances of a diagnosis of that cancer in a patient in Boston, USA.

Finding a breakthrough in this field no longer requires billions of pounds of investment, making innovation and entrepreneurship in health much more affordable. When I first met Sava Health, a company developing a much cheaper and sustainable continuous glucose monitor (CGM), they were working from converted accountants' offices in Shoreditch, London. This tall Victorian building looked like it belonged in a Dickens' novel, but the founders of Sava, Renato Circi and Rafael Michali, both graduates from Imperial College London, used each floor to develop different parts of their potentially game-changing medical device. Turning one floor into a certified wet lab, and another into a software development area, they are now in the process of testing a device which could make monitoring biomarkers like glucose accurate, painless and affordable for people anywhere in the world, with a fraction of the resources such a breakthrough would have required a decade ago.

Changing health outcomes doesn't mean you have to become a hardware expert. Software start-ups are also already making it increasingly cheaper to access care. Digital therapeutics company Kaia Health uses the selfie camera on your smartphone to monitor your movement as you perform stretches and exercises. Its 'computer vision' algorithms then make sure you are doing your physiotherapy properly and provides guidance as you recover from an injury. In clinical trials this approach has been shown to be twice as effective as regular in-person physio sessions, although the company still encourages patients to use a mix of in-person and digital care. Physiotherapists can also work remotely on their platform, taking on many more clients, while ensuring they are providing the best care combined with Kaia's AI.

In the near future, solo health care workers with access to tools like those mentioned above will be able to provide the same level of care as an entire specialist practice today. Entrepreneurial new companies like OneMedical in America and AVI Medical in Germany are already trialling this, offering traditional healthcare advice in a comfortable, in person setting but combining it with the offer of remote biometrics monitoring and 24/7 app-based care, giving patients and doctors the best of both worlds.

The impact of these recent innovations goes well beyond diagnosis, and encompasses treatment as well. Huge advances in research capabilities and therapeutics have allowed small teams of dedicated pharmacologists to achieve in weeks, what used to take large pharmaceutical companies decades. Just look at BioNTech, a German start-up that was able to develop the first COVID vaccine with barely 1,000 employees. They are now working on future cancer treatments using the same technology they'd developed in a fraction of the time and cost as was possible a decade ago.

As labs become more digital, and the machines they provide access to more affordable, a new generation of entrepreneurial biochemists and healthcare providers will emerge. Like BioNTech, an individual or a small group won't need large pharma companies to fund their research. Instead, they will be able to run their own experiments in virtual or fully automated laboratories. As Vijay Pande, an investor with the venture capital firm a16z, says, 'It's now time to build in healthcare.'

ARTIFICIAL INTELLIGENCE

As mentioned many times in this book, advances in the way AI models are built – in particular reinforcement learning, which teaches a model how to achieve a certain reward, and large language models (LLMs), which understand the statistical relationship between words – are quickly changing the ease with which individuals can get complex tasks done, and thus making it easier than ever for smaller companies and individuals to build smart products.

The impact these tools are expected to have on the economy is huge. Goldman Sachs says it was being conservative when it estimated that 'AI could raise annual US labour productivity growth by 1.5 percentage points over a 10-year period following widespread adoption,' but the team admits this figure could be much larger if AI and robotics prove capable of doing more difficult jobs. The final economic impact prediction? 'Generative AI could eventually increase annual global GDP by 7 per cent.'

There are myriad reasons to be both excited and anxious about the possibilities of AI models. Some worry about job replacement in the long run, but in the short run, as the writer Daniel Susskind argues, AI is far more likely to replace individual tasks than whole careers. 'There is a process of "task encroachment" at work, where machines gradually, but relentlessly, take on more tasks,' he writes. The question for entrepreneurs is thus how to use these new tools to make better products by optimizing such tasks.

How will this help entrepreneurs? As a first step, I asked the AI chatbot ChatGPT (using its GPT-4 model): 'How will advances

in artificial intelligence help entrepreneurs?' It responded with
four points:

1. Improved automation: Advances in AI will lead to increased automation of various
    business processes, which can help entrepreneurs save time and reduce costs. This can
    be especially beneficial for small businesses that have limited resources and need to
    streamline operations.
2. Better decision-making: AI can provide entrepreneurs with valuable insights and data-
    driven recommendations that can help them make better decisions. With access to large
    amounts of data and sophisticated algorithms, AI can help entrepreneurs identify trends,
    patterns, and opportunities that may not be immediately apparent.
3. Enhanced customer experience: By leveraging AI, entrepreneurs can create personalized
    customer experiences that can help build brand loyalty and drive sales. AI-powered
    chatbots and virtual assistants, for example, can help businesses provide 24/7 customer
    support and improve response times.
4. Increased innovation: AI can help entrepreneurs explore new business models and
    develop innovative products and services that can differentiate them from competitors.
    By leveraging AI to analyze market trends and customer preferences, entrepreneurs can
    identify untapped opportunities and create new revenue streams.

This is a useful summary but pretty generic. The accuracy rate of
such models makes them suitable for compiling quick answers or
first drafts, but not high-accuracy tasks such as writing a patient's
diagnosis or the crafting of legislation, where accuracy needs to
be 99.99 per cent. This is, however, the worst these models will
ever be. With each generation these models get more powerful,
and individuals become better at prompting and fine-tuning them
to their specific needs. The big leap for most of us will come when
these models move from generating content, to performing the
tasks themselves, known as actionable models.

One company leading the way on actioning AI is Writer.com.
Writer allows enterprises to create new product descriptions, or
internal knowledge guides, in their brand and style with the click
of a button using their proprietary AI model. Another is Levity.ai,
a platform where you can upload customer sales emails and tell it
which ones generated excited customer responses, and which ones
got little interest. Within minutes, Levity can plug into your email
provider and highlight similar emails from customers you may have

missed, and create new emails to send to future customers, trained on your own data and thus personalized to your needs. Using this service already saves me about 20 minutes a day responding to generic requests and cold emails – which adds up to a lot of time over the working year. Building a personal AI model to provide email responses like this would have cost over $100,000 just a few years ago. Today it costs less than $1000.

(This image from the *New York World* newspaper in 1923 didn't just predict machines would soon generate images for us – it even got the year right!)

Even more useful for budding innovators looking to use AI are agent frameworks like AutoGPT, a free piece of software which allows you to ask AI models to automate tasks through your command-line or web browser. These agents can be used like free and rapid researchers for entrepreneurs. For instance, an agent can already respond to commands like 'generate a plan to launch a novel type of walking boot' which it will do by using Google and summarizing market reports and consumer reviews of other walking boots.

We are still in the very early days of what new tools like generative AI and actionable models can do. What's undeniable, though, is that they will form the foundation of many millions of new products and businesses in the decade to come. If you're thinking about becoming an entrepreneur, experimenting with tools like those above is an obvious place to start.

ENERGY

Well before the 'tech bro' persona was associated with Silicon Valley, the cliché of a rich Californian was in fact an energy entrepreneur – an oil prospector who used the latest inventions in drilling and landscaping to identify new sources of 'black gold', turning their tiny energy start-ups into global titans of industry within a generation.

Modern day energy companies are a far cry from those cowboy days, and energy generation and transmission has become mostly centralized, dominated by a handful of heavily regulated providers, who in some cases abuse these oligopoly positions. The combination of regulation, political instability and oligopolistic behaviour has meant many energy bills have become more expensive in recent years. But we are now seeing a global shift in energy development so far-reaching that it could help us to tackle climate change, the cost of energy and rejuvenate our economies in the process.

Personal energy solutions are already a battleground for entrepreneurs. One big breakthrough has been in solar where, as in chip development and genomic sequencing, the cost of a photovoltaic (PV) cell has fallen almost exponentially in the last three decades. In 2022, small-scale solar for home and commercial use exploded, with China adding 51 gigawatts of capacity alone, that's as much as the USA, Germany and UK combined. This means an increasing number of individuals and businesses now control their energy usage and expenditure independently of the large providers.

In parts of the world where national infrastructure is not yet at the point that it can guarantee constant, accessible and green energy, entrepreneurs and start-ups are even more likely to benefit from decentralized energy provision – either through individual or community-scale projects. Mini solar grids are an increasingly popular way for remote towns to access cheap energy. One example of how small businesses are being set-up in this sector is Green Village Energy. This start-up has built a number of mini grids consisting of 126 solar panels for villages in Nigeria. This is enough to provide electricity for 340 households in an area, as well as powering small businesses, schools and a health clinic.

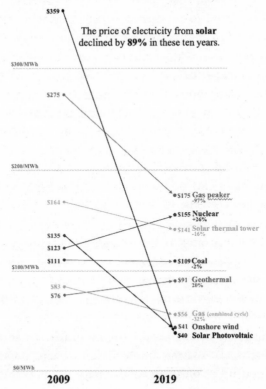

The price of electricity from new power plants

(Source: OurWorldinData.org, licensed under CC)

People with home renewable energy can independently manage their electricity usage to some extent, but solar and wind naturally fluctuate with the weather, making it difficult to predict when you will or will not have cheap power. Advances in batteries are now making home storage of energy a reality too. A battery the scale of a Tesla car battery would have cost almost $1 million in the 1990s, but costs just $12,000 today, another striking example of Wright's Law in action. Home batteries can now be purchased for a similar price and can store energy from solar when the sun is shining and release it when needed such as at night. In the not-too-distant future, it's feasible that in place of energy leviathans like EDF and ExxonMobil dominating our energy supply, there will be thousands of start-up businesses helping us balance and maintain our own energy generation solutions at home.

Even more powerful than home solar are small modular nuclear reactors (SMRs). They can range in size and can generate anywhere from less than 50 MW to a few 100 MW, compared to traditional nuclear reactors which typically have a capacity of over 1,000 MW. Because they are modular and simpler to construct, they are a lot more affordable and transportable.

SMRs are still in the development stage and are not yet commercially available. However, there are over 70 prototypes in development, and it is expected that SMRs will be able to provide electricity, heat and, potentially, input for hydrogen fuel. By the late 2020s SMRs could be providing energy to remote or off-grid locations or be a source of reliable and low-carbon energy for industrial processes, placed next to energy intensive projects like aluminium smelters. This means that rather than us all relying on a handful of large energy providers for the capital expenditure and operational expertise required to power industrial-scale factories, many small new energy companies could pop up in locations which couldn't previously access energy at reasonable costs.

Energy innovation isn't just coming from improved hardware like solar panels and batteries. Tibber is an energy company from Norway which gives individuals insight into how much energy they are using on a minute-by-minute basis via its smart mobile app. Their software can also automatically manage your energy usage. So, if you want to charge your electric vehicle or run the dishwasher, it will make sure these tasks are carried out when the renewable energy it supplies is at its cheapest. It will also balance usage and production for you if you've got solar panels or a heat pump. As Captain Planet, the blue cartoon hero, used to say, with Tibber 'The power is yours.'

Sadly, spreading innovation through new hardware and software in industries like energy is no easy task. Why? Because it is, according to the famous American investor Bill Janeway, a 'three-player game', a tussle between the market, finance and the state. Each one is required to enable the spread of new energy solutions, and in different countries different players in this three-way relationship can be blockers, making it a wicked problem to solve. The good news is that consumer demand, entrepreneurial zeal and finance for sustainable energy solutions exist in many parts of the world; the challenge will be getting the state on board as well.

In a period of much higher and more volatile energy prices, while we are also seeking to reduce our carbon emissions, it's understandable that entrepreneurs like those at Tibber or the many companies working on SMRs are looking for ways to generate clean, affordable and reliable energy as soon as possible. However, there are also several new energy technologies that are finally getting close enough to breakthroughs that could solve not just the world's current energy challenges but by the early 2030s solve all our energy needs going forward – and first and foremost among them all is fusion.

Fusion power has been a pipe dream for decades. The idea of generating energy by combining atomic nuclei has been around since the 1930s, when it was first proposed by physicist Enrico Fermi. However, it was not until the 1950s that scientists began to seriously study fusion as a potential source of energy, with the development of the first experimental devices. A series of recent breakthroughs has finally made the dream of fusion power feel more like a reality, and there have been several new start-ups launched to make this happen. Sam Altman, the CEO of OpenAI mentioned above, is an investor in one such company, Helion. The Washington-based company was founded in 2013 with the goal of producing low-cost clean electric energy using a fuel that is derived exclusively from water. Writing about Helion on his popular blog, Sam says that the company aims to '(produce) clean, continuous energy for 1 cent per kilowatt-hour, and manufacture enough power plants to satisfy the current electrical demand of earth in a ten year period.'

Given the uncertain timeline for fusion, you are probably better off investing in home solar energy or heat pumps in the meantime. If we can produce continuous clean energy at 1 cent per kilowatt-hour, however, the number of ways this will empower new entrepreneurs is endless. As Carl Sagan said, 'When we look up at night and view the stars, everything we see is shining because of distant nuclear fusion.' It may be coming down to earth sooner than we think.

HOUSING

On the more prosaic bricks-and-mortar level, housing has long been one of the sectors where individuals have made a living as entrepreneurs. Rather than being enabled by new technology most landlords and small property developers have been able to expand their business using another type of tool – cheap debt. As of 2018, independent landlords owned the majority of rental units in the US – 24 million units of the total 44 million – making property letting one of the most entrepreneurial pursuits in the country.

Property letting has been a lucrative business. As populations have expanded, and living arrangements changed, most rich nations haven't built sufficient houses to keep pace. In the last two decades alone, the average house price in America has soared by 130 per cent, and average rental value has increased with it.

In developed nations, the increase in the value of property has been driven more by a lack of supply, and the availability of financial products like mortgages, than homes becoming more luxurious or productive due to technical improvements. However, even where housebuilding has been increasing, in countries like China, prices have risen rapidly in the most desirable areas. According to data from the National Bureau of Statistics of China, the total number of new-build houses in China increased from 21.8 million in 2002 to 47.1 million in 2012, and then to 68.6 million in 2019. These figures may even be an undershoot because they do not include all houses built by individuals or by very small developers. Yet property prices in Shanghai increased by over 150 per cent between 2010 and 2019 as people wanted to move closer to high-paid work and the best amenities. In a recession, and with interest rates rising, these price rises are unlikely to continue and may even reverse, but even a significant fall in house prices will not fix the fundamental imbalance between supply and demand.

In the last few decades technological advances have done little to make home construction more affordable, at least in large cities. The average new home in the USA is 190 square metres (2,000 square feet), costs $300,000, not including the cost of land, and takes five months to build. Planning permission is another time-consuming hurdle which can spell the end of a project before it even gets going. The rise in costs of shipping during the pandemic and energy-driven inflation has also, temporarily at least, significantly increased the costs of materials, making constructing new homes even harder.

So now is an urgent time for improvements in the sustainability, speed and cost of constructing new homes. Fortunately, advancements in manufacturing techniques, such as 3D printing, smarter design software and robotics are finally making housebuilding more affordable, opening many new opportunities for tradespeople in the process.

While there have been many attempts to produce viable 3D-printed homes in the past, 2021 has seen the first successful examples: a Dutch couple became the first people in Europe to live in a 3D-printed home deemed to be legally hospitable. At scale, these homes take just five days to 'print', and massively reduce both the cost and the environmental impact of creating new properties.

The number of start-ups entering the housebuilding sector is accelerating. Austin-based 3D home printing company, ICON, raised over $207 million in 2021 to accelerate this trend. They made the first permitted 3D-printed house in the United States – a house 33 square metres (350 square feet) large which took 48 hours to 'print' – and the company has since claimed to be able to double that pace. Their ambitions don't stop at single homes. The company is now taking reservations for properties in a 100-property community in Texas Hill Country, all constructed using their huge 3D-printing robots.

More ambitiously, some entrepreneurs are working on building and reshaping entire cities. Ideas like charter cities – a city given a special jurisdiction to create a new governance system aimed at maximizing economic growth and innovation – have been around for a while. Groups like DoubleGDP, which has the grand ambition of doubling global GDP, have been set up to design software for such cities. They envisage new mixed-developments and cities where enhanced connectivity to energy and the internet will help deliver community and municipal services in startlingly more efficient and responsive ways.

The advent of new construction technologies with smarter cities should enable many millions more people to design and build homes themselves, reducing the cost of living, while utilizing advances in home energy services like home batteries, and personal internet providers, to lessen the load on local infrastructure as they grow. Reducing the largest cost in most people's lives – property – is not only good for our general well-being but will also give them the financial ability to invest in more entrepreneurial endeavours in the future as well.

SPACE

When there are so many challenges facing us here on earth, it is easy to dismiss the importance of expanding into space. But the final frontier is undergoing an entrepreneurial revolution at a much faster speed than even the great commercial explorations of the Indian Ocean or the Wild West, which could benefit us terrestrials as well.

Despite the dreams of a generation being ignited by the launch of Sputnik in the 1950s and the 1969 Moon landing, the massive complexity and costs involved in such endeavours meant getting stuff into space was, unlike the early days of flight, initially controlled by government.

However, the monopoly that governments have had on getting into space has ended, thanks to huge breakthroughs in new technologies and shifts in regulation. The Space Shuttle, NASA's most used space vehicle, entered service in 1981 and successfully launched 134 times before being retired in 2011. Each launch cost a staggering $1.8 billion, adjusting for inflation. As a result, the payload cost – the amount you had to pay to get stuff into Low Earth Orbit (LEO) – was $65,400/kg. But in the last decade private innovators have been allowed to compete to deliver payloads into space for the first time. The Falcon 9, developed by Elon Musk's SpaceX, can now send cargo to LEO for $2,600/kg, almost 30 times cheaper than the original Space Shuttle programme. The next generation of this launch system, Starship – another SpaceX designed rocket that looks more like a Jetsons cartoon than a space vehicle – intends to make transportation to space even cheaper. Starship will run on liquid methane, a much cheaper rocket fuel than liquid oxygen and kerosene, and is itself made from stainless steel instead of more traditional aerospace materials. As a result, if SpaceX can deliver this new rocket at its targeted cost of $5 million – and this remains a big *if* – it could reduce the cost of transportation to LEO to $10/kg – more than 100 times cheaper than even a Falcon 9 launch today.

What impact will this have on a new generation of entrepreneurs looking to build out-of-this-world businesses?

Companies like Orbital Insight are taking advantage of this dramatic fall in the cost of getting products into orbit by allowing more and more people to access data that was previously available only to the military, or to the very largest companies, using satellites. Now start-ups with even modest budgets can get detailed satellite data on almost anything – from the movement of cargo ships to working out where the best spot for their next high-street store is – based on traffic reports and land visualizations.

And on the horizon, entrepreneurs will be able to use this new spacefaring ability to sell much more than data. Varda Space Industries have raised over $50 million to accelerate manufacturing in space. Building on microgravity research conducted on board the International Space Station, Varda claims there are many high-performance products that can be made more effectively in zero gravity, including powerful fibre optics and breakthrough pharmaceuticals. They plan to launch their first 'space factory' in 2024. By giving people access to a factory in zero gravity, Varda believes they can enable a new wave of industrial applications. Their mission isn't *to boldly go*, but an equally grand, *to expand the economic bounds of humankind.*

Advances in space won't just mean we can travel to the stars, but also that we get around our own planet faster and more sustainably. In a paper imagining 'energy superabundance', created by technologies like Starship and fusion mentioned above, Austin Vernon and Eli Dourado calculate that, 'Flights that take 15 hours on a 747 could happen in an hour on a point-to-point rocket . . . Using new modes of suborbital travel, SpaceX's Starship launch system could take passengers from New York to Shanghai in 39 minutes.'

These are just five examples of industries that will be transformed by innovation and opened up to entrepreneurship in the coming years. Many of the innovations mentioned above, and the companies that are building them, will no doubt stumble. The few that do succeed, however, will be transformative. The entrepreneurial society is well and truly hurtling towards us. As referenced in the introduction, Michael S. Malone, in his 1985 book *The Big Score*, echoes again today: 'In the race for the world's technological leadership, it is increasingly coming down – as it should – to the solitary individual and his or her own imagination.'

As exciting as some of these innovations are, it will take much more than just technological breakthroughs to ensure that this future is one which supports *everyday-everyone* entrepreneurship. To make that possible we need to rethink some of the foundations of the world of work today, and the infrastructure on which we all rely. I think of these changes as the *digital scaffolding* of the twenty-first century, and it's what we'll look at next.

8

Digital scaffolds

As the number of traditional manufacturing and corporate jobs decline, and the tools at the disposal of entrepreneurs become cheaper, more powerful and more accessible, the rise of a more entrepreneurial economy seems inevitable.

But plenty of challenges remain to this innovation-led future. The global pandemic, growing political instability and economic volatility are combining in ways which have left most people understandably more worried about their employment than ever. In this global context, and with firms and factories shrinking, is the rise of a more volatile way of working going to be an unwelcome burden on people with no other choice?

Economic downturns are already correlated with a rise in entrepreneurship. One of the most detailed studies on business creation in America from the University of California showed that the financial crash of 2008 and the following Great Recession, saw the largest increase in entrepreneurship in decades. The formation rate of new businesses started to increase in 2007 before spiking in 2008. It hit its peak in 2009, when the rate was 17 per cent higher than it had been three years before. The only other significant spike reported in the study occurred from 2001 to 2003, the period following the dot-com crash. While I have no doubt most people saw positives in the opportunity to start a business in these periods, many were forced to, rather than chose to become entrepreneurs.

The challenge today is to work out how to make the coming entrepreneurial transition as successful, and equitable, as possible, while not repeating the mistakes of previous technological transformations, which saw swathes of society left behind or excluded altogether.

The rewards and opportunities for those countries that get this right are copious, and already evident in the booming pockets of entrepreneurship across the world, from the onshoring of high-end manufacturing jobs in the USA to the Chinese shopkeepers on Tmall. The coming chapters will explore how to ensure that as many people as possible benefit from this seismic shift in the way we will work, and how our education system, the welfare state and taxation, public services, businesses and indeed our very culture need to adapt. But before any of those changes can be made, the technological revolution that has fuelled this new era needs to be completed. To do that we must look at how the yawning *digital divide* that exists today can be bridged.

GETTING ONLINE

The digital divide – the split between people who have affordable access to the internet and the skills to use it, and those who don't – has been around for at least 30 years. It is an incarnation of a challenge that society has faced for many centuries, in one form or another. To be specific: *What are the tools and skills that every citizen needs to have a fair chance of thriving in the world around them? And what should civil societies do to ensure access?*

Historically the divide between those countries which trained and supported their populations to use the right technologies, and those that didn't, defined their very survival. Over the centuries the belief in investment in skills and infrastructure for every citizen, a social contract between us all, has provided universal access to new innovations from aqueducts to motorways, flushing toilets and radio stations. And so long as humans keep innovating, there will never be an end to the need to constantly invest in the latest advances, and support as many people as possible to access and utilize them.

The current digital divide is starker because of the speed of change, made clear by the inequalities in earnings and opportunities for those with access to the internet and digital devices – as well as, crucially, the skills to make the most of them – and those without.

The positive news is that in the last 20 years, this divide, at least in terms of internet connectivity and access to technology, has been closing. A large reason for this has been innovation and competition driving down the costs of devices and digital services, with the price of an entry-level internet-enabled laptop or smartphone falling precipitously over time (although the average costs of the 'latest' model of a smartphone has begun to rise again over the last five years). Similarly, digital connectivity has changed the world on a global scale in just 20 years; while fewer than 7 per cent of the world was online in 2000, over 50 per cent has daily access to the internet today, with penetration at over 90 per cent in the wealthiest countries such as the United States, the United Kingdom, Germany and France. (Interestingly, just two countries claim 100 per cent coverage: Monaco and Moldova.) Analogous trends can be seen in mobile phones. At the start of the 2000s, there were 740 million mobile phone subscriptions worldwide. Two decades later, by 2020 that number had surpassed 8 billion – there are now more phones than people on the planet.

A vast majority of this has been achieved through individual endeavour and corporate innovation. But dedicated government investment and philanthropic groups have played vital roles as well.

Take South Korea, the country with the fastest average internet speed of any major economy today. Astonishingly, in 1995 South Korea had only one internet user for every 100 people of working age. At the time, the government initiated the Korean Information Infrastructure project – a ten-year programme that started by connecting government buildings to the internet, and then financed the rollout of country-wide broadband by 1998. By 2000, within five years of the start of this infrastructure project, South Korea had connected 20 million citizens, almost 50 per cent of its population and more than Japan and France at the time, despite both being significantly richer and larger nations.

The Korean Information Infrastructure project worked by coordinating private finance and government bodies, rather than investing entirely out of the public purse. But thanks to its foresight, the overwhelming majority of South Koreans have access to the fastest internet network of any country on the planet today. So it is clear that government-directed solutions have already had a hugely positive impact on digital accessibility.

THE DIGITAL DIVIDE

While stories like this are a good reminder of how much of the world has been connected to the digital frontier in the last few decades, it would be too easy to get carried away and think that the revolution is finished. In fact, when it comes to even the most basic tenets of a digital-first economy, affordable and reliable access to the internet and internet-capable devices, a very real divide still exists today.

According to the Broadband Commission for Sustainable Development, which tracks internet adoption and advocates for greater connectivity, almost half the world still doesn't have access to broadband internet. In Low-Income Countries (LICs), a monthly broadband subscription costs 12 per cent of average national income, far higher than the UN target of less than 2 per cent by 2025. Similarly, the cost of a basic smartphone, which hovers at $150, represents more than 1.2 months' wages in LICs. And laptops, which are required for most productive aspects of online work, cost on average three to four times that. No wonder, then, that internet connectivity still lags even where there is coverage. The issue is so serious that the UN has incorporated access to the internet within Goal 9 of its 17 Sustainable Development Goals: 'Significantly increase access to information and communications technology and strive to provide universal and affordable access to the Internet'.

For those countries which are still struggling to reach mass connectivity, the need for help is clear. In 2021, on the thirty-second birthday of the invention of the Web, Tim Berners-Lee, its inventor and Rosemary Leith, the co-founder of the Web Foundation, argued in an open letter that in light of the dividing impact of the coronavirus and the following pandemic, investment in connectivity was both a moral and economic emergency.

They argue that internet access must now be recognized as a basic right in the same way that clean water and electricity was in the last century – achievements that improved both the health and livelihoods of billions of people.

But their argument was also an economic one, and a challenge that with focus and the resources of government and the private sector could be solved by 2030. Bringing the remaining three billion people without affordable and dependable access to the internet online in the next five years, in the same way Korea managed to do, would be a huge boon for the global economy.

The Alliance for Affordable Internet (A4AI), an initiative of the Web Foundation, calculated that $428 billion would be needed to provide everyone in the world with a quality broadband connection and basic devices. On its own, of course, that seems like an astronomical amount. But compared to the economic returns, it is an investment worth considering. The sum amounts to $116 per person for the more than 3 billion people who remain offline today.

Berners-Lee argues that giving billions more people access to the digital tools needed to learn, earn and create, should be seen as a down payment for future generations that would deliver 'incredible returns in the form of economic growth and social empowerment.' Their work suggests that just a 10 per cent increase in 'digital natives' would result in a 2 per cent rise in a LIC's GDP, which would translate to trillions of pounds of GDP growth globally. If those numbers hold, it would certainly be both morally wrong and economically incoherent not to put the A4AI plan into action.

The recognition that stable, open, affordable and fast broadband is a human right, as important a provision to people as clean water and energy, seems inevitable.

THE AGE OF AMBITION

Perhaps the most astonishing turnaround in a country's embrace of new technologies and entrepreneurship, even if it is far from a model in other regards today, is China. In 1977, *The New York Times* ran a headline about Chinese innovation that summed up their challenge as 'the long march to irrelevance'. The country had all but outlawed not just owning a business but, to some extent, owning anything at all. After painful decades of economic collapse, crumbling institutions and even hunger and starvation, small groups of farmers sought to take things into their own hands. And as these rebel groups managed to prove that some private ownership and individual responsibility could lead to better crop yields, the mega-liner that is the Chinese economy began to change course.

Individual-owned enterprises were legalized in China in 1981. By 1984, Chinese leadership was already beginning not just to embrace entrepreneurship, but broadly to promote it. The shift happened so quickly that Orville Schell entitled his 1984 book on China *To Get Rich is Glorious*, a quotation attributed to Deng Xiaoping, the leader of the People's Republic of China from 1978 to 1989. Although that phrase was a simplified version of the words Deng actually uttered, they certainly marked a shift in tone and spirit, with the future premier espousing a drive to wealth creation that had been sanctionable with imprisonment only a decade earlier.

While this embrace of entrepreneurship could have been seen as a short-term and pragmatic approach, it soon became a national obsession. In his book *Age of Ambition*, Evan Osnos of *The New Yorker* chronicles how, by 1990, the entrepreneurial firestorm in China was transforming not just the economy but the fabric of the country's entire culture. This was most powerfully encapsulated by the way the Chinese phrase for ambition, *wild hearts*, went in less than a generation from being considered a vice that should be chastised and eradicated, to a virtue whose importance was espoused by civic lessons in high schools.

Since then, many parts of this entrepreneurial agenda have continued to grow. In his 2016 address to the National People's Congress, Premier Li Keqiang mentioned the word *innovation* 59 times, and *entrepreneurship* no fewer than 22 times. In 2022, Li gave a speech promoting *mass entrepreneurship*, in which he celebrated the fact that new market entrants and start-ups create the majority of the country's 13 million new urban jobs every year.

Furthermore, the individuals who embraced new software and applied them to the Chinese market have benefited financially from this entrepreneurial surge unlike almost any group in history. Hundreds of millions of people have come out of poverty in China thanks in part to this renewed entrepreneurialism. There are seemingly endless examples where individuals have gone from grinding poverty to extreme wealth in a single generation by building Chinese technology businesses in particular.

One such person is Zhou Qunfei. Qunfei was born in Hunan Province, southern China, in 1970. After losing her mother at the age of five, she was brought up by her father, an injured soldier turned bicycle repair man, and dropped out of high school at 16. Following a stint working in Shenzhen at the age of 22, she set out to start her own company, which began with her brother, sister and cousins working together out of their three-bedroom apartment.

Armed with just $3,000 in life savings, Zhou started by refining watch lenses. But as the business grew, she spotted an opportunity in mobile phones. Lens Technology, which began in that small flat, went on to become a $70 billion company in just over a decade, manufacturing the touchscreens on mobile phones used by billions of people every day.

Zhou is just one of a new generation of exceptionally successful, and wealthy, Chinese entrepreneurs, who have created giant businesses from a standing start over the span of a single generation. Today China is the world's second largest producer of unicorns – non-listed companies valued at over $1 billion – with some of their breakthrough technology successes, including Baidu, Alibaba, Tencent and Xiaomi, now among the world's most powerful internet businesses. Although many of these now have uneasy, if not conflicting, relationships with the state, the previous policy of supporting entrepreneurship and helping hundreds of millions of people move from agricultural jobs to being part of a modern workforce must be recognized as an astonishing success in improving welfare and closing the skills divide with the rest of the world.

As in the West, an initial boom in superstar entrepreneurs was quickly followed by a broader shift in working habits towards personal entrepreneurship and creative projects, using the new technologies and platforms the previous wave unleashed.

For China, the cultural, economic and technical shifts towards a more entrepreneurial state have been transformative. While statistics are not always as reliable as might be desired, there are over five million new small businesses or sole proprietorships set up every year (the definition varies by industry and State Council, but broadly these are businesses with <250 employees.) While many of these small businesses paid a terrible toll during the initial period of the pandemic – with some estimates suggesting that one out of six self-employed businesses were closed in China – it appeared that work resumption rates for this segment had returned to over 80 per cent by the summer of 2022. In the face of a global pandemic more and more Chinese people are choosing entrepreneurial careers.

ANTI-VIRUS SOFTWARE

The digital divide is not just a challenge for lower income nations. It remains an issue across the globe. And nothing could have revealed the stark contrast between the digital haves and have-nots like the global pandemic of 2020 and 2021.

'We've seen two years' worth of digital transformation in two months'. That was how Satya Nadella, CEO of Microsoft, described the immediate impact of the coronavirus as the pandemic led to travel restrictions and stay-in-place orders across the world in the first half of 2020. As a huge swathe of the global economy shifted online almost overnight, access to stable digital infrastructure quickly moved from a priority to a necessity.

For higher-income nations, where digital penetration is high, the switch to remote work, with a majority of interactions done at home and online rather than in person, was remarkably smooth. Microsoft Teams, the company's videoconferencing platform, more than doubled in size to 115 million daily participants by October 2020, while Zoom, its largest competitor, saw daily participants grow from an average of 10 million in December 2019 to 300 million barely a year later.

While many sectors of the economy that couldn't 'go online' were severely disrupted by the pandemic, developed countries like the UK, which has a large service economy and a relatively high proportion of users with home devices and broadband internet connections, saw relatively low disruption to the work of its knowledge professionals. In fact, some sectors, such as companies in the technology sector, saw both record productivity and investment in 2020 and 2021.

But this experience was far from universal. Just as certain parts of the professional class saw little disruption, those on the other side of the digital divide saw their lives and livelihoods totally upended. Millions of workers in the hospitality, travel and industrial sectors were forced to stay at home and unable to work. And millions more people were asked to work but couldn't due to a lack of devices or support.

In response to the pandemic, the Federal Communications Commission (FCC), America's major telecoms regulator, recognized the scale of this challenge and committed to provide $10 billion of aid to support people who couldn't afford access to the internet or smart devices, calling it the 'emergency broadband benefit programme'. This level of response, matching emergency funds for some natural disasters in its scale and speed, acknowledged just how difficult life without access to digital services has become.

The digital divide was just as stark in the education system. Almost every child in the world had their education disrupted by the coronavirus. An August 2020 policy brief presented by the United Nations suggested that school closures and learning disruptions had impacted 94 per cent of the world's student population – an unprecedented event in modern history. And one of the most significant determinants of just how far a child's education was disrupted was their access (or lack thereof) to the internet and appropriate devices.

In his evidence to the UK's Lords Select Committee on the impact of COVID in late 2020 on education, Ian Macrae, a Director at the British telecoms regulator Ofcom, stated that '11 per cent of households in the UK do not have stable internet access', and of these, a further 10 per cent, or 280,000 households, cannot afford smartphone-enabled internet access. It was unclear how any child in these homes could continue with their education.

An even bigger challenge for students was access to the skills needed to use these devices to continue to attend classes while at home. Evidence given to the same Lords Select Committee in 2020 found that 28 per cent of pupils had inappropriate IT access in the home, rising to 43 per cent in schools with the highest levels of deprivation. This difference, between those who could access lessons and those who could not, has been estimated to have created an 18-month learning gap between classmates, for the want of a £200 laptop. While COVID certainly exacerbated the digital divide for students without appropriate home IT, it was just as critical an issue before the pandemic as well.

The Good Things Foundation, a UK based not-for-profit aiming to tackle the digital divide, reported in 2019 that 23 per cent of children in the poorest families in the UK didn't have home access to broadband and a laptop, desktop or tablet. This lack of digital access and skills doesn't just cost people in terms of future opportunities; it has an immediate impact on their current finances as well. Families with low digital engagement spend an average of £348 more per year on utility bills because of the added time of dealing with paperwork, associated administrative and travel costs and even fines resulting from not having stable internet access and the ability to use web portals.

Without access to the internet, essential services, like medical appointments and home schooling, became impossible overnight. Thankfully, within a few months of the lockdown being announced, the major internet companies in the UK, telecommunications providers and the government coordinated to offer cheaper internet access to those who needed it. And the UK government has now committed to achieving at least 85 per cent gigabit internet connectivity for the country by 2025.

This is an obvious issue to make a priority. In almost every way you measure it, making sure every child and household has access to a suitable internet-enabled device, and broadband internet would have made surviving the pandemic easier, and has many tangible benefits beyond that too.

But the solution to this digital gulf is not as simple as giving everyone a computer. Since 2005, Nicholas Negroponte, the founder of Massachusetts Institute of Technology's Media Lab, has been a proponent of the One Laptop per Child (OLPC) initiative, an ambitious attempt to provide every child in LICs with a durable, internet-connected device at the cost of just $100. At the time this was particularly ambitious, given the average cost of a laptop was closer to $1,500. The programme initially attempted to build dedicated devices and software specifically for education. But while over three million of its devices were shipped, it fell well behind the original goals. In part this was due to timing – neither the hardware or software were cheap enough when they started – and critical mistakes were made in the design of the devices. But arguably the biggest oversight was the lack of training and support given to students and teachers so they could understand how best to use the device once it had been delivered.

Where previous efforts to connect young and mature students with new digital tools have proven to be successful, it has been when those devices have been matched by equal efforts in changing the culture, training and incentives to develop the skills to make the most out of them.

As early as the 1980s, the UK led the world in giving students access to micro-computers, as they were then known, through the BBC Computer Literacy Project (CLP). As a 2012 review of the project by NESTA comments, the project had many facets, but at its core it had 'the grand ambition to change the culture of computing in Britain's homes'.

Launched in 1981, the effort to get educational computers into the hands of schools and homes started slowly, with 13,000 sales of a purposefully designed home computer – the BBC Micro – in its first year, but it quickly exploded. By 1985, three years after launch, around 500,000 Micros had been sold, and by 1986, a later version of the BBC Micro, the Master Compact, was being used in 82 per cent of primary schools and 92 per cent of secondary schools.

But the BBC Micro programme wasn't just designed to put devices into schools. Alongside the device, the project launched television programmes, dedicated content through magazines and software modules, and a broad teacher training programme. The BBC ran television and radio shows such as *The Computer Programme* and *Micro Live*. Individual programmes had audiences of up to 1.2 million and the NESTA review estimated that this programming reached 16 per cent of the adult population.

Despite the huge success in school rollout, the legacy of the BBC Micro programme is still mixed. For many people, the Micro was their first experience of a computer, and more importantly the first experience of being given any kind of digital training. The project had also hoped to be the foundation of a successful British computing industry. While many companies were spun out of projects associated with the Micro, most notably ARM, it was a small competitor from the US, Apple, which ultimately won the home computing market.

Modern efforts to close the digital divide must reflect on the successes and struggles of previous efforts like the BBC Computer Literacy Project and One Laptop per Child. One of the best blueprints for how this might be done can be found in Singapore. Before the pandemic, the Singaporean Ministry of Education had already planned to provide a laptop and training in digital skills, such as online payments, to every secondary-school child by 2028. This policy was put in place even though the consultancy

Roland Berger's *Digital Inclusion Index* already ranked Singapore top among 82 countries globally for digital inclusion in 2020. However, recognizing both the greater need for connectivity driven by the pandemic and a desire to be a world leader in digital skills they're already close to achieving this goal in 2023. Financing this new initiative was not the most controversial part of the plan. The Government had already distributed 20,000 laptops and 8,000 internet dongles to students in the first few months of the pandemic. The challenge, it seems, was making sure that the laptops were used to further education – and weren't just a distraction.

As the Education Minister Ong Ye Kung noted in the announcement, just providing a child with a laptop does little to close the gap, or prepare children for the digital economy into which they are likely to graduate. Equally important as the device itself is the support around the student. This may mean preloading software on the device, to make sure it is used as a creative and educational tool rather than for entertainment. It also means integrating the use of the device into the curricula, making sure capabilities are as much a part of learning as content. But it also refers to the support from teachers, parents and the community to provide direction and encouragement to develop and utilize these new skills.

PLAYING CATCH-UP

A foundation of digital skills as well as access to digital devices, a combination I refer to as *digital scaffolding*, is essential to everyone in modern society, but it is easy to overlook how often such supports are missing.

In their submission to the House of Lords' enquiry in 2020, the Cambridge Centre for Housing & Planning Research (CCHPR) argued that rather than thinking of the digital divide as a binary issue, it is better to think about digital inclusion and exclusion as a 'spectrum of digital engagement from internet access to skills, to being able to make use of online resources for beneficial outcomes'.

In other words, simply having an internet connection does not stop someone being digitally excluded. In 2018, 10 per cent of the adult population of the UK were estimated to be 'internet non-users', with access to broadband internet but the inability to use basic services. One recent analysis suggested 9 million people are unable to access the internet by themselves and 11.7 million lack the digital skills for everyday life.

It is increasingly clear that a lack of basic digital skills is no longer just a barrier to working in the modern economy, it cuts people out of large parts of social and civic life as well. In the UK, FutureDotNow is a charity aimed at supporting people to develop digital skills and works with 5,000 hyperlocal aides to help people access the internet and gain digital skills to navigate everyday life. At the start of lockdown, Liz Williams MBE, the chief executive, described the day of a single community organizer working at a community-run coffee shop near my hometown in Stockport, the northwest of England:

'Her day started with an 80-year-old woman who was in tears because she didn't know if she was going to be able to pick up her husband's prescription later in the week because they were both over 80 and didn't have access to the internet. Then there was a mum who was looking to order nappies [online] but didn't have access to the internet at home so used the facilities at the coffee shop.'

It cannot fall solely on the state or philanthropic donations from corporations to provide digital skills. We all have a responsibility to learn and to support others to learn as well. But as digital connectivity and skills are required to participate in even the most basic civic activities, more must be done to provide the digital scaffolding to help everyone adjust to this new world.

The Good Things Foundation, which partly funds initiatives like FutureDotNow, advocates for a great Digital Catch Up in the UK, which would cost around £130 million over four years, to help 4.5 million people reach a functional skill level. This would be delivered through *digital health hubs*, embedded in local communities, providing advice, support and training on everything from setting up a video call with loved ones to navigating the new world of online healthcare. If their costing is right, this would again be not just a socially positive step to take, but an economically valuable one as well.

Providing a baseline of skills to allow everyone to participate in our digital society is surely a prerequisite for a more entrepreneurial economy. But equipping people with the ability to thrive in that environment is another matter entirely – and to achieve that we must find a way to support people to make this transition financially and psychologically as well.

9

For better or worse

The financial and psychological stress that comes with a fast-changing work environment is already a reality for many of us, even in what were once thought of as stable professions. The average person already moves jobs every four years, and in the UK, 1 in 10 young people don't expect their job to exist by the end of the year. As job stability continues to deteriorate, more people will be self-employed, by choice or out of necessity. Whether they see themselves as start-up entrepreneurs, sole traders, gig workers or freelancers, they are going to find themselves building a career outside traditional support structures. But are we ready, as a society, for all the change this entails?

Making a successful switch from a life of steady employment and predictable income to the world of entrepreneurship is no mean feat. Anna Codrea-Rado is the author of *You're the Business: How to Build a Successful Career When You Strike Out Alone*, a practical, warts-and-all guide to the ups and downs of taking work into your own hands. She was a successful journalist, working in New York for the *Guardian*, when she began to realize that she was not sure she was cut out for a long career path within a large organization.

'I was ambitious,' she says. 'I wanted to progress in my career. But I'm a writer. I knew I wanted to write, rather than climb up through the company, become a manager and be paid for organizing and taking responsibility for other people. That's what gets rewarded in a big media group. It's a different skill set, and it's not what I wanted to do with my life.'

Journalism is one of those professions where freelancing has always been part of the mix. Every publication uses freelance contributors, but those on the inside, with secure, salaried positions, have always tended to see the freelancer as an outsider. Codrea-Rado was one of them. 'When I was a staff journalist, I probably thought, like everyone else, that freelancing was for people who couldn't get a proper job,' she admits.

In the end it took the shock of an unexpected redundancy notice to force her to confront her future. When the blow came, in 2017, she decided it was time to work for herself. She had good contacts and was confident of her own abilities, but she understood that trading a staff job for the independence, flexibility and autonomy of freelancing came with its own risks and insecurities. 'One of the first decisions I made was that I would have to move back to the UK. However successful you are, there is always the danger that you might become ill, and the cost of healthcare in America means any sickness or accident could quickly lead to disaster. In Britain, the fact that we have the National Health Service substantially reduces the risk for anyone working freelance or starting any other sort of business. People don't talk about that. Maybe we take it for granted. But it's a vital safety net.'

For Anna, this unexpected move gave her a number of new freedoms. She now writes about business, culture and technology for many leading journals in the US and Britain and co-hosted the *Is This Working?* podcast. For her, running what she calls 'a business of one' has been a hard-earned success. Yet it has turned out to be quite different from what she expected. 'I thought freelancing would be all the bits about my job that I enjoyed – the writing, doing the actual work – minus the boss and the office politics and the commuting. But that's not what it is. It turns out that you are the entire business. You're not just your own boss; you're your own employee, at the same time – the head of finance, the head of marketing, the IT manager, the bookkeeper, everything. It's like taking the company I used to work for and rolling it all into one person. And that person's you. It's hard to get your head around, until you actually do it.'

Journalism is a career in which the business of one is a well-trodden path. And there are a huge number of trades and professions where going it alone has long been the norm. Plumbers, roofers and locksmiths, window cleaners, gardeners and antique dealers, musicians, actors and accountants, taxi drivers and taxidermists, translators, consultants, piano teachers and upholsterers, dentists and photographers, small shopkeepers and many software specialists all work in areas where selling their specialized services can form the basis for a successful one-person business. The problem, traditionally, has been income security. How can you build that business into something which provides financial stability?

STARING INTO THE ABYSS

Alongside the financial challenge of entrepreneurship is the psychological challenge created by the uncertainty, responsibility and even loneliness of running a business by yourself. Elon Musk describes running a start-up as 'chewing glass and staring into the abyss'. Being an entrepreneur is difficult and rife with risk and uncertainty. Odds are, a start-up will fail. According to *Inc.* magazine, which claims to be America's small business magazine, half of all new businesses close their doors before they've been open five years. Dealing with this constant level of risk, according to Musk, is not something people are naturally designed to deal with psychologically. At a *New York Times* event in 2013 he put it like this: 'You have to put in incredible amounts of effort and huge amounts of stress – and it's much more painful than most people realize. And most companies die . . . we didn't evolve with companies; we evolved to respond to real death. And even though a company's death is not real, it's not like someone is physically dying, your brain doesn't quite understand that on the limbic system level.'

Of course, different types of work suit different personalities. Some people are naturally risk-averse. Some like structure and routine, a secure framework, a predictable income, the social pleasures of working as part of a team and the comforting knowledge that they are entitled to benefits like holiday and sick pay and, eventually, a liveable pension.

Others hate taking orders from anyone, have an unshakeable belief in their own skills and judgement and have always known they'd be happier working for themselves. They need money, too, of course. But their thirst for independence makes them more inclined to live with risk and uncertainty and more confident that they can make a business of one work for them.

Either way, providing ongoing support to entrepreneurs of any mindset is something that will have to be dealt with at scale in the *everyday-everyone* economy.

While far from solved, this is a challenge parts of Silicon Valley have begun to address. A large part of my job working on the board of multiple fast-growing but high-risk technology companies, is supporting founders as they deal with the immense pressures that being an entrepreneur can bring. Bernard Liautaud, a successful entrepreneur and my partner at Balderton, refers to this part of the job as *committed care* – a recognition of how personally difficult starting and running a business can be and the responsibility of investors to support them.

One way the technology community tries to support each other is through peer groups where individuals can share experiences and provide or receive emotional support and practical advice. Historically this was done in person, through groups like the Young Presidents' Organization (YPO) which brought together entrepreneurs to discuss the personal challenges of building their businesses. Today this is more commonly done online, with many public forums and private groups of founders supporting each other. Some self-employed technologists now advocate for *building openly*. This way of working entails putting your daily progress online for a select community, or the whole world, to see. Sharing their experiences and progress is useful from a practical perspective, as it can provide a sense of accountability, and helps founders get feedback to improve their product. Building openly can also be helpful for finding mentors and getting mental health support too. While some people worry that building this way may attract competitors and copycats, most who chose this way of working value the emotional support it brings.

It will take more than finding supportive online communities to help people make this transition. To tackle some of the psychological and financial insecurity this work entails will require legislative changes to protect entrepreneurial and freelance workers from the more extreme ends of this way of working as well. The gig economy has created many new jobs that appear to offer the chance of an independent existence – but in some cases, this is a mirage. Uber, for example, has always insisted that it is merely a technology platform, bringing together drivers and customers for their mutual benefit. In most countries, its drivers own their own cars and are classed as independent contractors, rather than employees and many work this way. But recent court cases across the globe have raised questions about this model and some countries have introduced the idea that long-serving drivers may be entitled to the national minimum wage and some benefits, such as sickness and holiday pay, that would normally be associated with a job on the payroll.

There is also growing opposition to the use of so-called *zero-hours contracts*, which have been a key element in the rapid expansion of firms in sectors such as deliveries, care work and hospitality, for similar reasons. A zero-hours contract does bring with it employee rights and benefits, at least in theory, though it doesn't guarantee a minimum number of hours' work (or income) per week and it does require the employee to work at a specific place and during specific hours, robbing them of the autonomy that contract work is supposed to offer in the first place.

The degree of independence that's actually available to a zero-hours contractor or, say, an Uber driver varies by platform. Whereas a self-employed plumber, for example, is free to turn down a job for any reason (if, for example, it would involve driving 30 miles), a gig worker can be penalized by the company's algorithms for turning down a similarly unattractive job.

To get a sense of the impact of such contracts, the British journalist James Bloodworth explored the realities of the gig economy by spending six months working undercover – as a care worker in Blackpool, as an Uber driver and as a warehouseman in one of Amazon's regional fulfilment centres. In his book *Hired*, he presented a depressing picture of the conditions in these jobs. Many of the workers Bloodworth came across were on zero-hours contracts, which meant they were waiting each week to be told the number of gigs they could expect in the week to come. Far from enjoying independence and autonomy, these workers were subject to disciplinary regimes, drug tests and airport-style security that made the experience feel exploitative for some, rather than empowering.

His conclusion was that many of the rights and benefits the labour movements and trade unions had won, over several generations – from sick pay and holidays to maternity and paternity leave, pensions and safe, civilized working conditions – had been undermined, not by political opposition but by technological innovation and ruthlessly demanding business models.

Even in higher-paid areas of work like freelance journalism, many people still face significant cultural and resource barriers to succeeding as an individual contractor. Unpaid internships, a common way to get started in the profession, effectively exclude youngsters from low-income backgrounds who cannot afford to work for nothing. People who are less able to take financial risks are often locked out by the creative economy's most popular business model, which involves building an audience by offering free content before eventually monetizing your service. As Money.com's Kristen Bahler put it recently, 'Devoting yourself to the life of a starving artist is a lot less risky if your family has enough money to make sure you don't actually starve.'

Entrepreneurial careers are not unique in being psychologically tough and stressful. The French philosopher Émile Durkheim wrote compellingly throughout his career about how capitalism in general makes us richer and yet frequently more miserable; in other economic models, people's identities are closely tied to belonging to a clan or a class. Their beliefs and attitudes, their work and status are determined mostly from the facts of their birth. But the strength of capitalism is, in theory, that the individual gets to choose almost everything: what job to take, what religion to follow, who to marry. We become authors of our own destinies. If things go well, we can take all the credit; if things go badly, there is no one else to blame. This is true of traditional careers but is exacerbated even further in entrepreneurial work.

Despite the additional psychological challenges, the idea of working for yourself, freelancing, or starting your own business still holds an enduring and magnetic attraction for millions of people who baulk at more conventional careers – or feel less than fulfilled by them. The experience of working from home, imposed by the recent pandemic, has been an eye-opener. Many of those who enjoyed the freedom and flexibility of working in a less supervised environment, and who felt no obvious decline in their productivity, are wondering why they should return to the office. It is only a small step from there to thinking, *If I am going to ditch the office, why shouldn't I ditch the boss, too?*

In those months of uncertainty, when many had no guarantee that there'd still be a job waiting on their return, people had plenty of opportunity to go back to first principles and take a fresh look at the relationship between their own ambitions and their employers' priorities.

Inc.com explains the record-breaking numbers of new start-ups being launched as an outcome of this reassessment. 'Working for someone else means your upside is always capped,' it declared. Getting an annual raise slightly above inflation is typically the best you can expect. Yet your downside is always huge. Getting laid off can mean your income disappears overnight – and in many countries you also lose other support such as healthcare as well as the psychological loss of the considerable effort, dedication and personal sacrifices you've made to support the company to date.

'Working for someone else? Limited potential upside. Massive potential downside. That's a reality people have been forced to come to grips with over the course of the year.'

That's clearly an oversimplification. Staff jobs can be well paid, enhanced with healthcare insurance, share options and other benefits, not to mention dependably secure – until they're not. But there's no doubt that the COVID pandemic has shaken people's faith and triggered a lot of radical rethinking.

A UK survey, compiled a few years ago by the Office for National Statistics, interviewed a representative sample of nearly 1,500 self-employed people about their motivations and experiences. It confirmed that having more independence, flexibility and enjoying greater job satisfaction were seen as the main advantages of being self-employed, and these traits were valued more highly than just earning more than a salaried job would pay. Despite the significant psychological challenges, and in some cases physical ones too, self-employment was seen as 'a positive choice' for the majority.

In fact, 84 per cent said *life was better when you worked for yourself.* Even among the one-third of respondents who believed they were financially worse off being self-employed, nearly three-quarters said their lives were better overall.

So while it is true that the psychological aspects of working as an entrepreneur can be extremely difficult, those who have made the leap come out of it on average feeling better off, mentally if not financially.

And money isn't everything. While I mostly argue that this shift in work to a more entrepreneurial society is an economically positive one, the day-to-day financial experience of most entrepreneurs is plagued with insecurity. A far less sunny study that focused on Britain's self-employed, produced by the Institute for Fiscal Studies in November 2020, found that over half of the solo self-employed and owner-managers surveyed earned less than £300 a week, though 11 per cent of owner-managers had 'very high earnings' of more than £62,000 a year (compared with 5 per cent of employees and 3 per cent of sole traders).

Despite the generally lower level of self-employed earnings, this IFS briefing found plenty of evidence that those who worked for themselves were happier, enjoyed higher levels of job satisfaction and reported lower levels of anxiety than employees. 'There may be non-pecuniary benefits that compensate for lower earnings, even for those who only became self-employed as a result of poor labour market opportunities,' it concluded. It also pointed out that the self-employed had 'more opportunities to engage in avoidance or evasion of tax' and could be shown to under-report their earnings by 10–13 per cent, based on random audits of tax returns and careful comparisons of spending and income. So, the slightly lower than average earnings of certain freelance professions may not be wholly accurate.

Despite the speed of change, people are also generally optimistic about the overall impact of new technology and the future of work. Research by the think tank Data for Progress shows that a substantial majority of Americans see large technology companies as more a force for good than not, despite reservations over the behaviour of some of today's tech giants, including labour practices, social media's hate speech and data privacy issues.

So while challenges remain, the data suggests that on average people are happy embracing tech-enabled, entrepreneurial work. By curbing the power of those who seek to take advantage of such workers, through improved hiring practices from online marketplaces to the reform of *zero hour* contracts (as detailed in the entrepreneurs' manifesto at the end of this book), we can offer more financial stability for this growing way of working. By helping people to find their online or in-person peer groups, we can help them navigate the psychological challenge of working this way too.

The next step in supporting people in the transition to a more entrepreneurial economy is to rethink how people get exposure to the skills needed to be an entrepreneur in the first place.

A new skills bargain

Almost 40 years ago, high school teacher Steve Mariotti decided to start teaching entrepreneurship to his students at a school in the South Bronx, an area which at the time had the highest poverty rate in New York City. Spurred into action by a school edict that discouraged teachers from talking about money in the classroom, and in Mariotti's own words, a welfare system that said: 'You may not own anything or else we won't support you anymore', the native Michigan was convinced that an entire generation of young people from low-income and severely deprived backgrounds were being held back from considering a more entrepreneurial career.

'Entrepreneurship is one of the most relevant skills to impart to high schoolers, and yet the subject was viewed with disdain,' he explained in a 2020 podcast interview. 'I remember one class I was teaching, I was struggling to get through to this class on maths. In the curriculum, there was just nothing there for them. Then I asked them a simple question: *How much would you pay for this wristwatch?* Every student in the class had an opinion.'

In 1987, Mariotti founded the Network for Teaching Entrepreneurship (NFTE), a non-profit organization which gives at-risk youth from low-income backgrounds opportunities to receive entrepreneurial education while at high school. While it may have started in New York, the programme is now global, reflecting both the appeal of the course itself and the demand for services like it. Today, China is its fastest-growing market, and some of his almost 30 books, which explain in very accessible terms the basics of starting and running a business, now run into their 40th editions.

The fact that Steve Mariotti and his extracurricular NFTE programme are so popular is just one example of how little the existing curricula in so many countries – even in supposedly more entrepreneurial ones like the USA – do to educate and encourage people to strike out on their own.

CEOs in the classroom

It is commonly claimed that you can't teach someone to be an entrepreneur, that it is instead something personal, a deep character trait (or flaw). This tendency to dismiss it as an academic subject, unworthy of being taught in schools, has seen entrepreneurship pushed to the edge of most curricula, resulting in education systems around the world that are primarily calibrated to teach 4–18-year-olds the foundational skills required for specific categories of employment and civil society rather than focusing on providing the skills that students may need to build their own businesses in a much more volatile economic environment.

I believe that this is the wrong way round. To paraphrase Picasso: 'All children are born creative, the challenge is to remain creative as we grow up.' As we age, our entrepreneurial opportunities increase, but without proper support from a young age, our confidence to take risks, think creatively and look for novel solutions can be stunted. This is why education is so critical to entrepreneurship.

So we must start providing such support early, which demands a change to our education system. If Henry Ford were teleported to a modern automotive factory, he would barely recognize the machines and processes operating today compared to the assembly lines he built. Similarly, Florence Nightingale would be astonished by modern operating theatres, compared to the ones she set-up in the nineteenth century. But if you teleported a teacher from the last century into a modern classroom, they would see little in the way of change, and could even pick up some textbooks and continue the lesson, such has been the pace of change in education.

In the coming decades it is clear that the skills needed to survive and thrive in the world of work will be radically different to those provided by most schools today. Providing the digital scaffolding for people to get online is an important first step. But, even more importantly, people will need to develop the skills needed to use this new infrastructure and adapt to a more volatile and demanding job market throughout their lives.

While few countries have fully embraced this need, there are plenty of examples of programmes today which help students develop the robustness and creativity required through exposure to entrepreneurship. Take the Junior Achievement (JA) Programme, which has been running in Europe since 1919 and is the most widely taught entrepreneurship programme in the world. Each year over 350,000 high school students enrol and take a business idea from inception through to liquidation, guided by trained teachers. A study that followed 9,731 Swedish participants in the programme over 16 years found that they were not only more likely to start a business than non-participants but were likely to be better at it as well. Those who participated in the project as teens went on to earn on average 10.2 per cent more from entrepreneurship a decade later compared with entrepreneurs who hadn't – and more than their peers who had pursued other career paths.

Or take Germany's highly successful CDTM programme, which has been around since 1998. The Center for Digital Technology and Management (CDTM) offers students an interdisciplinary add-on study programme that combines digital technologies with management theory and practice. The CDTM curriculum is designed to give students the skills and knowledge necessary to become successful innovators, offering courses on topics such as business model development, digital marketing and venture capital. In addition, the CDTM provides students with access to a network of entrepreneurs, innovators, investors and mentors. As of 2022, the programme has seen over 1,000 graduates start a total of 240 companies, which have raised a combined $5.4 billion from international investors for their companies. It's distinct from a traditional MBA programme, being an add-on to other studies and focusing specifically on high-innovation businesses. Other universities should take note.

On top of the clear financial benefits for the participants of these programmes, they also focus on the entrepreneurial character traits that every entrepreneur, from global successes to one-person businesses, needs to develop over a specific technical or financial skill set.

The EntreComp entrepreneurship competition, an EU-wide programme experienced by tens of thousands of students, states explicitly that it is about developing 'the capacity to act upon opportunities and ideas to create value for others.' In fact, there is evidence to suggest that dedicated entrepreneurship programmes help students improve their scores across the curriculum. In their *Educating Future Founders* report of 2020, the excellent UK-based think tank The Entrepreneurs Network argued that 'the psychological traits developed through enterprise education, such as creativity, analytical thinking, persistence, and confidence, have clear applications in other subjects . . . a student might persist to solve a difficult maths problem when in the past they would have given up. Alternatively, the confidence developed through an entrepreneurship education programme may lead students to raise their hand and participate more in lessons.' Giving a student a sense of ownership and agency, the key qualities of any entrepreneur, could clearly have positive effects across their academic career even if they never start a business.

Such programmes needn't be about starting your own business specifically but rather seek to instil some of the fundamental skills that form the foundations of a more entrepreneurial mindset. Synthesis, an online school created by executives from SpaceX, offers twice-weekly courses for students with a cohort of peers focused on team-building games, teaching concepts such as risk management and skills such as negotiation, qualities few modern academic courses cover.

A review of the NFTE in 2016, some 30 years after Steve Mariotti originally founded it, revealed the primary benefit its alumni claimed to have gained from the experience was the 'Ability to be self-reliant and responsible'. In a world of much greater volatility, this is perhaps the most important skill anyone could have.

Adding dedicated entrepreneurship programmes, which focus on encouraging students to think creatively of how to solve problems *and* then put those ideas into practice, would be an impactful way to help young people prepare for the new world of work, and far more useful than the baseline of ICT skills taught widely today which can quickly go stale.

LIFELONG LEARNING

Many people who have left formal education are now facing a combination of forces that are reshaping the landscape of work like never before. Automation is already reducing demand for many existing jobs, while the increased pace in technological innovation means that even highly valuable skills that were expected to last a generation, can lose their relevance in a matter of years. Helping people to navigate these changes requires an even more fundamental change in the way we think about skills development beyond the school.

The rise of automation, and resulting mass unemployment, has been a concern for centuries. From the nineteenth-century Luddites, who smashed textile machines during Britain's Industrial Revolution for fear of job replacement, to protests by horse-and-carriage operators in the early twentieth century against the motor cab, technological change has been met with both fear and anger by segments of almost every industry. And while globalization and failed political ideologies have undoubtedly been the cause of most periods of high unemployment in the last century, it's clear that the speed of change in the latest technological upheaval, driven by smart, connected and automated solutions, will have a significant impact on the type of skills people need in future.

A 2018 McKinsey and Company report, which aligns with similar research papers in the field, claimed that up to 800 million existing jobs, or a third of the global workforce, could be automated by 2030. It also acknowledges that many people will move into different roles within the same or similar industries. However, it still concludes that as many as 375 million people globally – including 23 per cent of the workforce – will see their current job titles disappear altogether and will need to seek entirely new professions. 'This will require training at the mid-career level at a scale we've not seen in this country [the USA], or any other country before,' says Susan Lund, a Director of Research at the firm.

And the people being affected aren't just older, manual workers who have often been most disadvantaged by historical advancements in areas like robotics. Carl Melin, a research director at Futurion, a Swedish think tank funded by trade unions, says: 'We see the average age (of workers needing retraining) going down every year,' and adds: 'Increasingly, workers in their mid-30s are finding their skills are out of date.'

Sweden is arguably one of the best-prepared countries in the world for mass automation. The country spends a significantly higher proportion of its GDP than average on employment transition services, known as job security councils, which promise individualized support for each person made redundant. If Sweden is worried with such high levels of investment already in place, it is fair to say we ought all to be concerned.

While automation, the replacement of human-led jobs with automated robots or software, is clearly a huge challenge, just as big a challenge is skill redundancy – i.e. the replacement of one skill with another, human-led skill. Historically, many economists argued that innovation-led economies had higher demand for STEM-educated workers, resulting in increased earning inequalities while those without STEM skills sought to catch up.

However, the increased speed of technological change now means that even the most sought after and highly paid technical skills today can become completely irrelevant in a matter of years.

A seminal study run by Harvard economists David Deming and Kadeem Noray showed that, contrary to received wisdom, STEM skills are becoming obsolete within increasingly shorter time frames. The researchers looked at 22 million job vacancies between 2007 and 2019 and showed that for vacancies posted by the same firm for the same high-paying (over $100k per year) occupation, almost 30 per cent required completely new skills by 2019. Even more startlingly, 16 per cent of computer and mathematical job vacancies in 2007 listed a skill that had become entirely obsolete by 2019. Simply learning the latest programming language is in no way a guarantee you will be in high demand for more than a few years.

They concluded that college graduates majoring in career-oriented fields such as computer science, engineering and economics earn higher starting wages because they learn job-relevant skills in school, but that for high-ability college graduates, the advantage to majoring in STEM is *completely erased by age 34*, versus majoring in any other subject.

These findings will ring true for many recent entrepreneurs. As the tools we use to build businesses and products change, the key skills required move further away from mastery of a specific skill set, such as using Python in data science, or operating a genetic sequencing machine, and rely more and more on the individual's ability to identify an opportunity, learn a new skill and solve a problem.

LEADING THE WAY

Given the increasing velocity of technological change, simply shifting our existing educational system to focus more on scientific, technical and digital skills will not be anywhere near enough. Instead, we first need to set in place the foundations for a more entrepreneurial approach to the world of work, and then provide adaptable, effective and lifelong learning opportunities for people to understand how to build products, solutions and businesses as well as to keep up with this pace of change. The era where someone's formal education ended at high school or graduate level is truly over.

The good news, however, is that while it may sound like a revolution in education is required, much of this shift is already underway.

A 2022 survey from the consultancy ECMC found that only 51 per cent of Gen Zs want to pursue a four-year college degree, down from 71 per cent just a few years ago. Instead, 56 per cent of this young generation believed that a skill-based education would be more valuable in the future. It also found that over half a billion people already use online resources like YouTube to learn new skills for free – lifelong learning is already happening at scale.

This movement goes well beyond the under 25s. Sarah, 46 and a single parent of three, knew she wanted to go back to work when the right moment came, but didn't know where to start. 'I'd been bringing up children for such a long time and I was really well away from the labour market,' she said in a 2020 interview on the state of online learning with UK think tank Demos. 'So it was quite a struggle to think where to begin.' She accepted that she needed to develop her skills, but studying in person wasn't viable given her family commitments. 'Being in the position I am, it's quite hard to actually go and do a course. I hadn't got time, I had children, I'm on my own and I hadn't got any money. So it's not like you can just up and do a course, you've got to learn another way'.

Sarah found herself facing the same challenge as many people in the modern labour market, and in particular women with caring responsibilities. So she did what many mums do, and turned to Mumsnet, a leading online community for mothers. 'There were lots of women who were obviously more developed in their careers than I was,' she recalled. 'But I found I could still talk to them, and I was able to learn things just by talking about what they did.' From there she started building a network through Twitter, and via those connections began working as a freelance copy editor of national press articles. 'Just to know that I'm good enough was a huge confidence boost.'

Sarah is just one example of the estimated 20 million people who have used online platforms, communities and courses to help with work or find a new profession in the UK alone. While the extent to which people already develop new skills online varies, from watching the odd YouTube guide to completing remote courses, initial research into this often self-directed and self-funded approach suggests it is highly beneficial. In the Demos study of almost 20,000 respondents, more than three quarters of people who learn online (77 per cent) say it boosted their mental health. Their research also showed that 30 per cent of the UK working population have used internet-based learning to raise their pay, with a median pay rise being equivalent to £3,640 per year for a 35-hour week, while almost 33 per cent have already used online learning to help them get a new job or start their own business.

As far as a winning solution goes – finding an approach to learning that improves mental health, raises pay and helps people retain or start a new job – can hardly be beaten. And new ways to learn are being developed at a rapid pace, with ever-improving online solutions for people to develop even highly technical skills and start new businesses.

Labster is a Danish company which started in 2011 with the goal of making learning laboratory work accessible to everyone. It was founded by Mads Tvillinggaard Bonde, who trained in labs while studying for his PHD in synthetic biology. While there, he was frustrated that even at world-leading institutions like Harvard and Denmark's Technical University, access to the laboratories and the machines he needed was very limited. 'These were some of the best funded laboratories in the world, that spent tens of millions of dollars on equipment, but I had to wait days sometimes to do even basic tasks, and had very little time to learn or experiment.'

So he and his co-founder set out to change the way people could learn in laboratories, by making them virtual. 'We started off with online models of the simplest machines, you could click along on a website and follow the graphics, it was pretty basic, but much better than the static textbooks,' he explains. After much iteration, the pair developed one of the first 'virtual' labs – an immersive, 3D laboratory that helped students to learn online how to use the latest machines, from preparing cancer samples for mass spectrometry to exploring the potential of new gene therapies. After raising over $100 million in venture capital, the company is now used by 2,000 institutions across the globe, giving 3 million people access to virtual labs and courses that were previously both inaccessible and unaffordable.

While solutions like virtual reality labs, and gamified biology lessons, may sound niche, innovation is happening in more traditional areas of education as well. For example, Jolt, an Israeli online learning company founded in 2016, builds personalized courses to replace traditional institutions offering MBAs, a popular postgraduate accreditation. Rather than require people to take one to two years out of their career, and part with an average of £30,000+ to get an MBA, Jolt's on a mission to provide highly effective, live learning experiences around people's current work commitments.

By being online, Jolt can connect students with teachers anywhere in the world. This means the professors leading each course are often in full-time work as well but enjoy teaching around the side. On their platform you can choose to join live lessons from current or recent employees from Tesla, learn about the modern supply chain, or explore the latest in marketing technologies with employees from Google. The platform's scheduling software means that it always tries to find the best time for a lesson or lecture, based on the attendees, and continues to connect students as they learn with mentors and job opportunities, based on their profiles and performance. By utilizing software, and avoiding the overheads of large campuses or full-time professors, Jolt is able to provide all of this to students at less than 10 per cent of the cost of a traditional MBA. The company was acquired in 2022 by education group Global University Systems to take its technology international.

Even AI – often positioned as the cause of possible job insecurity – is now being used to support students of all ages to learn new skills, although not all institutions have embraced its educational capabilities. Only a few months after their launch, services like Bard and ChatGPT were being adopted so quickly by students that New York City's Department of Education banned them from use in schoolwork or being present on student's devices. It's hardly the first-time students have adopted new technology faster than schools could integrate them. 'Maths teachers have been through this before, with the calculator long ago and the Photomath homework smartphone app more recently. History teachers weathered the storms of Wikipedia and Google,' wrote Anne Bruder, the academic dean and an English teacher at an independent school in Massachusetts. 'Now, it's time for English teachers to gather their wits and jump into the fray.'

'In just the first few days after it was released to the public, I watched my students ask this AI bot to interpret Emily Dickinson's poems and write whole essays about those same poems in her elliptical, enigmatic style.' Quite the achievement for a service that was made open to the public just a few months earlier.

Anne was right to recall the early days of the calculator becoming affordable for students. A survey in the mid-1970s found that at that time, 72 per cent of teachers did not approve of the use of calculators for children in seventh grade. Once they had become widely available, and more teachers had seen students using them, professional and public attitudes quickly shifted with over 84 per cent of teachers in a similar survey approving of their use in classrooms for older age groups by the late 1970s. It still took until the mid-1990s for calculators to be a part of most curriculum in the United States.

Much like the calculator and Wikipedia, most uses of ChatGPT appear to be to help people learn new skills, not cheat on their English homework. A popular use is to develop code for specific applications. You can ask it, for example, to give you a step-by-step guide of how to create a website and mobile application for a new product, and it can generate the results instantly and in simple language, massively reducing the time needed to learn how to get a product online.

Other AI models, like Meta's Galactica, have been developed to help summarize scientific papers, to make them far more accessible to millions of keen minds. The company eventually pulled the

AI after a brief launch in November 2022 due to consistent inaccuracies, and Sam Altman, the CEO of OpenAI, the creator of ChatGPT, also said in a tweet in December 2022: 'It's a mistake to be relying on it for anything important right now. It's a preview of progress.' However, it's clear such models are not far off being fantastic learning companions to help anyone accelerate their understanding of a new field.

YouTube and Labster, ChatGPT and Galactica are just a few examples of how new solutions are being found to broaden access to education, reduce costs and provide choice for a generation of self-directed and more entrepreneurial learners. But despite a high level of interest from people in using online platforms to learn new skills, and many innovative new solutions coming to market, there remain significant barriers to serving the needs of this new generation of independent, lifelong learners.

AN A* POLICY

Most countries, and many political parties, have recognized the challenge of adapting education for a new world of work, both in schools and throughout life, and say that it is a priority – but action has been slow. In my opinion there are three 'A's any government needs to get to grips with to pass the test posed by lifelong learning: *accessibility*, *affordability* and *accreditation*.

Tackling accessibility and affordability in particular should be top of mind for any government keen to take on this challenge. Demos' study of online learning revealed that of those people who do go online to improve their skills, only 17 per cent, under one in five, do so with the support of their employers, while even fewer are incentivized to do so with any financial support or time off from work. Finding the motivation to take on a challenge like developing a new skill is tough at the best of times, but having to find time to do this around existing work commitments, and scrabbling to find the money to pay for such courses, can be a huge deterrent.

Where do people, in particular those people on low pay, with long hours or with care commitments, find the time or support to train? Even if new technologies mean that it doesn't take 10,000 hours to perfect a skill, as Malcolm Gladwell once suggested in his book *Outliers*, it's certainly a significant commitment. And this isn't just a challenge for people in low-pay roles. In their 2019 book *Ghost Work*, anthropologist Mary L. Gray and computer scientist Siddharth Suri argue that despite the apparent cultural norm of high-paying and elite firms giving employees time to explore new ideas and skills, the lived reality for even high-paid roles is very different. 'A common complaint among tech founders and recruiters trying to hire programmers . . . is that no one can seem to find good hires who have all the skills and experience they want, yet no company wants to invest in training up workers because no one expects anyone to stay at the same job for more than a few years.

'Every job expects programmers to work day and night on tight deadlines to ship products, leaving them burnt out and with no time or energy to develop their skills.'

In other words, developing new skills, even in the highest-paying roles, is a major challenge. Even though everyone would benefit few people have the time, resources or desire to put in the extra effort for it to happen.

To avoid this skills trap – where employees may not have the time to learn new skills or try out new ideas and in return contribute more to their company as well as their own well-being – we need to find a way to normalize lifelong learning and reskilling. One obvious way to fix this challenge is to make learning part of any employment contract. In an economy where skills depreciate more quickly over time, and firms seek to make savings by replacing skilled employees with automation, it makes more sense than ever that an employer should contribute to their workforce's skill set because they stand to benefit greatly from upskilled teams.

Just as the labour movements in periods of previous technological innovation sought new settlements between employees and bosses for rights such as sick pay and maternity and paternity support, the right to train and learn ought to be considered an essential part of the employment contract of the twenty-first century. Many governments have already experimented with similar concepts. But instigating a minimum of 40 hours' paid leave a year, the equivalent of five days, to be used for any accredited skills course – either by supplementing time outside of working hours or as days off from regular work – would be enough to enable even people in some of the most precarious roles to learn new skills.

While providing 40 hours of paid leave would be a game changer for many people *in employment*, for the many and growing number of people who are freelancing, sole traders or unemployed and looking to learn how to start a new venture, provisions from employers aren't much help. To give entrants into the entrepreneurial economy a chance of developing new skills, we must find other routes to making training accessible and affordable, which in turn means adapting how existing further education is funded to reflect this new demand for skills.

Who pays for what when it comes to education is always a thorny issue. Compulsory, state-funded education in the United Kingdom has existed for only 140 years, a relatively small period given the immense impact it has had. Debates have raged in every generation over how much current taxpayers should fund the next generation's education, from the rights and wrongs of grammar schools, university tuition and even the school meals children are offered, in term time and holidays. Yet the biggest shift in educational funding in the last two decades has been the steep rise in the cost and scale of graduate education, and the resulting debt burden for students – particularly those in the USA. The average cost of attending a four-year degree in America was $26,120 per year in 2018, or $104,480 over four years. The comparable cost for the same four-year degree in 1989 was half of that – $52,892 adjusted for inflation. This figure would be completely unaffordable without student loans, which are designed to cover the costs of attending university and are then paid back over the lifetime of the student as they enter the workforce.

However, with decreasing returns to specific skill sets developed at university, the wage premium assumed to come with this expensive level of education has waned over the years. At the same time, these astronomical costs have put students from poorer backgrounds off the idea of going to university in the first place. Concerned about taking on such levels of debt, they miss out on many other life-changing opportunities.

While the USA is an outlier in terms of the sheer scale of its student debt, with total outstanding student loans now surpassing all other areas of borrowing except mortgages it is certainly not alone in the challenge of financing further education. The UK, too, has seen the average debt with which a student leaves university treble in the last two decades.

But the future world of work will require regular retraining, and new and innovative approaches to learning are being developed all the time, so it is clear that focusing educational investment heavily on the three to four years of expensive, graduate education at university is a model that will continue to work for only a minority of people.

Instead, to make lifelong learning more affordable, especially for freelancers and entrepreneurs, we need to repurpose the student loan facility to be a lifelong government-backed learning loan that can also be used for accredited modular, part-time and virtual courses, repayable once a borrower's earnings pass a certain level, as is the design of many typical student loans today. By repurposing student loans in this way, and opening them up to many more providers than just universities, future students could get access to courses as and when they need them throughout their lives – whether they be recent returners to the workforce like Sarah, aspiring biologists using Labster, or on-the-job reskillers using online courses like Jolt. It would also inevitably bring down the cost of reskilling, by introducing competition for this tranche of education spending.

QUID PRO QUO

As well as making services more affordable, we also need to ensure that ground-breaking new technologies are accessible, to give students the ability to experiment and new entrepreneurs a chance to compete with incumbent companies.

One example of how students and aspiring founders can be given access to technologies is in the availability of laboratories in technical areas such as biotech, quantum computing and high-end manufacturing. Historically, access to expensive equipment was limited to employees at large organizations, academics at universities or in government-owned research and defence facilities. As detailed in this book, in many fields such as biotech and advanced materials, the machines required to test and produce new products have fallen rapidly in cost, making them more affordable, but still far from free. Space in a wet lab – where chemicals, drugs and biological matter are handled – is estimated to cost around ten times more per square foot than a traditional office, driven in part by the need for new machines, but also by dated regulations and planning limitations, which artificially inflate the price. Even in universities, which receive huge sums of public funding, only a handful of people are allowed to access cutting-edge facilities, despite the knowledge of how to use such machines becoming much more widely available online.

Changing this should be a priority for any society keen on supporting a new wave of entrepreneurship. Just as the mass availability of personal computers and the internet had huge societal benefits, so will opening up access to new facilities in emerging industries. In the PC-era, supportive policies and innovative business models were required to make these machines available in schools, libraries and internet cafés, before they became so cheap that people could afford to have one in their homes or offices. The same is undoubtedly true of many new technologies today. There are plenty of models already up and running that show how to get this right. Manchester's National Graphene Institute, which cost £60 million, was designed to provide access to the knowledge and infrastructure that innovators in advanced materials, specifically graphene, will need to launch products on top of breakthroughs in university-led research. Building similar centres of excellence for other frontier technologies is an obvious policy choice.

Governments could lean into this opportunity further, by making access to their national markets dependent on a set amount of any new technology being made open to all. For instance, should a major pharmaceutical company wish to build a new lab, or an automotive company open a new automated manufacturing plant, then some time must be dedicated to providing access to the machines to *qualified* students and entrepreneurs. This is especially important when it comes to AI. In order to ensure new AI models enable entrepreneurship, not stifle it, then the software developers behind these models must be mandated to open up the *weights and biases*, the information which determines the output of a model, to the public, perhaps after a certain period of exclusivity.

PASSING THE BAR

While financial support to learn, and access to new facilities to experiment, may be both desirable and effective in opening up lifelong learning, we will only solve the problem of accessibility and affordability if we overcome the final test in education: accreditation.

Let me first acknowledge that many entrepreneurs are flippant about the value of accreditations and certificates. There is rightly far more of a focus on the *potential* of a candidate than on what they have achieved to date. For instance, Tobias Lütke, the founder of $100 billion software company Shopify, said in 2021 that 'we hire on future potential . . . we all have to requalify for our jobs every year'. So looking back at someone's CV is far less important than looking forward at what they can achieve, at least to tech start-ups

Indeed, there are already signs that historical accreditation is becoming less important in the new world of work. TestGorilla provides online tests which employers can build in a matter of minutes to assess a candidate's abilities in anything from basic accounting to warehouse logistics. Its 8,000 clients have decided to drop the CV as part of their assessment process and instead look for current skills. By ignoring a candidate's education history and looking only at what an applicant can achieve in live tests and interviews created by the TestGorilla software, employers can reduce biases and according to their research – coordinated with the consultancy Bain – find better and more diverse candidates as well.

However, in many professions, accreditation, such as a formal degree from a recognized university or trade body, is still a fundamental requirement when applying for roles. And this is especially true for freelancers, where new relationships have to be regularly built with clients looking for validation of your skills.

So as we move towards a more entrepreneurial economy, making sure accreditations such as formal degrees are accessible to people outside of traditional learning routes is essential. This will be especially important for the increasing number of people pursuing degrees at later stages of their lives, who already have other caring or work commitments.

One short-term fix would be to encourage universities to open up their accreditation schemes for remote learners (for a minimum fee to cover administration). This would mean that a self-directed learner, of any age, could sit exams for existing degrees, such as Materials Engineering at M.I.T, Mathematics at Cambridge or Digital Design at the Royal College of Arts even if they hadn't studied there in person. While they wouldn't have the same experience of being a full-time and in person student, opening up examinations and thus accreditation of these courses would incentivize people to learn new skills without the demands of going back to being a full-time student. Multiple universities have been experimenting with this type of co-branded accreditation scheme, with varied success. As more and more people look to change roles in the modern workplace, demand for such offerings will be certain to follow as well.

Another way to provide skills and improve access to accreditation for this new world of work is to broaden the number of organizations which can offer degrees. In 2018 in the UK, only 175 bodies were able to award graduate-level degrees, with around 2,700 across Europe as a whole. These institutions have increased the number of places offered to match demand over the last decade but are now creaking under the volumes. As a generation of students were both encouraged and given finance to seek degree-level qualifications, the supply and choice in where to get them has not kept pace with demand. If the whole working population must now be considered as perennial students, far more accrediting bodies will be needed.

In the UK, a handful of new accredited bodies have been given parliamentary assent in the last few years, offering students exciting and challenging new ways to learn. One example is the Dyson Institute, a joint venture between Dyson, a global engineering company, and Warwick University designed to bridge the UK's engineering skills gap. Speaking at the launch of the affectionately named *Dyson degree* in 2020, Sir James Dyson stated clearly that the venture would offer a very different university experience. 'This is not a traditional university education, it is not for the faint-hearted,' he said. 'Technology is developing at such speed that rigorous academic study benefits from immediate application.'

Unlike traditional degrees, students at the Dyson Institute of Engineering and Technology are paid to attend (there are no tuition fees, but students do pay for their accommodation), and have a mixture of academic, in-work and hands-on training.

The more hands-on approach to learning a skill is particularly important in trades which are often overlooked as careers by people with little personal experience of them. Despite steep increases in demand for tradespeople like construction workers, the Makers Index, an annual survey run by the tool-manufacturer Stanley Black and Decker found big perception gaps amongst students remained. While 85 per cent of young people did see value in a skilled trade career, only 16 per cent were 'very likely' to consider trying one. The gap between interest and expectation of working in a skilled trade is put down to a lack of exposure to people working in the industry, and opportunities to try such roles. Providing more routes into trade, through schools, apprenticeships and specialist institutions like Dyson's is a sure way to tackle some of this gap.

By introducing entrepreneurial mindsets into the classroom early we can give students the broad base of skills and experiences they will need for this new world of work. By offering people guaranteed time to learn as part of their employment contract, broadening the use of the student loan, and opening up access to facilities and accreditation, we can help them build on this mindset throughout their lives.

Even with this support structure, however, we need to look again at the rights of the self-employed to make sure even those armed with the skills needed to thrive, have a chance to compete in the new economy.

Keeping the balance

The economic value of entrepreneurship is still, in my opinion at least, a topic that gets less attention than it deserves in policy circles. Academic debate on entrepreneurship seems to reference the Austrian School of nineteenth-century economics more often than it does the recent rise of new technologies, platforms or cultural shifts when assessing the value and impact of the self-employed. Even now, it's possible to get a PhD in economics without ever coming across the word.

You cannot say this of one student of economics, though: the great political economist Joseph Schumpeter, the grandfather of the study of innovation. The son of a factory owner who died when he was still young, Schumpeter rejected the idea that you could describe the economy as a static, mathematical model, which many classical economists did, contending instead that it was a dynamic, almost organic entity. In one of his most famous works, *Capitalism, Socialism, and Democracy* (1942), he described the nature of entrepreneurship and innovation as 'incessantly revolutioni[zing] the economic structure from within, incessantly destroying the old one, incessantly creating a new one.'

For many solopreneurs, the grandiose and abstract notion of being part of a constant wave of creative destruction feels very far removed from the realities of the daily grind and the near constant jeopardy involved in keeping a business running. But they are nonetheless part of this cycle, and large corporations and slow-moving institutions will always lobby against these disruptive forces. As we transition to a more entrepreneurial society, the balance of power between corporations and manufacturers, and the growing army of freelancers and entrepreneurs, who are both their contractors and their competitors, will begin to tilt in the latter's favour. Yet the transition will not be an easy one because today much of our regulations and financial institutions are still based on the twentieth century model of work.

From complex regulatory bodies that refuse to engage with small businesses, to government contracts which still prioritize large companies with huge revenues, despite pledges to level the playing field for SMEs the deck is still stacked against the 'little guy' in many ways. To make this transition as smooth and equitable as possible, we need to rethink protections for gig workers, freelancers and start-ups to enable them to compete on something approaching level terms with the goliaths in their industry.

TIMELY INTERVENTIONS

'As an employee, if you got your pay packet a day late, you might get a bit worried about what was going on in your company,' explains Anna Codrea-Rado, as she recalls her time as a full-time journalist. 'Today, getting paid late is the default. As a freelancer, somehow the obligation is on me to be paid for my work.'

Late payments are just one example of how large and medium sized corporations can push solopreneurs to the very brink. Even as improvements in technology mean that corporates seek to work with freelancers and SMEs more often, and while they have increasingly better software to automate these payments, the problem hasn't abated. Bonsai, a US-based platform that provides digital tools to help freelancers manage their businesses, found in a survey of its 100,000+ users that 29 per cent of invoices were paid late. And while 90 per cent were eventually paid within a month of the original due date, up to 10 per cent were paid later or not paid at all. In the UK, the British Government estimates that late invoices to the value of £23 billion are owed to freelancers and small firms at any one time. Even more alarmingly, Bonsai found discrepancies in payment to women over men, with female freelancers paid late 31 per cent of the time, versus 24 per cent of the time for male freelancers – a gap beyond statistical error. As a result of these poor practices, the UK's Federation of Small Businesses (FSB) estimates that at least 50,000 businesses close every year due to late payments.

Historically, if such large numbers of salaried workers were paid late it would have been countered by political intervention, press pressure and organized labour or trade unions. While entrepreneurs, tradespeople and freelancers do have different federations and lobby groups varying in power by country, none match the strength of previous institutions that protected workers' rights.

Some groups are coming together to provide ways for solopreneurs to find joint solutions to this type of corporate bullying, enabling them to find a shared voice and suggest solutions to abuses of power such as late payment. In 2017, Freelancers Union, a voluntary group based in New York, managed to lobby for – and successfully get passed – the Freelancing isn't Free Act (FIFA). This piece of local legislation put into law a requirement for 30-day payment terms, and established penalties for violations of these rights, specifically including 'statutory damages, double damages, injunctive relief, and attorney's fees'. Individual cases are now being adjudicated in state court.

Progress like FIFA, and the UK's Prompt Payment Code (although at the time of writing, this is still voluntary) are steps in the right direction. But as any tradesperson will confirm, late payments from clients, including large businesses, have been a pernicious but consistent problem forever. And as technology develops, a small number of large platforms will have even more control in determining the rights of entrepreneurs, the amount of work they can take on, and ultimately their commercial success. Solving these challenges will be a lot more complex than fixing slow accounting systems.

PLATFORM PROBLEMS

One of the main reasons that more people are able to set up their own businesses is the rise of online marketplaces and platforms. Whereas once you had to rely on word of mouth, catalogues like the Yellow Pages or a local agency to source specialist support for anything from niche legal expertise to expert plumbers, access to such talent is now available at the click of a button. The infinite scalability of the internet means that skilled people can offer their services online and participate in a huge, sometimes global marketplace for their services, building reputations through reviews, and finding work without having to leave their living room. Indeed, these platforms have revolutionized the lives of tens of millions of people, and because they are digital-first, they are often much easier to work with than traditional companies, thanks to instant payments and clear contracts built in from the start.

But the biggest platforms have now become so powerful that there clearly needs to be a new settlement to protect the entrepreneurs and freelancers who rely on them. A settlement which ensures that their users aren't so reliant on them that they are susceptible to unfair practices.

Among the most prominent of these platforms (although by no means the largest in terms of the number of people who work on them) are so-called gig economy platforms like Uber, Lyft, DoorDash and Deliveroo. These services are predominantly focused on using logistical excellence to serve customers, and notable because of the high demands placed on their contractors – in terms of both physical labour and time even when gig workers aren't being paid, such as when waiting for new orders or rides to pop up on their screens. The trade-off for gig workers, the drivers and riders on these platforms is supposedly clear. If they were full-time employees rather than gig workers, they would of course lose some of the flexibility around when and how much they can work – and perhaps the chance to pursue other jobs simultaneously – but they would also be afforded the protections, such as minimum wages and sick pay, that previous generations of manual workers marched for and, in some cases, gave their lives to win.

As surveys have shown, on average gig workers are happy with this trade off. But as more examples come to light of how some gig workers have been mistreated by these platforms, governments across the world have begun to introduce new legislation to ensure that they are given rights similar to employees, and not contractors as they are often defined. In 2018, California's AB5 law (which was eventually gutted by a state ballot) sought to introduce tests that would have defined many Uber drivers as full-time employees. In September 2020, Spain's Supreme Court ruled that riders for the country's leading food-delivery app, Glovo, were employees, not freelancers, clearing the way for them to request formal labour contracts and the associated benefits and costs to the platform. In February 2021, the UK's Supreme Court ruled that Uber was akin to an employer, because their drivers could not set the fare and could be penalized for choosing not to accept jobs, meaning that they were therefore de facto employees, not contractors, and the platform was liable to taxes like VAT and providing employee rights. This slew of pro-worker legislative decisions, alongside a tough macroeconomic environment, has resulted in the share price of these companies falling drastically in the last few years, with some well-known platforms having to shut their doors as a result.

It is undeniable that these global, digital platforms are both creating new opportunities for entrepreneurs to find work and exploiting outdated regulations on what it means to be an employee to their own advantage. However, the approach of most legislators to this new era of gig working seems to be based on the previous social contract between employees and corporations, putting most of the cost of supporting employees onto the company, an economic model that is already under strain. This approach risks robbing millions of people of freedoms that come with gig work, and that first taste of entrepreneurialism. And it also risks putting the barrier to entry of starting a new platform to challenge these larger players so high that it inadvertently entrenches the winners, preventing competition that would have benefitted gig workers in the long run.

Instead, the state needs to develop new ways of protecting and financing the rights of this new class of solopreneurs, while also addressing the new challenges that these platforms pose.

In particular, we need to consider the significance of the two new methods that these digital giants deploy to shift the balance of power away from entrepreneurs, in ways that are much more worrying than the straightforward reclassification of their employment contract.

THE BOT-IN-THE-MIDDLE

Historically, the transactional costs of finding freelancers or accessing solopreneurs outside of a firm were kept high for a variety of reasons – but a key one was the middleman. The middleman ran the local taxi firm, the local recruitment agency or pizza delivery franchise. Sometimes they played an essential role in sourcing, managing and coordinating large numbers of workers. But many just took a cut for making introductions. Traditional taxi firms, such as my old local taxi service which operated out of Stockport, for example, took over 20 per cent of the fare simply for answering the phone. There was no shortage of complaints from the taxi drivers, but they had little choice but to accept it.

Today, global platforms like Uber have replaced many of these small taxi agencies as the 'bot-in-the-middle' connecting rider and driver, just as Airbnb has become a global travel agency, and Amazon's marketplace has replaced many high-street retailers. The human middleman, often seen as a rent-taking burden, has been cut out. But the take rate – the cut these tech giants take of transactions on their platform – has remained high.

Uber and Lyft can take 20–30 per cent of the cost of a ride. Amazon marketplace can charge up to 15 per cent commission on the cost of products sold on their platform. And when the goods being sold are products with particularly high margins, such as software, the take rates get even higher: Apple and Google, for instance, have by any definition a duopoly over smartphone software, and Apple takes 30 per cent of any sales made through apps on their app stores. For an entrepreneur looking to launch a new software service, having a presence on iPhone or Android is often a necessity. The upside is that as gatekeepers, Apple and Google offer access to billions of potential customers, with a stable and well-documented approach to the code needed to achieve this. However, the demand for 30 per cent of any revenues generated is a take rate that would have made even the struggling taxi agencies of Greater Manchester blush.

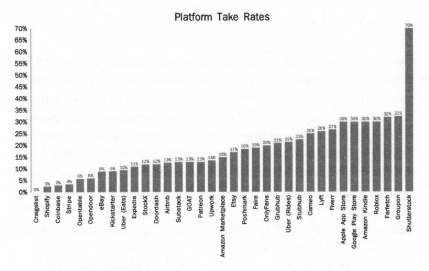

Platform Take Rates

(Source: Public filings; Company websites; estimates by Tanay Jaipuria, Wing Venture Capital)

Private companies are already pushing back on these egregious pricing strategies. Epic, a popular gaming company that owns the teenage gaming mega-hit Fortnite, took Apple to court after the technology giant removed its game from the App Store for trying to circumvent their fee system. Epic argued that the App Store was an effective monopoly, and although the court largely ruled in Apple's favour, the Fortnite publisher was still pursuing a similar case against Google on the same basis in spring 2023 (the game was kicked off Google Play at the same time as the Apple App Store).

As these platforms grow in scale and fall in number, the power they have over the supply side – the entrepreneurs using the platform – has grown to the point where these companies become as important to their businesses as other utilities like internet access and transport infrastructure. As such, regulators need to start weighing in on what represents a fair take rate, in the same way that most countries have regulations on what water and power companies can charge. The pressure seems to be working, with Apple announcing a programme for small business owners and independent developers that would mean they were charged only 15 per cent on the first $1 million they earn on the platform, a welcome concession for the many millions of single-person developer companies that rely on the company for distribution. Cloud computing, an equally important general purpose technology provided by software giants like Microsoft, Google and Amazon, has long been run with great success on the basis that initial fees for usage was low, even if the fees ramp quickly as companies scale. As increasingly disruptive tools, such as AI models, become available, being quick to manage potential oligopolistic behaviour will be essential for regulators. If governments want to help new entrepreneurs thrive in a digital world, capping the fees that solo-preneurs and microbusinesses have to pay to get up and running would be an easy place to start.

BOSS-WARE

One of the other changes in the modern workplace is the increasing role that algorithms play in our professional lives. While normal code can be said to do what you tell it – i.e. send this email when I click this button – algorithms can be used to optimize for an outcome – i.e. send this email to the *right* person when I click this button, based on similar emails I have sent before.

Today, fine-tuned algorithms determine a vast majority of our interactions with digital products. Our photos and video calls are optimized for quality and in some cases beauty, our word processing software tries to guess the next word we want to type, while our maps are designed to work out the best route to our destination and even guess where we want to go. And while in many multitudes of ways these powerful new tools have radically improved our lives, there have also been plenty of unforeseen and worrying outcomes when algorithms are given significant roles in deciding how we live and work.

Mistakes are common. In 2014, Amazon developed an AI recruitment tool that appeared to discriminate against female job applicants. In 2018, it emerged that an algorithm that analyzed the risk of repeat offending by millions of defendants on trial in the USA made as many mistakes as a human with no training in criminal justice. In 2020, Apple's credit card policies were called into question when the co-founder of Apple himself, Steve Wozniak, claimed that his female partner received lower Apple Card credit limits than he did simply for being a woman.

How much a specific algorithm can be blamed for such mistakes depends heavily on the context. An investigation by the New York State Department looked at 400,000 applications and found that Apple's banking partner, Goldman Sachs, did not actually discriminate based on sex. And of course, decisions made by human managers on things like hiring and promotions have been proven regularly to be full of hidden (and sometimes overt) biases as well, suggesting that in many cases algorithms, when properly trained, may be even fairer, especially for traditionally marginalized groups. Yet concern that autonomous algorithms, trained on opaque data sets and with millions of parameters, determine more and more aspects of our lives is clearly justified. Jamie Susskind, a barrister and author of *The Digital Republic*, goes further to say that 'code is now the law' – meaning that certain aspects of how code is implemented need to be reviewed just as one might review new legislation.

It is not just large software platforms that rely on algorithms to make critical decisions about us. Some of the most well-publicized misuses of automated decision software are in traditionally low-tech areas of work such as warehouses and call centres. Warehouse workers, for example, have reported quotas so stringent that they don't have time to use the bathroom and say they've been fired – by algorithm – for not meeting them. According to an opinion piece for Wired.com by leading researchers from the Bonavero Institute of Human Rights at University of Oxford, 'Algorithmic management has also been documented in retail and manufacturing; in software engineering, marketing, and consulting; and in public-sector work, including health care and policing.' They point out that while there has been much written about the threat to employment of workers, it is increasingly the bosses and middlemen who have been automated by software, often leaving the workers with harder, less private and less secure working conditions as a result.

As algorithms increasingly determine how work is commissioned, priced and assessed and whether people keep their jobs, entrepreneurs bidding for this work need to be given the opportunity to understand how these decisions are being made, and protection from the worst incursions on their privacy. What chance are we giving people in the gig economy, or on online marketplaces, if they're not told how their algorithmic commissioners decide who gets what work, when?

There is no easy way to introduce, much less retrofit, transparency into the process of decision-making for algorithms that can be trained on billions, and sometimes trillions, of data points. Putting the principles in place that at a certain scale algorithmic decisions must be explicable and shown to have no malignant bias should at least be an aspiration for governments who want to protect entrepreneurs put at their mercy. An example of how to do this is Spanish Supreme Court ruling on gig workers in 2020, which included a secondary clause that made it mandatory for all businesses to inform their food-delivery riders about how algorithms and artificial intelligence affect their working conditions, hiring decisions and layoffs. 'Now algorithms are going to be put at the service of the majority in society,' said Yolanda Díaz, Spain's Minister for Labour.

Putting laws like this into practice is no mean feat and will require multinational efforts, and close cooperation with private sector players, entrepreneurs and experts to make sure they protect workers without excessively hampering innovation. Much like the sophisticated algorithms that make millions of tiny decisions for us every day, the devil will be in the detail. But as policymakers consider how to make the transition to a more equitable, entrepreneurial society possible, ensuring that take rates and algorithmic decision-making are as fair and transparent as possible is just as urgent as dealing with traditional problems like late payment and worker classifications.

SAVING (FOR) THE FUTURE

Even in steadier economic times, saving and managing a pension was a challenge. There are countless examples where the mismanagement of pensions, on both a corporate level and by government, have meant millions of people have struggled to retire. In a world of increasing change, as employment becomes more volatile, saving for the future is going to be even more challenging, especially for the self-employed and those working in small businesses.

A study done by the private pension manager PensionBee in the United Kingdom in 2022 found that while the vast majority of employees are paying into a pension, the figure among self-employed workers was only 18 per cent. A Pew Research study of 2019 found a similar position in the USA: for the solo self-employed the figure was just 13 per cent. This number is, of course, skewed by the type of work done. For people making over £100,000 a year, the chances of them saving into a private pension pot is much higher. For those entrepreneurs earning median wages or less, the savings rate is significantly lower and the number contributing to their pension pot has fallen rapidly in the last decade, by as much as two thirds from 1998 to 2018 according to the Institute for Fiscal Studies.

Of course, individuals have to be responsible for their own private savings and make adjustments where they can between day-to-day financial demands. This is no easy task, and in traditional employee roles, many countries around the world make contributing to a pension compulsory, as well as providing a state pension after a certain age paid for via taxation. But given the scale of the challenge facing a new generation of entrepreneurs, ensuring they have the right support in place for themselves well into old age is critical, both to give them additional confidence to try something new and to feel they are not being prejudiced against for choosing this path, versus a traditional career.

One fair settlement between the government and the self-employed would be to mandate the self-employed, earning over a certain threshold, to have a private pension provider with a minimum contribution made each year. Given that starting a digital pension pot is now free or comes with de minimis fees, this seems like a low enough bar to not be a burden. As a quid pro quo, the government can extend tax breaks on entrepreneurs making these long-term savings tax-free, as the Individual Savings Account (ISA) scheme is in the UK, to encourage them to save in the same way that pension contributions are mandated for many millions of employees in traditional careers. This wouldn't guarantee all individuals would have enough saved for retirement, but it would be a fairer settlement in a system which was set up at a time when far fewer people were self-employed.

In his writings on capitalism, a system that had been practiced for barely a century when he was born, Schumpeter both championed capitalism and predicted its demise. That demise would come as a result of corporatism – the increased cosiness of large corporations and the political establishment, and the consequential suppression of the competitive nature of entrepreneurs and the regulatory system that keeps said corporations in check. The net result of this, Schumpeter warned, would be that capitalism would inevitably morph into cronyism and give rise to oligopolies.

Whether he has been proved right is moot. To make sure this is avoided in future, though, will require a rethink of how the state operates not just as a regulator, but as a provider of welfare too. This will require a rethink of how governments take risks, empower public servants and adopt new technologies to avoid stultification and corporatism. Getting this right won't only support entrepreneurs, it should result in the improvement of government and vital public services too.

12

The public innovator

The public sector – services funded and mostly delivered by government – employs anywhere between 15 per cent and 30 per cent of the working population in capitalist countries. From teachers and nurses to our waste collectors and civic planners, millions of people work in organizations that make up some of the largest coordinated efforts on the face of the planet. In fact, while many multinational businesses have been shrinking headcount over recent decades, governments have generally ended up employing more people. In a list of the largest employers in the world, only two private companies, Walmart and McDonalds, make the top 10 at the time of writing, with the American Department of Defense, the Chinese civil service and the British National Health System employing millions of people each.

As institutions focused on the public good, and not motivated to make profit or needing private investment, these organizations don't necessarily face the same type of pressures from technological change and a growing entrepreneurial class as their for-profit counterparts. But that doesn't mean they do not need to innovate and improve. With a global cultural and technological revolution empowering the individual underway, it seems both inevitable – and for the best – that civil servants will also seize on new tools and mindsets to radically improve our public services as well.

For as long as we have had public services, there have been those who have complained that they are too bureaucratic and need to be more entrepreneurial. And for a long time lip service has been paid to the idea that the solution is to empower the public servants toiling on the front lines, over the large centralized bureaucracies that direct them. In 1991, then UK Prime Minister John Major said: 'departments and agencies should be given greater flexibility to develop programmes for improving efficiency which best meet their own needs . . . with less detailed central oversight.' Some 20 years later, another Prime Minister, David Cameron, said his goal for public servants was 'to free [them] from top-down micro-management and targets . . . liberating the hidden army of public service entrepreneurs.'

But despite these calls for a more entrepreneurial public service, little has materially changed in the past two decades. In fact, many people continue to believe the very notion of *public entrepreneurship* is an oxymoron. Public servants are often delivering critical services, under intense pressure, to millions of people, who expect to be treated in a uniform way – and that isn't an environment which lends itself easily to taking risks and trialling new ideas. Or so the rationale would go. As a result, sometimes public-spirited entrepreneurs feel the need to leave the public sector altogether to build innovative services for it.

Take Sam Chaudhary and Liam Don, cofounders of ClassDojo. Sam had worked as a teacher in Britain, and Liam had been studying a PHD in computer science before coming up with the idea for the online engagement platform for students. Frustrated by the lack of tools to help teachers build relationships with their students and their families, they set out to build a solution using software. 'We found that improving student behaviour is one of the biggest problems teachers face,' Sam told me from the ClassDojo headquarters in San Francisco. 'Forty per cent of teachers say they spend more than half of their time managing behaviour rather than teaching. And one of the main reasons teachers give for low morale, and leaving their roles, is the lack of support in managing students' behaviour.'

Instead of relying on once-a-term written forms for teachers to share feedback on a student's behaviour at parents' evening, with little engagement with the student themselves, Sam and Liam built a dynamic, private, child-friendly platform that enables teachers, children and families to share what was happening in the classroom each day. 'We try to shift the focus to expecting and reinforcing positive behaviours from children, instead of punishing them for being bad,' Sam explains.

ClassDojo has been a huge hit with teachers, and fans claim that their features have helped demystify what happens in the classroom for parents as well. The platform is now used by tens of millions of students across 180 countries, and has partnered with the likes of Yale University to provide more mental health support for K–12 students, even running the world's 'first-ever global mindfulness lesson'.

Could this have been built within the public sector? Sam says there was no lack of skills among the teachers he worked with; but there was a distinct absence of support. 'I don't think teachers have the time or resources to experiment with these kinds of ideas in the current way of working.'

And it's not just teachers who feel hemmed in by the rigid, managerial culture which pervades much of the public sector.

'It's always surprising how much small, dedicated teams can get done when they have freedom and focus,' says Dr Jean Nehme, founder and CEO of DigitalSurgery. Like Sam and Liam, Jean and his co-founder, Andre Chou, were previously public servants, spending years training as surgeons and working in the UK's NHS before deciding to leave to set up Digital Surgery, a software platform which provides training and AI assistance to medical students and surgeons. The platform they built has won global accolades and been adopted by healthcare institutions around the world from Harvard to Imperial College London, helping tens of thousands of surgeons to train digitally, and supporting them in theatre.

'In medicine, like in many things in life, you've got a clear path,' Jean reflects. 'You know what you're going to be doing in five years. It's laid out for you. You've got boxes that you've got to tick, and if you achieve each one of these positions and these statuses, you climb this ladder.

'But entrepreneurship isn't like that, it's not a straight line, you have these ups and downs – it's not something that's easy to do within the risk-averse processes of the public sector.'

Entrepreneurs, like Dr Nehme and Sam Chaudhary have been hugely successful, building tools that have benefited millions of people. But they had to leave their institutional roles behind to develop tools to improve public services. In this new entrepreneurial era, does it really have to be this way?

Many people believe so. Taking risks, and thus risking failure, is something that few public sector workers can ever afford to do. After all, when it comes to the provision of care or welfare, errors – however well-intentioned the action from which they result – can cause huge stress and sometimes jeopardize human life. And even where innovative approaches to public service delivery are actively encouraged, it isn't realistic to expect doctors and teachers, already under huge strain, to also take on the burden of developing new solutions themselves.

Mark Zuckerberg's now very dated mantra that entrepreneurs should *move fast and break things* simply cannot be applied to the public sector when people's livelihoods, health and welfare depend on tried-and-trusted systems and procedures.

If we're going to empower public sector workers to embrace innovative solutions and develop a more entrepreneurial approach while staying within the state system, we must explore different ways of providing them with the structures and tools required to do it.

THE START-UP STATE

One of the most common and arguably successful examples of introducing a more entrepreneurial mindset into the public sector is the *moonshot*. Popularized by President Kennedy's agenda to put the first man on the moon, a modern moonshot is considered to be an ambitious mission with a large, audacious goal that needs an innovative approach. It often also requires considerable interaction with entrepreneurs and the private sector. The moon landing, for instance, was a massive partnership between the government, private sector and academic institutions. It is estimated that more than 400,000 people (around 94 per cent of them external contractors) were involved in getting the first man to the moon and back.

Moonshots have come to embody innovation in the public sector due to their occasional success of rallying huge resources around a single, tangible goal. In her 2020 book *Mission Economy: A Moonshot Guide to Changing Capitalism*, Mariana Mazzucato, Professor in the Economics of Innovation and Public Value at University College London, goes even further than the idea of a moonshot, advocating for the government to take on 'earthshots' – which have a similar scale of ambition to moonshots for the great challenges of our time such as achieving net zero and building solutions for meeting the UN's Sustainable Development Goals. Professor Mazzucato stresses that the key to government supporting innovation and being more entrepreneurial, however, must be driven 'not only (at) a rate, but also (with) a direction'– in other words, they need to use government's purchasing power to promote innovation for a broad range of public goods, and take a more systemic approach rather than focus on a single outcome.

Moonshots are not just an American innovation. Genomics England is another example of how more entrepreneurial approaches can be taken for the public good. A British company owned by the UK government, it was set up in 2014 to sequence 100,000 human genomes of NHS patients with rare diseases and cancer to support scientific research. Provided with resources, a clear target and critically independence to operate outside of the usual healthcare structure in the UK, it achieved its goal in 2018. It has been such a success that they have now set themselves a new target, to sequence 500,000 whole genomes by 2024. The ability to sequence genomes at scale was one of the reasons why the UK was able to be a global leader and contributor to understanding the effects of COVID-19.

There are many more moonshots in the making. The Quantum Technologies Flagship Fund is one of the largest research and innovation initiatives in the European Union. Backed by €1 billion in funding, the Quantum Flagship is a long-term research and innovation initiative that aims to put Europe at the forefront of quantum computing, an effort to harness quantum phenomena. In 2016, the then vice president Joe Biden kicked off his own moonshot, with the aim of making a decade's worth of advances in cancer prevention, diagnosis and treatment in five years. Some early evidence suggests that this has helped accelerate the development of personalized therapies for certain cancers.

Of course, almost by definition, not all moonshots are successful. In 1969, buoyed by success on the Moon, NASA said it would put a man on Mars within 15 years, but budget cuts and other technical challenges saw this target scrapped soon afterwards. However, the mission to put a man on Mars has since been revived with a slight twist on the traditional model. In the light of more entrepreneurial outfits entering space exploration, made possible in part by the US government's willingness to underwrite space transportation rather than be a sole deliverer, private space companies like SpaceX and BlueOrigin are now helping the government to reach its goals.

This modern model of enabling entrepreneurialism in the delivery of public goods, like healthcare and space travel, is a departure from the traditional moonshot model where government ultimately owned much of the delivery of services. Instead of being a monolithic and sole provider of a solution, government can encourage innovation by setting a price for it, initially generous enough to cover the inevitable early failures, and allowing entrepreneurs to sell the first versions of their products, whether it be new types of energy generation, biotechnology or space transportation. This *price-setting model* for innovation is becoming increasingly popular globally. In the USA, the CHIPS and Science Act and the bipartisan Infrastructure Investment and Jobs Act, which were both passed in 2022, provide routes for entrepreneurs to gain funding and payment for new products in strategically important areas such as semiconductors, solar power and cyber resilience.

And possibly the most impactful way that government is going to incentivize more entrepreneurship in the coming decades will be in setting the price for the replacement and removal of carbon. Reducing climate-changing carbon emissions is a classic dilemma for innovation-led capitalist economies. While more and more entrepreneurs wish to help tackle the climate crisis, the willingness to pay for the removal of carbon in the private sector is still very nascent. If you discovered a new technology that reduced the need for carbon-intensive products such as jet fuel or aluminium, you would still have to invest heavily to make the product price-competitive with existing solutions or rely on the goodwill of businesses to buy your services, as few companies are currently negatively affected commercially by the carbon emissions they produce. While carbon taxes and shifting consumer behaviour are slowly changing the commercial interests of big companies and forcing them to look for new, low-carbon alternatives, a far more effective way to stimulate innovation in this field and work with entrepreneurs is for government to step in and set a price for services, as they have done previously in fields as broad as solar panel energy production and space transportation. By setting prices in this way, it gives people the confidence that if they are successful in creating a technological breakthrough, they will be able to build a business out of it, and it won't be another world-changing invention left sitting on a laboratory shelf. Done well, this approach promotes both entrepreneurship and green innovation.

A prime historic example of this approach was the introduction of feed-in tariffs – as part of Germany's Renewable Energy Sources Act (2000) – which was a key driver of the country's investment in renewable energy. In practice it meant that producers of renewable energy received a fixed price from the national grid for each kilowatt-hour they generated, over a period of 20 years. That offered certainty to consumers and businesses, leading to a flourishing renewables sector in Germany and creating an estimated 280,000 jobs. The legislation's impact helped ensure that the share of renewable energy in the overall power mix in the country rose from 5.4 per cent in 1999 to 40.3 per cent by 2017 – depending on the weather, of course. A huge policy win by any standard.

If the state is to embrace the start-up century, setting the price for services – whether carbon removal, quantum computing or personalized cancer treatments – in order to catalyze the market seems like a good place to start. It would allow many more publicly minded entrepreneurs, like those mentioned above, to get to work solving some of the great challenges of the decades to come. However, some services, like education and healthcare, by their very nature, will always need to be coordinated and delivered by state-led organizations, and so we must consider what public servants can do to embrace this more entrepreneurial era within the existing system.

SHARING IS CARING

One of the fundamental differences in this new age of the entrepreneur is the amount of knowledge and data available to help people make informed decisions. In the corporate world of the twentieth century, finding out even the most basic facts often took hours of phone calls and paper shuffling, but today data can be tracked down in milliseconds online. Data sharing in public institutions is often more complex, however, partly due to the scale of operations but also often due to the additional personal nature of the data that practitioners need to share.

One example of how the entrepreneurial spirit is being disseminated throughout the public sector is Apolitical, the civil service social learning network. The start-up connects 150,000 public servants and policymakers, across countries and functions, to share knowledge, evidence and case studies on how the state can tackle some of the greatest challenges of our age, through breaking out of the more traditional knowledge hierarchy. Some advice and online training courses on Apolitical are high level, on topics like how to manage change in large organizations. However, many are specific to digital skills, such as better data visualization, giving civil servants the same support, training and – with the right investment

– tools as start-ups would offer their own employees. Explaining her motivation for starting Apolitical, its founder Robyn Scott said in a 2020 interview: 'It seemed crazy that in a world where we can find the best hotel room for our holiday in a few clicks, policy makers could not find out about how people on the other side of the world were dealing with similar problems.' Adopting a knowledge portal like this – or, better yet, allowing companies to compete to develop national and international solutions like Apolitical – would be a quick win for any organization, especially those of the size and importance of the state.

The best way the state could encourage innovation, and support entrepreneurs would be to share its needs, and be willing to purchase solutions, more openly. Ask any public servant what they need to change to deliver a better outcome for their departments, and most could fill a book with ideas. The challenge for any large institution, and in particular hierarchical workplaces like government-run bodies, is routing the ideas for a solution, from improving local bus routes to better deploying billions of pounds on national infrastructure projects to the people who can best solve the issues.

Instead of keeping such challenges, and potential solutions, locked up in government, local councils and state departments should be encouraged to publish a list of challenges they are facing and the price they would be willing to pay to find solutions. Government already does this at the highest levels, with RFPs (requests for proposals), but these are mostly for very large projects. How different might the relationship between local government and entrepreneurs be if they laid out problems at a hyperlocal level – such as the waiting times at a local GP's office – with the appropriately censored data to explain the issue, and then encouraged entrepreneurs to submit bids for how to solve them.

Mitchell Weiss, author of *We the Possibility*, argues that to get more effective public services, public servants have to start thinking more like entrepreneurs, and convince voters of that approach too. 'We are going to need public officials who are willing to take on riskier projects and scale them,' he writes. 'But we are also going to need members of the public who are granting them their permission, encouragement and even co-participation.'

WITH GREAT RESPONSIBILITY,
SHOULD COME GREAT POWER

Beyond price setting and knowledge sharing, there's a much more radical option for supporting state-led entrepreneurship. This is to turn the current decision making hierarchy upside down when it comes to the tools used and the goals set, and give public servants on the front line the permission, power and resources to take the initiative in pursuit of our common good. But can this more entrepreneurial mindset – one that has worked when rallied around ambitious projects like *moonshots* – be as effective when focused on the more day-to-day, challenging, physically and emotionally draining tasks of delivering front-line public services?

This is not a straightforward question to answer, as most of the important work that front-line workers perform is hard and human-centric. From providing career advice in job centres to organizing waste collection and caring for the elderly, these roles won't have a moment when it's possible to declare 'Mission accomplished' – unlike, say, achieving net zero or delivering a vaccine roll-out during a pandemic. But that doesn't mean public sector workers can't benefit from the shift to more self-directed ways of working. And by empowering them in this way, we could introduce more innovative and better services for the public, while also providing these hard-working public servants with more autonomy and dignity in their profession.

In 2010, while in my early twenties, I spent a few months working in Tower Hamlets, an area of east London. I was working with the Social Business Trust, a UK-based charitable group which was looking at ways to support health visitors, the professional nurses who provide in-home care for mothers who have recently given birth. For almost a week I was asked to shadow Claire (I have changed her name for privacy purposes), a district nurse who had worked in the NHS since arriving in London from Ireland three decades earlier. As we sat in the kitchen of a young family that had moved to London from Bangladesh, Claire was working with a translator to provide support that ranged from nutritional guidance to advice on nappy rash.

To deal with these challenges, Claire relied on her years of experience as a community nurse. The only tools she had to hand were her wits, notebook and the little red book that parents and caregivers use to keep track of their child's early years health data. She had no access to online resources for guidance while on the move, no way to arrange prescriptions online, nor to connect with the family digitally to provide reminders or extra support. She had her own mobile phone which she paid for herself, and which could access email, albeit slowly, but her local NHS Trust hadn't given her the ability to access digital communications on their platform from anywhere but her office on the other side of the borough. And even if she could have found the information she needed remotely, the family she was talking to did not have reliable access to the internet anyway.

When we talked about how new technologies and government spending on IT projects had changed her job over the years, she replied that the main difference was that she now had to wait for her archaic computer to load up once a week to copy her rota down into a notebook, and that it had been much quicker taking the details down directly from the cork noticeboard they used a decade ago. She knew new technologies could potentially help with her job, but she didn't have the resources, institutional support or permission to try them. The many new tools available at a click of a button to most people in the world had done nothing to support the work of this community nurse or any of her colleagues.

That was over a decade ago, but things haven't changed all that much even now that most people have smart devices and reliable internet access in the UK. Even before the increased challenges of the pandemic and the resulting lockdowns, clinicians in the UK were widely using the chat tool WhatsApp to coordinate efforts and communicate about patients' needs. 'We use WhatsApp for everything, [including] reminding other nurses about problems with patients,' one unnamed NHS nurse told the anti-censorship website Reclaim The Net in 2019. 'Having a group chat for a ward can be quite useful to keep everyone up to date on what's been going on.' They added: 'Lots of doctors take photos of patients' wounds and x-rays and share them with other doctors on WhatsApp.'

Using the chat app clearly has many advantages for patients and carers, including speed, efficiency and flexibility. But until very recently, using a chat app like this could have cost clinical staff their jobs. This is because despite the obvious benefits, the health administrators took years to decide which, if any, mobile app could be used for communications by staff. Fortunately, the NHS is now supporting health practitioners to use such services where they are secure, and even allows them to use their own devices where sensible. Empowering front-line carers, even in this small way, to make sensible decisions on which tools to use for themselves and their patients benefits health outcomes, and makes the work of clinicians easier as well, for no extra cost. If the state is only now allowing carers to make such simple decisions as which chat app to use, it's clear there is a long way to go before they feel empowered to drive service change from the bottom up.

THINK GLOBAL, ACT LOCAL

It is easy to argue that the state's functions are so important, and its operations so large and complex, that centralized direction and procedures are a necessity – a lesser of two evils – even if this actually stunts more innovative thinking. Such approaches may reduce the upside of more localized decision-making, but in the long run, so the logic goes, it protects against complete failure. Sadly, however, that view has been tested to destruction.

Just consider the case of Carillion, the UK construction firm that collapsed under a debt pile of £1.5 billion in January 2018. According to the Public Accounts Committee report into its failure, the UK government 'allowed a culture to develop in which a small number of large companies that believe that they are too big to fail pursued new business with little apparent consideration of their ability to deliver the right service at the right price.'

If centralized decision-making can still result in such large errors, with so much taxpayer cash wasted, it seems well worth the risks of giving front-line workers more autonomy in certain areas to procure the services and use the tools they think are best, even if it occasionally leads to inefficiencies and mistakes.

Elinor Ostrom, the Nobel Prize-winning economist, and one of the earliest and most consequential writers on public entrepreneurship, put it this way: 'There is no reason to believe that bureaucrats and politicians, no matter how well meaning, are better at solving problems than the people on the spot.' In my view it is usually the provider of a service, and the recipient, that are best placed to solve their issues with new and innovative solutions. Empowering them to do so can not only result in better outcomes but is also the basis for a more innovative and problem-solving culture.

This may seem obvious, but it runs counter to much of the current approach taken by developed countries to the running of public services. This culture can be broadly termed as *managerialism*, the view that management itself is the most essential and desirable element to effective administration and government. In particular, advocates of New Public Management (NPM) argue that the public sector should import management ideas from the private sector, focused on results-based outcomes, pay incentivization, internal markets and many other adaptations of the concepts that made some of the largest organizations of the late twentieth century successful. But as we've seen, many of these companies are under increasing pressure themselves, if they have not already failed. And the watered-down versions put into place in the public sector have little chance of seizing on a new world of entrepreneurial opportunities – leaving the public sector, and all of us who rely on it in different ways, worse off.

Rather than focusing on the inputs, as NPM does, or on the number of tasks completed, or the number of boxes ticked, public sector leadership needs to pivot to look more at the outcomes they want and give public servants more freedoms to achieve them. We must also treat the future of public service delivery with the same urgency that we treated the global pandemic. At the onset of the crises in 2020, the NHS adopted digital innovation at high speed – and scale – proving that large bureaucracies can be innovative in moments of crisis. 'Hospitals are on the front foot here, they are being really proactive and taking change management into their own hands,' Tom Whicher of DrDoctor, an online patient platform, told the *Financial Times* at the time. Start-ups like DrDoctor, and the extreme efforts of front-line workers, boosted efficiency overnight in an organization that has a reputation for being lumberingly slow to embrace change. Seeing change happen this quickly on the front lines, albeit at times at the cost of longer-term care, shows what is possible.

This model, of focusing on the experience of front-line employees and working upwards to a solution, rather than relying on top-down implementation, has precedent in governments across the world. The global consulting group BCG calls this model Smart Simplicity, and they say that they have been helping put it into practice for years. They give the example of an Australian government-owned railway that wanted to get their trains running on time. Through hundreds of interviews, they discovered that train drivers weren't being given the reason for delays when they saw a red signal; they just knew that they had to stop and wait. As BCG wrote about the case, 'Drivers were frustrated at being out of the loop and unable to explain delays to passengers. The interviews also revealed that drivers were frequently assigned to different routes and shifts from one day to the next, making it difficult to track their performance.' Understandably, this left drivers and passengers waiting in anger.

The railway responded by installing a new communications and public address system, giving drivers more details on why a delay has occurred, and reducing shift changes. As a result, they claim that the railway's on-time percentage increased from the low 80s to the mid 90s, and train drivers were a lot more engaged in fixing and communicating the problems, rather than just being the rule-takers when they saw a red signal.

Hardwiring innovation throughout the public sector is a near-insurmountable task, and governments of all stripes have struggled. Giving public sector workers and civil servants more choice over which tools they adopt, and enabling them to become rule makers and not just rule takers, is undoubtedly a good place to start. However we can't rely on the state, even a more innovative one, to fix all the challenges of moving to a more entrepreneurial economy. To make sure start-ups and entrepreneurs thrive in the decades to come, the private sector must play a role too, and one of the most important ways it can do this is through properly funding innovation.

13

Funding the future

Open any broadsheet newspaper from the last decade and within a few pages you're likely to be reading the story of an astronomical IPO, or the spectacular collapse of a tech start-up. The increased interest in software-enabled businesses – high growth, high risk and often unprofitable – has been astounding, even to those of us who work in the industry. The stories behind the boom of companies like Apple and Google (Alphabet), as well as the busts like Theranos and FTX, and their charismatic anti-heroic founders, are now quite literally the stuff of blockbusters, with podcasts, books and even films and television series dedicated to them. While these narratives are often overly dramatized, they nonetheless reflect a renewed global interest in a certain type of entrepreneurship, and in the rags-to-riches – and sometimes back to rags – stories behind them. Underpinning many of these tales – and indeed those of giants like Facebook (Meta) and Amazon – is a relatively novel form of financing: venture capital.

The history of venture capital (or VC), my own field of expertise, stretches back centuries. As Sebastian Mallaby argues in *The Power Law*, his 2021 book on the venture capital industry, this financial asset class has been around since at least the great sailing expeditions of the seventeenth century. Buccaneering investors were happy to provide capital in return for equity in highly risky, but potentially highly rewarding, nautical adventures. Venture capitalists also financed the exploration of the oil wells of Texas at the turn of the century, as well as the rebellious spinouts of silicon chip manufacturers in California in the mid-twentieth century.

It is an asset class well suited to financing entrepreneurs. Unlike traditional lenders, venture capitalists do not ask for personal collateral or interest payments. Knowing that their house or personal savings aren't on the line if they fail allows founders to take more risks in pursuit of their vision. Also, unlike lenders, venture capitalists aren't looking to take capital out of businesses' cash flow, but rather to make money from selling shares in companies further down the line. This means the cash generated by the company in its early days can be reinvested into talent and research and development, rather than being used to pay off investors. In short, in exchange for a part of your business, VC lets you take more risk, and invest more into your product than your profits initially.

VC is differentiated not only from debt but also from other forms of finance provided by equity investors, such as private equity (PE) investors or public market traders. Venture capital firms raise money from their investors, known as Limited Partners, with the intention of returning many multiples of that capital in ten years' time or even longer. This decade-long time frame is important, as it means venture capitalists can take very long-term positions in businesses, unlike more short-term investors such as private equity funds, who have a holding period of closer to three years, or crypto token or public market investors, who may target a meaningful return within a year, month or – in some cases – microseconds.

The length of an investment period matters for entrepreneurs starting up new companies because it determines how long they can experiment with new ideas, or invest in initially unprofitable technologies or products, before having to have their performance judged on a public basis in the form of share prices. In the long run, every business should plan to produce profits consistently; that is, after all, the best indicator you are making something people want. Yet being given years to do this, rather than months, makes a big difference to an entrepreneur's ability to build something truly innovative. As a result, venture capital is, in theory at least, one of the most entrepreneur-friendly forms of finance out there.

No surprise, then, that as many more people choose to become entrepreneurs, the VC industry has exploded correspondingly. The speed at which the industry has grown over the last decade has surprised even the most bullish estimates. Investment into American VC expanded 500 per cent in the 2010s, from around $26 billion of annual investment in 2010 to $128 billion in 2021. In Europe the increase has been even more impressive, with the total amount raised by European venture funds in 2020 over ten times greater than in 2010, expanding from $4.1 billion to $46 billion. In 2021, venture capitalists ploughed a record $621 billion into start-ups globally. Although macroeconomic shocks in 2022 saw a downward correction, the VC industry raised more, during this, the worst year for the performance of public technology stocks in decades, than it did in 2020.

But as we prepare for an economy not just influenced but dominated by entrepreneurs, this growth will need to continue to meet new levels of demand. VC still makes up a tiny proportion of the total amount of capital invested into businesses annually. The $128 billion of VC raised in America in 2021, for example, is likely to be the top of the most recent market cycle, but is a fraction of the daily volume of capital traded in Nasdaq-listed companies, which averages around $200 billion a day; and it pales into insignificance compared to the trillions of dollars of debt raised by American businesses each year. Despite the column inches and its increasing profile, VC still makes up only a small percentage of capital available to business builders today.

A fair criticism of the VC industry is that while it has led to the creation of some of the most important technology businesses in the world, with 43 per cent of all public companies in the USA using VC since 1979, it can also result in poor governance and financial frenzy – the very types of frenzy described by Carlota Perez in the introduction. This was undoubtedly on display in the period of venture investing between 2019 and 2021, an era I now refer to simply as *the madness*. The rush to deploy capital into any entrepreneurial endeavour that labelled itself as a technology company in those years defied economic sense. And the fallout is far from over; no doubt there will be many more stories like WeWork and FTX in the years to come, where silver-tongued founders oversold their businesses and investors bought into the hype. After the frenzy of 2021, and the collapse in growth and late-stage technology company valuations in 2022, there will surely be many who lose faith in the venture model as a sustainable way to finance a more entrepreneurial society.

I believe that would be a mistake.

The success of venture firms who did invest in the most impactful and successful businesses continues to outweigh those who made bad judgements. While there are certainly instances of individual greed and misconduct, investments into even failing technology companies mostly go into funding the training of more productive developers and operators, who will have the chance to pick up the baton as entrepreneurs in the future. So even in failure, VC is an asset class that fuels entrepreneurship. The boom and bust cycle in VC is not the most desirable model, but that doesn't mean it doesn't work.

Despite the froth and frenzy of the last few years, supporting a new generation of ambitious entrepreneurs to take on some of the greatest technical challenges that face humanity in the next decade, from improved healthcare to renewable energy, does mean we are going to need even more VC than in the last decade. Yes, you read that correctly. Even after record increases in VC funding in recent years, and the subsequent plunge in company and stock market valuations, a growing entrepreneurial class will demand multiples more funding to start and scale their businesses.

Calculating the exact demand for financing of this sort is near impossible. Not only are there many virtuous circles in investing in technology that mean deploying capital drives even greater demand, but simultaneously destructive investments can put people off VC just as quickly. However, almost every developed nation has set targets to increase the availability of VC to improve their national technology ecosystems. For instance, if Europe wanted to match

America for venture dollars per capita, it would still need to deploy twice as much per year – and that's assuming American VC per capita stood still, which it is unlikely to do.

VC funding per capita for leading nations:

Country	VC funding in 2021 ($ Billion)	Funding per Capita
Singapore	$8.3	$1,398
Israel	$8.3	$959
Estonia	$1.2	$915
United States	$269	$808
Sweden	$7.2	$700
United Kingdom	$32	$472
The Netherlands	$6.2	$358
Denmark	$2.0	$340
Switzerland	$1.8	$316
Finland	$1.7	$303

(Source: Crunchbase.com March 2022)

GUARDIAN ANGELS

For all its impact, VC is still just one small cog in the capital machine needed to support the entrepreneurial class. Venture investments best suit entrepreneurs who are looking to build highly productive but very large-scale solutions, not least because venture capitalists themselves need to make significant multiples on their winning investments to justify their many failed ones. But for those entrepreneurs who are just getting started, or for those who don't want to build a business on a global scale but have a more local or limited target market in mind, then other types of financing make more sense.

Before founders approach organizations like Balderton, the first step many of them take is to raise money from *angel investors*. The term has expanded to mean many things over the last decade, but generally encompasses investment from individuals – often wealthy people interested in funding innovation and diversifying their portfolios by taking high risk for potentially high return investments. It also encompasses other types of financial support, increasingly that of accelerators and crowdfunding, all of which are needed to support new business creation.

Accelerators in particular have proven themselves to be an effective way to help new entrepreneurs, and play a key part in helping countries start new technology ecosystems. These are institutions which provide small amounts of capital to help entrepreneurs go from idea to their very first product, and possibly first customers, while connecting them with other founders in the same situation. Some accelerators, such as San Francisco-based Y Combinator and London-founded Entrepreneur First represent these models par excellence. Y Combinator helps hundreds of entrepreneurs a year with an investment of around $100,000, so they can build a minimal viable product (MVP), or first iteration of their service, and has helped start businesses like Airbnb, Stripe, DoorDash and Dropbox. Entrepreneur First, meanwhile, provides support at an even earlier stage, helping entrepreneurs to come up with an idea in the first place, and find other entrepreneurially minded individuals with whom to start a company. It provides them with a small investment of around £70,000, an amount they describe as enough to 'get any idea going'. Founders who have met each other through EF, as it is known, have created businesses worth many billions of dollars in the last decade and more importantly solved some huge technical challenges. While not all accelerators have been as successful as Y Combinator or EF, they are nonetheless an integral part of any start-up ecosystem, and broadening access to resources, capital and simply other people with similar aspirations has been proven to be a catalyst for many businesses.

As a result of the success of some of these models, the number of accelerators has exploded. According to the Centre for Entrepreneurship the number of business incubators and accelerator programmes doubled between 2017 and 2022 in the UK alone, with over 750 start-up programmes supporting an estimated 19,600 firms a year – which means that almost 1 in 20 new companies found support through this approach. The rapid expansion in the number of accelerators and incubators for new businesses can be put down in part to surging demand, with more businesses being formed than ever before, and in part to supply, thanks to an increase in government-led funding, which makes up around a third of the funding for such programmes in the UK and Europe.

There are many reasons for the success of this model, with a major one simply being the proximity of entrepreneurs to each other. A recent study by Harvard University and the Georgia and Massachusetts Institutes of Technology suggests that the exchange of ideas increased when the founders of start-ups sat closer to other start-up founders in co-working spaces, even when those companies were operating in different sectors. Increasing the number of accelerators and incubators that help budding entrepreneurs with the time, space and network to get a company up and running has many positive externalities for society as whole, and should be a focus point for any country looking to build a more entrepreneurial workforce.

However, even in countries like the USA and UK, where these models are more prevalent, there are still a number of areas where significant funding and policy changes are required to provide the scaffolding for building a more innovative economy.

ENGINEERING SERENDIPITY

Putting like-minded people together and giving them resources to innovate is hardly a new idea, and in fact it is one of the foundational ideas of most universities across the world. This approach to technological innovation has been around at least since imperial Germany in the late nineteenth century, if not earlier. In its current incarnation, modern research universities such as MIT and Stanford have played a disproportionate role in technological progress over the last century. Stanford University, for instance, was founded in 1885 by California senator Leland Stanford and his wife, Jane, 'to promote the public welfare by exercising an influence on behalf of humanity and civilization', a concept it has pursued by supporting a huge number of entrepreneurial spinouts from its research. In which case why not just build more universities?

With notable exceptions, today's universities are not the crucibles of innovation they once were, and across the world governments are experimenting with new ways to help academics and entrepreneurs co-mingle and access the resources and infrastructure they need outside of the traditional university system. One of the most popular ways that governments are trying to do this is with advanced research funds, such as DARPA and ARPA-E in the USA, and the newly formed ARIA in the UK. The Defense Advanced Research Projects Agency, DARPA, was set up in 1958 by Dwight Eisenhower's administration to provide funding to entrepreneurial researchers to experiment with ideas thought to be too far out, or too important to the nation's defence, to be left to the constraints and considerations of university-funding alone. While DARPA provided grants to thousands of projects, many of which went nowhere, it has also been credited with being the initial funding for research which resulted in weather satellites, GPS, drones, voice interfaces and the internet – a history-making string of achievements.

The US Government also funds BARDA, the Biomedical Advanced Research and Development Agency, which proved to be a vital intermediary and catalyst for the development of the Moderna vaccine, and continues to play a role in the development of many other important vaccines and bioweaponry defences.

This model of a government body providing grants for research on frontier technologies has subsequently been borrowed by many other nations across the world. Germany has launched two similar institutions in the last few years, Japan has launched a moonshot fund, and in 2021 the British Government announced an £800 million fund which will 'focus on projects with potential to produce transformative technological change, or a paradigm shift in an area of science'. This might seem like a vast sum of money to spend on outlandish research projects, many of which will come to nothing, but if just a handful of such initiatives turn out to be as impactful as the internet or

RNA-based vaccines, they will, in the long run, pay back the taxpayer many times over.

BACKING THE BOLD

Whether it is by expanding support for university research programmes or creating new pipelines for research through government-funded bodies like DARPA, financing research is a powerful route to delivering a more innovative and entrepreneurial economy.

But as this book has already emphasized, invention is not the same as innovation, let alone entrepreneurship. While a central tenet of my argument is that it has become cheaper and easier to become an entrepreneur, this does not mean it is free or easy, and there are more radical solutions to help people start a business than just extending existing entrepreneurial support.

While VC, accelerators and government-led research agencies all play a role in supporting entrepreneurialism, only a tiny proportion of start-ups are likely to be supported by such institutions. And although the founders who do get such support may turn out to be disproportionately successful, in an economy where many more people are likely to be self-employed, building companies to cover their cost of living, not make millions, there will need to be a much broader shift in the type of financial support available to them.

One critical if intangible part of a business is data, and the government in particular could help those starting a business by sharing the vast quantities of information it already collects. One way to do this is to open up data gathered by tax authorities. Capturing details on the performance of every business in a country annually is a colossal undertaking, so why not then reuse this treasure trove of data, properly anonymized, to help tax-paying entrepreneurs and the wider economy?

In a 2018 experiment led by the ScaleUp Institute in the UK, HMRC, the UK's tax body, analyzed their data sets to identify scaling businesses, and then messaged them with introductions to local support groups. The businesses in question had to meet specific criteria, such as being more than five years old, and have reported increases in turnover of at least 20 per cent over a three-year period. The pilots took place at locations where people had been trained to help companies grow, and there were dedicated support centres. HMRC sent messages via letter and email to each company explaining the support available to them, and those that responded and joined local centres went on to benefit through winning more local contracts or discovering grants that were previously unknown to them.

This simple messaging trial had a positive impact. Yet given the sheer amount of data harvested by tax authorities, a much more direct campaign could have an even greater effect. By looking at tax and other public data, authorities like HMRC could help entrepreneurs identify cost savings by showing averages in their industry and geography for services like computer equipment or office space. They could connect newly registered companies with relevant mentors, either local or globally, to help people kick-start new projects, and connect new entrepreneurs with others in their local area going through the same process, thereby creating instant peer groups which have been shown to have a positive impact on business success rates.

With such a policy in place, the first contact you would get when founding a business might no longer be targeted advertising but rather data-driven advice – with the added bonus that you may be less fearful of opening messages from the tax authorities in future as well!

But why stop at simply providing static advice? Local government could also provide ongoing mentorship for founders of new companies, with hyper-targeted support through business scouts. In the world of sports, the best football clubs have scouts traversing the world, and combing through every junior football team's match report to find and develop the next great talent. But there are very few equivalent examples in business. In our experience at Balderton, having a board of experienced investors and business builders makes a huge difference not just to the success of a company but to the mental health of founders, who know they have other people around them to share their burdens. Assembling a directory of experienced business builders, who may be interested in investing or simply supporting a founder in a sector or the local area they are passionate about, could enable more entrepreneurs to scale their company – and, once again, tax authorities could easily play matchmaker here, by alerting interested parties to new businesses based on their tax code and company registration.

Even more critical to the success of a business than an experienced board or advisor is access to a strong community of peers. We need to create more networks aimed at people who want to get started in many different fields. Academic evidence demonstrating the importance of professional communities to the success of businesses is overwhelming. Writing in the *Harvard Business Review*, Gary Pisano and Willy Shih coined the term *the industrial commons* for an industry-specific network that can include, among other things, 'R&D know-how, engineering, and manufacturing competencies related to a specific technology.' And they stressed the importance of these commons in the success of ecosystems such as Silicon Valley.

While there's plenty of evidence that these commons benefit from having an in-person context, perhaps sharing the same space or building, online communities can be highly effective as well. There are now a growing number of for-profit and not-for-profit businesses building virtual platforms for entrepreneurs who are looking to get started or to level up their operations. As mentioned in a previous chapter, such services have existed within the technology community for years, with platforms like Stack Overflow providing free advice for software developers looking to troubleshoot problems or share snippets of code that helped them save time, creating a virtuous circle of support. Newer platforms like Primer, Polywork and others are now being set up to help people start businesses and pursue ideas in many emerging industries. These online groups provide a combination of content, network and active experts to help young and old alike navigate opportunities to replicate the benefits of the physical spaces that entrepreneurs spinning out of universities, research labs and corporates enjoy.

Such policies – including an increase in business education, targeted data, directed support, and online and offline communities – are all relatively cheap ways for the government and private sector to expand the number – and improve the productivity – of start-ups. However, as any entrepreneur will tell you, the single biggest challenge to the success of any new venture is the availability of capital. While capital certainly doesn't solve all problems, and in some cases too much capital can skew a business's priorities, a lack of funding will often prove fatal to a new company's chances. Increasing the availability of relatively low-risk capital is therefore essential. And one big way to do this would be to give every entrepreneur in the country access to a start-up loan, in the same way that many countries offer student loans.

In the 1990s, university education was identified as a critical way for individuals to improve their life outcomes through enhanced social mobility and salaries from graduate jobs. But further education came at a price, and governments were unable to foot the bill for a generation of students to be given such education for free, resulting in a huge expansion of university loans. The university loans system was generally designed in such a way that only those people who earned a certain amount of money paid back the loan with interest.

As well as expanding this programme to cover lifelong learning opportunities, such a funding model would be even better suited to people who are looking to start a business. Giving aspiring entrepreneurs a one-off loan of a similar quantum, say up to $50,000, with a repayment schedule that would kick in only once the business reached a certain level of revenues or profitability, would give millions more people the chance to go from idea, to product, to company in ways that only the more fortunate or well-connected have been able to do in the past. Such an intervention in the business world is not a novel one. Many countries took a similar approach during the COVID pandemic, when lockdown resulted in a huge shock to the economy and many millions of businesses would have gone under without emergency support.

It was certainly right to use such a fiscal intervention to avoid disaster, but there's equal justification for intervening in a similar way to support entrepreneurs. Adapting the existing university loans scheme to fund a business – a business in which the government could share in the upside through loan repayments and increased tax returns – would allow many more people to become sustainably self-employed.

Ask the average person what they would prefer – a university degree, or targeted financial, advisory and community support to launch the business they have always dreamed of – and I'd wager you'd quickly learn just how popular these policy changes would be. Moreover, they would help smooth the transition away from traditional corporate careers to more entrepreneurial ones, and in the process boost economic growth and productivity.

The final piece of the puzzle in unlocking an *everyday-everyone* entrepreneurial economy lies beyond legislative, educational and financial reforms. The most important, and perhaps hardest, challenge will be overcoming the many decades of cultural resistance to this new world of work. Navigating that will require leadership, not just funding and legislation.

14

How to change the world

On what principle is it, that when we see nothing but improvement behind us, we are to expect nothing but deterioration before us?
THOMAS BABINGTON MACAULAY,
REVIEW OF SOUTHEY'S COLLOQUIES
ON SOCIETY, 1830

With most decisions in life, it's worth carefully weighing the positives and negatives, and coming to a balanced conclusion. This is how a vast majority of the best decisions are made. In venture capital, however, the scales are stacked differently. If we make the right decision on an investment, we help start businesses that can produce world-changing technologies, create huge numbers of highly paid jobs and return many times our investment. If we get it wrong, we lose only our initial outlay, while hopefully also funding the development of new technologies, and training of new developers, in the process.

As a result of this imbalance, alongside the usual weighing of pros and cons, we train ourselves to focus on the scale of the opportunity should the best possible scenario play out. In short, a critical question that we ask ourselves about any investment is: *What happens if this goes right?*

Of course, asking this question without truly understanding the risks can lead to some pretty bad decisions. Such considerations must always be matched with reality. Yet all too often, in recent decades the question of what society could achieve has been outweighed by the question of what we stand to lose. Risk aversion, and a concern about widespread change, is perhaps a natural position for people and societies that have sacrificed so much for what they have, and still feel so vulnerable to change. If you are working every hour in a job you hate, in the knowledge that unemployment means you can't keep the heating on or put food on the table, talk of a utopian, entrepreneurial world of self-employment matters little. If you're a pensioner, who has worked hard all their life to retire on your savings, in the home you love, the prospect of financial and societal upheaval could of course make you anxious. However, maintaining the status quo is equally unacceptable. That's a future of propped-up large and failing corporations, top-down managerialism of declining state services, and a generation robbed of the dignity of independent and self-directed work. Rather than unleashing waves of transformative ideas, such a future would also put the brakes on higher productivity driven by risk-taking innovation and entrepreneurship, with a chilling effect on our economies and a continued heating of our climate. So to convince people of the benefits of change, we should start by asking a simple question: What happens if this goes *right*?

Let me offer a glimpse of just such a scenario.

'THE HUSTLER'

Harry toiled in sales roles for most of his twenties. He started by cold-calling for a recruitment firm, before progressing to an account management role. By the time he was 30, he'd become a team manager, hiring other cold-calling newbies to follow in his footsteps. The company he worked for paid reasonably well. He had plenty of friends in the office, with whom he enjoyed Friday office drinks. It wasn't a bad gig overall. But soon after his thirtieth birthday, he felt a nagging sense of restlessness. He wanted more of a challenge. More autonomy. A chance to build something for himself. So, he did something his mum and dad had never once so much as considered in their careers: he quit.

Harry had been thinking about building something new for a while. It began with him spotting that successfully filling vacancies in biopharmaceutical companies took four to five more candidate application compared with other industries. The extra time and effort involved meant that he and others on his recruitment team had started turning down work in that particular sector. But given how rapidly the biopharmaceutical industry was expanding, and how the corresponding demand for high-quality candidates was ramping up – with firms paying handsomely for the right people – he sensed an opportunity to start his own business.

On quitting his job, he received his pink slip confirming the end of his employment, via the government's holistic online portal, which seamlessly managed employee information from social security payments to pension plan options, and also sent him a message giving him ten free credits for a range of online education platforms. Right away he zeroed in on a particular class: How to set up your own company. It began with a ten-minute interactive video, an AI-led but completely fluid and interactive conversation running through the key details of the process. By the time the video had ended, Harry had told the service exactly what he wanted to achieve with his new company, and the entire legal entity had been set up and registered in his name by the afternoon, for the princely sum of $10.

Next, Harry searched for online classes on launching a company, many of which came with easy access to the tools they provided training on, and by the end of the afternoon he'd set up his own interactive webpage, social media presence, and infrastructure such as email and payments systems. With the help of the latest AI, a large language model that specialized in new company branding, and a few prompts from Harry himself ('Happy scientist, vector graphics, Celtics' green'), he'd created a brand, LabAssist – and even had time left over to make a video pitch on his state's crowdfunding website, all slickly edited by an AI service.

Within 24 hours of leaving his old role, and with the digital ink barely dry on his resignation, Harry's new business felt very real. It was one thing mulling over his idea with colleagues over lunch; it was quite another now that it had a website and a logo. The initial admin largely out of the way, he felt genuinely invested in making it work. After listening to a podcast about automating people searches, he found a tool that could identify people looking for work who had opted in to share their information on a professional networking site using a wide range of parameters. After a few days of experimentation, Harry had narrowed down the traits he believed the most successful candidates for biopharmaceutical roles shared, and gradually trained this new tool to find more people with these criteria. Soon he had a basic version of the tool, which produced the names of candidates his employer would never have considered let alone recommended for these roles – all high potential people with very different backgrounds, across a wide variety of geographies.

Excitedly, Harry began contacting these candidates and introduced them to his biopharmaceutical customers. With bated breath and champagne on ice, he waited for the first few candidates to give him feedback. But none of them were successful. It turned out that while his clients liked the applicants personally, they lacked some basic areas of knowledge about the sector which made assessing them too difficult.

As the week ended, a dispirited Harry sank back into his home office chair wondering whether he'd made a huge mistake by turning his back on a stable job with decent prospects. But just then he received a notification from the government's 'new business assistant'. This state-built automated bot was reminding him of the Founders' Collective, a service that connected entrepreneurs with experienced business builders. He signed up and quickly found an expert in biopharmaceuticals, Sophie, who had built a successful business in that sector before. After a few meetings, Sophie decided to help Harry design an interactive training video for candidates to go through before the interview process.

The video adapted automatically to the candidates' differing styles of communication and backgrounds, and helped explain key terms, distilling Harry's knowledge of recruitment and Sophie's industry experience into concise, clear language. Sophie was so impressed in these meetings that she offered to invest in Harry's business, which alongside a few hundred thousand dollars that had come from the local crowdfunding site, gave him just the shot in the arm he needed.

The very next month, after further fine-tuning, Harry relaunched the platform. This time, when the search tool he had trained started spitting out candidates' names, those individuals received automated messages highlighting the benefits of working in biopharma companies, and interested parties went through Harry and Sophie's refined training video remotely. The first batch of new candidates went for interviews just a week later, and over half of them got the job. Harry's new service was now placing candidates at twice the rate of his former company, at a fraction of the price, and with just one employee: the owner himself.

'THE ENGINEER'

William had always loved Chemistry. From his sixth birthday, when his parents had got him a children's chemistry set, the very idea that you could make a brand new substance or get a fizzing reaction by mixing different elements together, had thrilled him. He'd done well at college, studied the subject at university, and went on to work at a major chemistry company, where he produced huge quantities of incredibly pure cobalt, with its bright blue hue, for industrial buyers. At first, he'd loved the role. But five years into his career at the multinational, he hadn't really progressed at all, while his ideas for improving the production processes were routinely overlooked by his increasingly stressed superiors. No one in the company seemed to be interested in trying something new. With prices for chemicals falling, it all felt a bit stagnant.

So, when William and his partner had their first child, Louise, he decided to go part-time, while his other half worked. He loved those three days a week he spent with his daughter; caring for her was infinitely more rewarding than the huge corporate that was steadily smothering his ambition and passion for work. But then, while browsing using his AR headset during naptime one afternoon, he came across an article on the rise of biopharma companies, aided by a breakthrough in new miniature bioreactors. Large chemical reactors were Will's particular area of expertise; he'd thought for years about how to make them smaller and the benefits that would bring – so the article naturally piqued his interest. However, the piece went on to report that a major problem for these new miniature bioreactors was temperature control – even more critical in biological processes than in chemical reactions.

Intrigued by this knotty problem, William set aside time each evening to experiment with designs for a smart-heat valve he'd seen work in cobalt reactions, to find out whether it could be used in bioreactors as well. At home he could access a range of cutting-edge solutions, including virtual reality design tools and artificial physics engines that his workplace wouldn't sign off on due to the 10-year contracts signed by management with huge but inflexible software providers.

As his daughter started going to school, William had more time to work on his idea until, after months of experimentation, he finally cracked it. The simulation of his new valve performed perfectly. But what was he going to do now? He considered selling the rights to his model to a bioreactor company. However, according to blog posts he'd read from many of his favourite entrepreneurs, he knew it wasn't a good idea to sell out too early. What's more, after a few years of working part-time, he also knew he didn't have the resources himself to start production of his valve immediately. Even though advances in 3D manufacturing had cut the cost of production by 80 per cent, versus a few years ago, it was still high-tech equipment, and each valve would be expensive to make.

Fortunately, a family friend who had also started a company suggested he approach the Business Loan Company, a government-funded programme that offered terms similar to his wife's old student loan. After registering his company in the morning, he was told the same afternoon that he could use the facility to start producing his first few valves, assisted by risk-assessment algorithms.

It was the next step that had worried William the most. While he felt comfortable with designing products, and even raising finance, he had never worked in sales and marketing. He needed someone to join him on this entrepreneurial journey but couldn't afford to pay a salary. And although he'd met with a few candidates from a large recruitment company, none of them were a good fit, and the company's fees were far too high.

Then he got an automated outreach from LabAssist, a new recruitment service and thought the targeted model, and the lower fees, were worth a shot. After many conversations with the second candidate, they sent him, William hired his co-founder, Nabeel. And the pair set to work.

After five years in a dead-end career at a listless corporate, and now that his daughter was old enough for school, William was fired up about launching his own business. Within months, his 3D printed valves were flying off the shelves.

'THE MONEY'

Hannah loved trading. It didn't really matter what she was buying or selling, she lived for the thrill of the deal. After excelling at school and university, she had considered going into carbon trading, a fast-growing industry that had exploded in the mid-2020s. Instead, she took what she thought would be a more stable job as a quant trader at a well-known hedge fund based in New York. She designed some of the firm's best performing algorithms, trading currencies across the world.

Everything was going well until one day her boss pulled her aside to say the firm was being reorganized. Specifically, they needed more computing power, and fewer people. Hannah soon found herself unemployed, struggling to pay her extortionate New York rent – and worst of all, cut off from her love of trading.

She was down, but she certainly wasn't out. Some of her university friends had moved to a beautiful town outside Austin, Texas, which had recently upgraded its communications infrastructure and built data centres that were powered by the Lone Star State's ample solar farms. As a result, Texas was offering free, superfast internet access and cheap computing power to anyone who moved there and paid state taxes. Deciding to cut her losses in New York, Hannah moved in with some friends there, using her savings to access a state-of-the art, AI-driven cloud computer, now just $5,000, which could analyze vastly more data than the traditional systems her former employer had used.

Talking to acquaintances in Austin one evening, she heard about the huge advances in biopharma, and decided to spend a few months immersing herself in the sector. Combining her previous experiences, the cheap data infrastructure that Texas offered and immense data sets scanned using her new computer, she started picking out patterns in the data emanating from the biopharma industry.

While sifting through these reports she stumbled upon an incredible reading; so incredible in fact, she had to double-check it. She'd found a small group of bioreactors which were operating at a 50 per cent higher efficiency than average. Suspecting this was a data error, she called the owners of the sites in question. One by one they explained that they had recently been contacted by an excellent sales executive from a company called LabAssist, who had sold them a smart valve that was performing miracles. Hannah instantly felt the trading-floor rush she had always loved. After a quick search she found the founder's name and set-up a video call with the inventor behind the wonder valve. Within 30 minutes, she knew she wanted to invest. She struck an agreement with William and Hannah started a crowdfunding project to secure the capital. They went on to raise over $10 million from venture capitalists, excited to be part of the new bioreactor breakthrough.

Despite never meeting in person, and all working for themselves, William, Hannah and Harry, the inventor, financier and hustler, had kicked off a small revolution.

BACK TO REALITY

While this story may sound fanciful today, it could be a common example of how entrepreneurs work together in the years to come. Not everyone wants this future though. The economic and social benefits of a more entrepreneurial society, one where more people are self-employed or work in small firms versus large corporate ones, or government bodies, is still hotly debated. In their book *Big is Beautiful*, the economists Robert Atkinson and Michael Lind argue that, if anything, policymakers have focused too much on entrepreneurs and small businesses, when large companies drove much of the productivity gains and created the new jobs of the twentieth century. The idea that self-employed citizens are the foundation of a dynamic capitalist economy is a relic of the Jeffersonian dream of an agrarian society, they argue. But much of this scepticism concerning entrepreneurs, and praise for the impact big businesses can have, is based on a theory of the firm that no longer holds for many industries and dated ideas of entrepreneurship.

Multiple studies have shown that start-ups and small, high-growth firms disproportionately contribute to job creation. As entrepreneurs are able to build solutions in industries which play a much bigger role in our lives, such as housing, health and transportation, their contribution to productivity and employment will also rocket.

On his excellent blog on start-ups, Paul Graham, the founder of the influential start-up accelerator Y Combinator, argues that entrepreneurs and early-stage start-ups are 'probably the most productive part of the whole economy.' But this type of productivity – finding product market fit, testing new technologies and discovering what customers want – isn't easily captured in official statistics. In start-ups, there's chaos, with 'offices strewn with junk at two in the morning . . . This is what real productivity looks like.' Suffice to say I'm confident that with the right support, the next generation of entrepreneurs won't just have more personal choice in their careers, they will create a more productive economy too.

So, what more can we do to drive this change? Yes, policy, institutional reform and financial innovation all matter. But more important than all those things is culture and the people that define it. At the beating heart of every social movement is hope, aspiration, and scores of individual leaders who are able to inspire others to make change happen. This entrepreneurial movement is no different.

To grasp the influence of culture in this narrative, you need only turn to recent history. As mentioned in the introduction, this book is being published on the fiftieth anniversary of what is widely seen as a turning point for economic productivity in the twentieth century. In the third quarter of 1973, productivity growth fell by 3.7 per cent. It was the first of five consecutive quarters of negative productivity, and the beginning of the end of an almost unparalleled run of economic growth following the Second World War. Today, half a century later – despite all of our advancements in bringing more people into the workforce, the globalization of the economy, the advent of the internet and increasingly powerful smartphones – developed economies are still growing more slowly than they did in that golden age. Moreover, the median wage has stagnated, leaving many people worse off than their parents were a generation ago.

The economist Tyler Cowen's 2011 pamphlet 'The Great Stagnation' argued that much of the growth from the boom years was driven by easy wins such as expanding education, bringing women into the workforce, cultivating free land and the exploitation of cheap fossil fuels (which would later be recognized to have come at a great cost). Much of the Great Stagnation – the last 50 years of lower productivity – was partly inevitable therefore as these wins dried up.

From the role of technology to money supply, energy costs and government policy, there are myriad explanations for this multi-decade decline in both economic growth and the fall in entrepreneurship which accompanied it. However, I believe one of the most underestimated challenges was the cultural shift away from the risk-taking mentality that drives innovation. Much of the end of the golden era of progress was accompanied by a cacophony of criticism aimed squarely at innovators, entrepreneurs and technology leaders and the unforeseen effects of regulations aimed at maintaining the status quo.

Innovation and entrepreneurialism during this time came under attack from many angles. The anti-Vietnam War movement in the USA closely, and often correctly, criticized the role of industry and scientific research in creating the weapons used to such devastating effect on the Vietnamese, imbuing a sense of suspicion of technological innovators, encapsulated by what President Eisenhower described as the 'military-industrial complex'. The environmental movement, which rightly sought to limit and reverse the impact that new industries were having on the natural world, chose to align themselves with an anti-innovation agenda, seeking to stop growth rather than find more sustainable technologies to enable it. In 1973 the Oxford-trained economist E. F. Schumacher published his instant hit *Small Is Beautiful* – a series of essays that called for limits to entrepreneurial zeal and endless consumption to protect the environment. It was quickly named one of the 100 Most Influential Books written in the post-war period, setting the tone for the argument that progress is anti-environmental, rather than an essential part of finding solutions.

Meanwhile, in Europe and the UK, green movements, such as the Campaign for Nuclear Disarmament, chose to correlate, erroneously, the development and potential use of nuclear weapons with civilian use of clean nuclear power. At the same time, multinational corporations, financial institutions and a larger state all settled into a post-war consensus with regulations protecting large companies from disruption. This left little room for entrepreneurs and had the effect of ossifying the economy. Even as late as 2010, Germany's DAX 30, the country's leading public equity index, contained only two companies that were founded after the 1970s. Today France's CAC 40 has only one. In fact, if you compile a list of Europe's 100 most valuable public companies, none were created in the past 40 years.

The writer Brink Lindsey argues compellingly that in the 1970s, technological progress was purposefully frustrated, writing that in the latter decades of the twentieth century 'Capitalism didn't just stumble; capitalism had its legs broken.'

What would have happened if the environmental movement of that era had instead chosen innovation as the route to a greener world rather than anti-capitalism? Or if governments had sought to level the playing field for entrepreneurs and enforce anti-monopoly policies, rather than entrench large companies? While we can only speculate, I strongly suspect it would have resulted in more prosperous and sustainable economies today.

SETTING THE TONE

The problems that beleaguered the post-1973 era – the Great Stagnation – seemed to have found respite in the 2000s and 2010s in certain parts of the economy. The rise of companies like Apple, Google, Amazon which overthrew established multinationals not only improved productivity, but inspired and enabled millions more people to find entrepreneurial work. But the shadows of the 1970s loom again.

The dizzying success of the entrepreneurial culture of Silicon Valley, and the global digital movement of the last decade, is now being re-evaluated in the light of harsher macroeconomic circumstances and the disappointment, deceit and in some cases outright criminality of once celebrated technology founders.

This will undeniably have a negative impact on a still emerging pro-entrepreneurial culture. Investment into new technology companies, ushered in by the huge success of the internet, cloud computing and mobile technology, has already started to cool. With rising inflation, fluctuating energy costs and shifting political sands, the barriers to starting a business are returning in a strikingly similar way to the 1970s, making entrepreneurship a riskier career path, even as traditional careers pay less and no longer offer the stability they once did.

Lip service is often paid to entrepreneurship by politicians of all stripes, but once in government too little is done to lighten the burden on those looking to start a business, or to invest in new energy infrastructure, housing or child care, the underpinnings of a more entrepreneurial society. A much-needed resurgent environmental movement often conflates caring for the environment with stopping innovation, prioritizing their concerns about capitalism over finding technological solutions for climate change. And ever present are a small but vocal group of people who, for whatever reason, will always challenge those who are brave enough to try something new, to dream slightly bigger, and to go it alone.

The transition to *everyday-everyone* entrepreneurship will not be an easy one.

To get there the most important shift must be a cultural one. At the height of the 2020 pandemic, the entrepreneur and investor Marc Andreessen wrote in his piece 'It's Time to Build' that: 'Every step of the way, to everyone around us, we should be asking the question, what are you building? What are you building directly, or helping other people to build, or teaching other people to build, or taking care of people who are building?'

To my English sensibilities, that directness is a bit much. But in response to such great challenges – a declining sense of personal purpose, global economic stagnation, climate change, declining living standards, inequality and the rising threat of automation – his call to action hits the mark.

While cultural change feels intangible and elusive, there are real things we can do to set the tone. We can celebrate tradespeople, freelancers and entrepreneurs who have set out on their own as role models. We can encourage the virtues of creative thinking, ingenuity and resilience. We can create and distribute more content showing how millions of people are learning new skills and experimenting with new technologies as was done with programmes like those developed for the BBC Micro. We can encourage more public awards, like the French *Légion d'honneur* and the British Royal Honours system (of which only 6 per cent a year go to entrepreneurs today!) to recognize individual efforts in driving innovation. We can champion the idea that blue-collar workers are entrepreneurs too, that crafts and trades are just as valuable as office jobs, that front-line carers deserve to be empowered and that you don't need to work in a FTSE 100 company to change the world. Local public servants can call out for help from start-ups in their area, seizing on new tools to make a difference in our civic life. Small business owners can be sent congratulations by the tax office on milestone achievements, reminding them of the great things they've funded through the taxes their businesses generate. We can prioritize celebratory and entrepreneurial events, like the Great Exhibition of 1851, the first of a series of World Fairs that showcased over 100,000 new inventions and entrepreneurial endeavours, to spread the contagious idea of starting a business oneself.

The perhaps breathless list of ideas above would cost little but could provide the nudge required to kick-start an entrepreneur's dream. We need to support entrepreneurship in every way we can, for as many people as possible, to give everyone the tools, the impetus, purpose and power to build. Once that's accepted as a cultural norm, the institutional, regulatory and financial reforms needed to make it easier will surely follow. In short, we need to let more people know that if they want to make a meaningful difference in the world, in a way that brings a sense of personal fulfilment, even if it is extremely hard work – then a route exists: start a business.

That will make this century the start-up century.

An Entrepreneur's Manifesto

As more of us work in the entrepreneurial economy, all countries will have to consider how they make it easier for people to develop new skills, access resources, and find work as a sole trader or as a microbusiness. Government cannot solve all these challenges, but it has a role to play. The starting point is to embrace the concept that supporting business, and in particular entrepreneurs, both in the private sector and on the front line of public service benefits all of us.

There are many ways to do this in practice, and I have summarized the ideas in this book into three commitments, or guiding principles, which will smooth the transition to more entrepreneurial work: a commitment to help people find work, to fair work and to fulfilling work. A longer list and an exploration of these ideas can be found at www.startup-century.com.

FIND WORK:

- Provide funding on top of existing benefit payments for people who are out of work but in the process of setting up a business (See the UK Government's former efforts with the New Enterprise Allowance);
- Provide a one-off loan, in a similar model to student loans and Covid relief programmes, for people with a registered microbusiness and qualified business plan to help them expand;

- Accelerate the creation of new universities, in particular those with a technology, engineering and entrepreneurial focus;
- Have employers provide paid time for training through qualified providers;
- Offer tax breaks for investors who hold their stake for a significant (over five years) period in a new business, or who become company advisors or board members, to encourage patient, hands-on capital over short-termism.

FAIR WORK:

- Commit to providing a universal level of digital devices, skills, and resources (the digital scaffolds) to all citizens through educational institutions;
- Enforce on-time payment to freelancers and microbusinesses by law, guaranteed by businesses' bank accounts;
- Lower the revenue requirements for businesses bidding on public service contracts to allow entrepreneurs to compete for contracts to provide essential services;
- Ask local councils to make public requests for innovative solutions to local problems;
- Open up tax authority data to provide insights and advice to entrepreneurs and small businesses.

FULFILLING WORK:

- Make entrepreneurial skills, such as sales, negotiation and business planning a part of young people's education;
- Provide benefit payments for the self-employed to cover sickness or maternity and paternity leave based on a percentage of the last 12 months' earnings;
- Empower public servants to make choices about the tools they use;

- Allow civil servants to take sabbaticals from work after a minimum number of years of service to experiment with new solutions;
- Establish online and offline community business hubs to connect new entrepreneurs with each other and prospective mentors;
- Establish Banks for Entrepreneurs by providing public capital to support new banks, with the mandate to provide overdrafts, working capital, personal mortgages and pension products for entrepreneurs and freelancers.

Notes & Bibliography

The many notes and references in this book are detailed below in order of appearance. For readability I have avoided numbering each reference in line. You can find the full list with links where available at www.startup-century.com. The names of several founders and start-ups were changed and some of their quotes edited and amalgamated, where they preferred not to reveal their company strategy or data for commercial reasons.

INTRODUCTION

'How did starting a business become easier than ever?' – The World Bank, December 2017.

Entrepreneurship during the Covid-19 Pandemic: A global study of entrepreneurs' challenges, resilience, and well-being by Stephan, Ute; Zbierowski, Przemyslaw; Pérez-Luño, Ana et al of King's Business School

Invention: A Life. James Dyson, Simon & Schuster, 2021

'A $100 genome? New DNA sequencers could be a "game changer" for biology, medicine'. Elizabeth Pennisi, Science.org, June 2022

'The lack of VC funding to women is a Western societal shortfall' – Dominic-Madori Davis, TechCrunch, October 2022

'The State of the Global Education Crisis: A Path to Recovery' – UNESCO, Unicef and the World Bank, December 2021

Technological Revolutions and Financial Capital by Carlotta Perez, Edward Elgar Publishing, 2003

The Big Score: The Billion Dollar Story of Silicon Valley. Michael S. Malone, Doubleday, 1985

CHAPTER I BUILDING SOMETHING NEW

The Employment Situation – Bureau of Labour Statistics, December 2022

'The Great Formation' – AVC.com, December 2021

Entrepreneurship at a Glance – OECD, 2017

To some extent this trend is still the case today, with the amount of total entrepreneurial activity – i.e. the number of people either starting a business or running a small one – ten times higher in the Dominican Republic where the informal economy makes up most employment, than in Norway, whose GDP per capita is ten times larger.

The Exponential Age by Azeem Azhar, Random House Business, 2021

'Number of people starting a business in the UK hits record high' – Dan Martin, February 2022

'Start-Up boom in the pandemic is growing stronger' – *New York Times*, Ben Casselman, August 2021

'2023 Side Hustle Statistics and Survey Results' – Sidehustlenation.com, 2023

'Young people are more entrepreneurial than ever' – CentreforEntre preneurs.org, 2016

Business Formation Statistics – US Department of Commerce, 2022

'The strange case of China's self-employment statistics' – Andrew Batson, 2022

'Searching for the American Dream' – Steve Gillon, HuffPost, December 2014

'Is the UK a meritocracy?' – Economics Observatory, Juliette Brown, 2021

'Elon Musk and others urge AI pause, citing risks to society' – Reuters, Narayan, Hu, Coulter and Mukherjee, April 2023

Ark Investment Management LLC, 2023

'The AI road not taken' – Daron Acemoglu, MIT.edu, August 2021

Poll: 'Americans say even the legal breaks for college admission are rigging the system' – *USAToday*, 2020

'U.S. Lost Over 60 Million Jobs, Now Robots, Tech And Artificial Intelligence Will Take Millions More' – *Forbes*, Jack Kelly, 2020

Bullshit Jobs: A Theory by David Graeber, Allen Lane, 2018

See the Pew Research Center attitudes to work survey, 2016

'Map Of The Month: How Many People Work In Agriculture?' – Emily Cassidy and Amelia Snyder – May 2019

Dignity at Work by Randy Hodson, Cambridge University Press, 2001

CHAPTER 2 THE MAKINGS OF AN ENTREPRENEUR

'The Rich List: At last, the self-made triumph over old money' – *The Sunday Times*, May 2018

'Why encouraging more people to become entrepreneurs is bad public policy' – Shane S. Small Business Economics, 2009

Freshbooks entrepreneurship survey – 2019

'Entrepreneurship in the Future: A Delphi Study of ETP and JBV Editorial Board Members' – Marco van Gelderen, Johan Wiklund and Jeffery S. McMullen – May 2021

For more details on employee equity grants in start-ups, you can find the Balderton Equity Guide on www.Balderton.com

Ownership: Reinventing Companies, Capitalism, and Who Owns What by Corey Rosen and John Case, Berrett-Koehler, 2022

'How technology is redrawing the boundaries of the firm' – *The Economist*, January 2023

You can follow Pieter's extraordinary story of living and working as a *digital nomad* at nomadlist.com

The characteristics of those in the gig economy – BEIS report, February 2018

'Does the gig economy promote entrepreneurship?' – Chicago Booth Review – Michael Rapoport, October 2020

Zero to One: Notes on Startups, or How to Build the Future by Peter Thiel and Blake Masters, Currency, 2014

The Innovator's Dilemma – When New Technologies Cause Great Firms to Fail by Clayton Christensen, Harvard Business Review Press, 1997

Super Founders: What data reveals about billion-dollar start-ups by Ali Tamaseb, PublicAffairs, 2021

'The future of entrepreneurship: the few or the many?' Springer Science and Business – Donald F. Kuratko and David B. Audretsch, July 2021

'The "idea" of being an entrepreneur' – New Things – Matt Clancy, August 2021

'Business owners struggle to ease work-life imbalance' – *Guardian*, September 2015

You can find many more great pieces on how entrepreneurship is 'contagious' on The Entrepreneurs' Network website, https://www.tenentrepreneurs.org/

'Mind the Gap: The role of gender in entrepreneurial career choice and social influence by founders' – Vera Rocha and Mirjam van Praag, January 2020

'Who Becomes an Inventor in America? The Importance of Exposure to Innovation' – *The Quarterly Journal of Economics*, May 2019

See De Wit and Van Winden, 1989, Uhlaner et al., 2002 – On the lack of relationship between education and entrepreneurship.

'Impact of Media on Entrepreneurial Intentions and Actions' – Global Entrepreneurship Monitor – Jonathan Levie, Mark Hart and Mohammed Shamsul Karim, November 2010

In fact, The Entrepreneurs Network found in their 2019 survey of 544 parents in the UK that 97 per cent of parents of children under 18 would be supportive of their children starting a business, a rapid turnaround in the last few decades.

For more on the topic of how role models influence entrepreneurship, I highly recommend subscribing to Matt Clancy's substack, 'What's new under the sun'.

'Global EdTech started the last decade with $500m of Venture Capital invested in 2010 and finished 32x higher at $16.1B in 2020, nearly 2x the previous investment record in 2018' – Education Intelligence Unit, January 2021

CHAPTER 3 GROWTH CURVES

'Underwear in the Mediaeval Period.' – Melissa Snell, ThoughtCo, December 2022

'The Pace of Technology Adoption is Speeding Up' – HBR.org, Rita McGrath, 2013

For more examples of building critical infrastructure at speed, like Renkioi Hospital, I always find it inspiring to see the list of projects kept by Patrick Collison at www.patrickcollison.com/fast

The Wealth and Poverty of Nations: Why some are so rich and some so poor by David Landes, W. W. Norton, 1998

See William D. Nordhaus' extensive work on the cost of lighting in his Cowles Foundation Papers, 1998

Florence Nightingale: The Woman and Her Legend, by Mark Bostridge, Penguin, 2020

'Pandemic Speeds Americans' Embrace of Digital Commerce' – *WSJ*, Harriet Torry, November 2020

The future of work after COVID-19 by McKinsey & Company, February 2021

'Telemedicine Arrives in the U.K.: "10 Years of Change in One Week"' – Benjamin Mueller, April 2020

A great example of how Wright's Law scales, and the impact this can have on the climate crises can be found in Anand Gopal's piece for *Project-Syndicate:* How Wright's Law can right the climate

See OpenAI.com for the latest developments with ChatGPT

See www.copy.ai for more examples

'Explained: What is ChatGPT?' – World Economic Forum, December 2022

CHAPTER 4   OF FARMS AND FACTORIES

See www.infarm.com/vision

'Desktop Metal Becomes the World's Only Publicly Traded Pure-Play Additive Manufacturing 2.0 Company' – www.desktopmetal.com, December 2022

An Enquiry into the Nature and Causes of the Wealth of Nations, Adam Smith, New York: Random House, 1937

Ibid pp. 734–5

It's testament to just how important these roles in society were, that so many people are still named after the craft their families were known for. Smith and Cooper are still very popular names in England today. There are very few people named after the roles they played in the mills and factories of the industrial revolution.

Visit https://openbionics.com/

Farming and Farm Income Data – https://www.ers.usda.gov/

See https://www.highersteaks.com/

'Vertical farms nailed tiny salads. Now they need to feed the world' – Wired UK, November 2022

CHAPTER 5   THE FALL OF THE FIRM

'Rise in sales of second-hand party outfits' – BBC News, December 2022

www.pointfranchise.co.uk provides a summary of the cost of setting up many high-street businesses

The Wal-Mart Way: The Inside Story of the Success of the World's
   Largest Company
'The Nature of the Firm' by Ronald Coase, 1937
The Organization Man by William H. Whyte Jr, Simon & Schuster, 1956
'How did starting a business become easier than ever?' – Worldbank.org,
   December 2017
'Elon Musk slept on his office couch and "showered at the YMCA"
   while starting his first company' – CNBC, June 2018
Tetrapak Company History, for more see www.Tetrapak.com
'OpenAI releases Point-E, an AI that generates 3D models' –
   TechCrunch, December 2022
*A World Without Work: Technology, Automation and How We Should
   Respond* by Daniel Susskind, Allen Lane, 2020
   See https://mattsclancy.com/new-things-under-the-sun/

CHAPTER 6 A CREATOR'S ECONOMY

'Self Made Women: Teri Ijeoma Of Trade and Travel on how she started
   with nothing and created a million dollar business.' Interview with
   Sara Connell June 2022
Number of self-employed workers in the United Kingdom from May
   1992 to October 2022 – Bank Of England
'Li Jin on the future of the creator economy' – *The Economist* 2022
'Sole Survivors: How the Internet is Saving Bespoke Shoemaking' –
   Derek Guy, April 2023
'44 per cent Of Global eCommerce Is Owned By 4 Chinese
   Companies' – John Koetsier, *Forbes*, 2020
'China's small and medium-sized enterprises rebounded after the
   COVID-19 lockdown, but economic problems linger' – Xiabo
   Zhang, 2020
See www.upwork.com and their 'Freelance Forward Economist Report',
   2021
'TikTok Rich List' – HopperHQ.com
'How Much Do YouTubers Make? Facts and Figures for 2022' – Intuit
   .com, December 2022
'Future founders, Understanding the next generation of entrepreneurs'
   – Octopus Group
'Entrepreneurship, Economic Conditions, and the Great Recession' –
   Robert W. Fairlie with the Kaufmann-RAND Institute, April 2013

'U.S. newsroom employment has fallen 26 per cent since 2008' –
Mason Walker, Pew Research Centre, July 2021

'Trade Group Probing Stock Sales of 3 Firms'– Bob Schwartz, *LA Times*,
June 1991

'How GameStop found itself at the centre of a ground breaking battle
between Wall Street and small investors' – *Guardian*, Ed Helmore,
2021

StackOverflow Developer Survey, 2021

Rebel code: the inside story of Linux and the open source revolution by Glyn
Moody, Basic Books, 2002

'DoNotPay's "first robot lawyer" to take on speeding tickets in court via
AI' – USAtoday.com. January 2023

'Creating in The Era of Creative Confidence' – Scott Belsky, December 22

'Generative AI could raise global GDP by 7 per cent' – Goldman Sachs
report, April 2023

See The Federation of Master Builders annual State of Trade Survey
(www.fmb.org.uk)

'Building Products with AI' – Tariq Rauf, January 2023

CHAPTER 7 NEW FRONTIERS

'Moore's Law is Dead, now what?' Przemek Chojecki – 2022

Innovate Finance – 2022 Report

'Pee is the magic number, as Withings puts a urine analysis lab in your
toilet' – Haje Jan Kamps, 2023

'Kaia Health's Digital MSK Therapy App Effectively Reduces Pain' –
Kaia Health Team, July 2020

See www.sava.health

See the A16Z Biotech & Health Blog at www.a16z.com

'Work and meaning in the age of AI' – Daniel Susskind, Brookings
Institute, February 2023

See www.Levity.ai

See www.AutoGPT.net for more coverage of what this software can do.

'Renewable electricity is growing faster than ever' – IEA.org, 2021

The data for this comes from China's National Energy Administration
and GOV.UK, however I would recommend subscribing to www
.exponentialview.co for great coverage of the shift to renewable
energy

'What are Small Modular Reactors (SMRs)?' – Joanne Liou, IAEA
    Office of Public Information and Communication – November 2021
How solar mini-grids can bring cheap, green electricity to rural Africa –
    ODI.org
'Doing Capitalism in the Innovation Economy' – William H. Janeway
    – 2012
'Helion Needs You' – Sam Altman, July 2022
'Electric vehicle batteries would have cost as much as a million dollars
    in the 1990s' – Hannah Ritchie, December 2022
Shanghai Municipal Statistics Bureau – 2022
'Dutch couple become Europe's first inhabitants of a 3D-printed house'
    – *Guardian*, April 2021
See https://www.doublegdp.com/
'How much did it cost to create the Space Shuttle?' – Planetary.org
'Space factory startup Varda secures NASA partnerships ahead of demo
    flight next year' – CNBC, September 2022
'Energy Superabundance: How cheap, abundant energy will shape our
    future' – Austin Vernon and Eli Dourado, 2023

CHAPTER 8 DIGITAL SCAFFOLDS

Entrepreneurship, Economic Conditions, and the Great Recession by
    Robert Fairlie, 2011
'To build a better world from the COVID crisis, we need a global push
    to connect the world's young people' – Web Foundation – March
    2021
'The State of Mobile Internet Connectivity 2019' – Connected Society
'COVID-19 Committee Beyond Digital: Planning for a Hybrid World'
    – House of Lords, April 2021
'Children and parents: media use and attitudes report 2019' – Ofcom,
    2020
'Mobile phone prices soar over 20 years' – Ray Ali, July 2020
'Five reasons South Korea has the fastest internet' – IDG Connect, July
    2017
'FCC begins rollout of $10B in connectivity aid through emergency
    funds' – Devin Coldewey, May 2021
'Watch out Zoom: Microsoft Teams now has more than 115 million
    daily users' – Owen Hughes, October 2020

'The challenges facing schools and pupils in September 2020' – Caroline Sharp, Julie Nelson, Megan Lucas, Jenna Julius, Tami McCrone and David Sims

'Blueprint for a 100 per cent Digitally Included UK' – Good Things Foundation, 2020

'The Charisma Machine: The Life, Death, and Legacy of One Laptop per Child' – Morgan Ames, 2019

'The Legacy of The BBC Micro Effecting Change in the UK'S Cultures of Computing' – Tilly Blyth, May 2012

'Commentary: Laptops for every student – a lot could go wrong' – Lim Sun Sun, October 2020

'Bridging the digital divide: Improving digital inclusion in Southeast Asia' – Roland Berger, 2020

CHAPTER 9   FOR BETTER OR WORSE

Jimmy's Jobs Podcast, based on Focal Point Data, January 2023

See https://www.ypo.org/

See https://www.annacodrearado.com/

'Elon Musk Says The Human Brain Cannot Cope With Business Failure. Is He Right?' – INC.com, Christine Lagorio-Chafkin, November 2013

Hired: six months undercover in low-wage Britain by James Bloodworth, Atlantic Books, 2019

'Want to Be an Artist? Hope Your Parents Are Loaded' – Money.com, April 2019

Suicide: A Study in Sociology by Emile Durkheim, 1897

CHAPTER 10   A NEW SKILLS BARGAIN

EntreComp: The entrepreneurship competence framework: Bacigalupo, M., Kampylis, P., Punie, Y., & Van den Brande, G. 2016.

A history on CDTM – https://www.cdtm.de/about-us/

'How Entrepreneurship Might Be Genetic' – INC, Adam Heitzman, January, 2015

'Earnings Dynamics, Changing Job Skills, and STEM Careers' – The Quarterly Journal of Economics – David J Deming, Kadeem Noray, June 2020

See www.synthesis.com

'The Learning Curve: How the UK is harnessing the potential of online learning' – Demos, 2020

See www.crunchbase.com/organization/labster

See www.jolt.io

'What ChatGPT Means for How We Teach Writing' – Anne Bruder, January 2023

'Complexity and the Ten-Thousand-Hour Rule' – *New Yorker*, Malcom Gladwell, 2013

'ChatGPT banned from New York City public schools' devices and networks' – Kalhan Rosenblatt, January 2023

'Meta's Galactica AI can write scientific papers, but is it any good?' – *New Scientist* – Matthew Sparkes, November 2022

The Carnegie Trust UK

'Price Of College Increasing Almost 8 Times Faster Than Wages' – *Forbes*, Camilo Maldonado, July 2018

See www.dysoninstitute.com

2022 Makers Index: What's keeping young people from the skilled trades? – Stanley Black & Decker

CHAPTER 11   KEEPING THE BALANCE

Capitalism, Socialism, and Democracy by Joseph Schumpeter, 1942

'U.S. Federal Government Tax Revenue, who really pays the bills?' – *The Balance*, Kimberley Amadeo, December 2022

'Taxing work and investment across legal forms: pathways to well-designed taxes' – IFS – Stuart Adam and Helen Miller, January 2021

'How often do freelancers get paid late? It depends if you're a woman or man' – Matthew Brown, December 2022

Department for Business, Energy & Industrial Strategy, Small Business Commissioner, The Rt Hon Kwasi Kwarteng MP, and Paul Scully MP – January 2021

'Why are small businesses struggling to win Government contracts?' – SmallBusiness.co.uk, May 2018

'Spain's Supreme Court rules food delivery riders are employees, not freelancers' – Reuters, September 2020

'Uber drivers are workers not self-employed, Supreme Court rules' – BBC, February 2021

'Epic v. Apple keeps coming back to the gap between ignorance and
    inconvenience' – The Verge, Adi Robertson, 2021
'Apple scores legal win over Epic in Fortnite lawsuit: What you need
    to know' – Ian Sherr and Daniel Van Boom, CNET, September 2021
'Marketplace take rates factors' – Tanay's Newsletter – Tanay Jaipuria,
    January 2021
'Computer Vision in 2023: In-Depth Guide' – AI Multiple, Cem
    Dilmegani, January, 2023
'Algorithms Need Management Training, Too' – Wired Magazine, 2023
The Digital Republic: On Freedom and Democracy in the 21st Century by
    Jamie Susskind, Bloomsbury Publishing, 2022
'How Amazon automatically tracks and fires warehouse workers for
    "productivity"' – The Verge, Colin Lecher, April 2019
'Retirement saving of the self-employed' – Institute for Fiscal Studies,
    Crawford, R and Karjalainen, H, 2020

CHAPTER 12   THE PUBLIC INNOVATOR

'Students Around the World Practice Mindfulness Together as Part of
    ClassDojo and Yale "Mindful Moment' Initiative" – THE 74 – Kate
    Stringer, May 2019
Mission Economy: A Moonshot Guide to Changing Capitalism by Mariana
    Mazzucato, 2020
'Quantum Technologies Flagship' – European Commission 2020
'Turning the Word Upside Down: How Cantillon Redefined the
    Entrepreneur' – Mark Thornton, June Penguin, 2021
'President Biden's Bipartisan Infrastructure Law' – The White House 2022
'Renewable Energy Act (EEG)' – BWE
Creating a global network for change – Robyn Scott Interview, 2019
We the Possibility: Harnessing Public Entrepreneurship to Solve Our Most
    Urgent Problems by Mitchell Weiss, Harvard Business Review Press,
    2021
'Using mobile messaging' – The NHS, December 2022
'The Smart and Simple Way to Empower the Public Sector' – BCG, Jason
    LaBresh, Mark Watters, and Sachpreet Chandhoke, January 2017
'Challenges in using data across government' – Comptroller and
    Auditor General – National Audit Office
Handling of the Windrush situation, Session 2017–2019, HC 1622,
    National Audit Office

'German hospitals to get €3 billion funding boost for digitalisation' –
Healthcare IT News, Tammy Lovell, September, 2020
'Coronavirus opens up the NHS for health tech entrepreneurs' –
Financial Times, Hazel Sheffield, April 2020
One of the original meanings of the word *entrepreneur* was someone who
contracted with the government, albeit on a crony-like basis, before
the economist Richard Cantillon morphed it to its current form.

CHAPTER 13   FUNDING THE FUTURE

The Power Law by Sebastian Mallaby, Penguin, 2021
'These Countries Have The Most Startup Investment For Their Size' –
Crunchbase News – Joanna Glasner – November 2021
'A growing number of governments hope to clone America's DARPA' –
The Economist – June 2021
'20,000 businesses per year benefit from near doubling of startup
programmes' – Centre for Entrepreneurs
State Of Venture 2021 Report – CB Insights, January 2021
See Universitylabpartners.org
'About the NGI' – University of Manchester
'Unlocking HMRC data to engage with scaling companies – the
practical impact' – Scaleup Institute, 2020
Restarting the Future: How to Fix the Intangible Economy by Haskel and
Westlake, Princeton University Press, 2022
'How Much Does Venture Capital Drive the U.S. Economy?' Stanford
Business School, Ilya A. Strebulaev and Will Gornall, October 2015

CHAPTER 14   HOW TO CHANGE THE WORLD

'The Great Stagnation' – Tyler Cowen, 2011
'Learning from Founders' – Paul Graham – January 2007
'What's driving the decline in the firm formation rate?' – Ian Hathaway
and Robert Litan, 2014
'The Anti-Promethean Backlash' – Brink Lindsey, November 2022
'Europe is now a corporate also-ran. Can it recover its footing?'
The Economist, June 2021
'It's Time to Build', Marc Andreessen, www.a16z.com, 2020
For more on the Great Exhibition, read the The Entrepreneurs Network
paper by Anton Howes

Acknowledgements

Much of my thinking in this book comes from the conversations I have had with the thousands of entrepreneurs I have met over my career. It is a privilege to have a job which entails meeting so many ambitious, intelligent, and passionate people; I hope I have done those discussions justice in this book.

I would like to thank the Balderton portfolio companies mentioned throughout, and especially those where I currently or previously sat on the board. Our investments referenced in this book include Depop, Infarm, Hubs, Labster, Digital Surgery, HigherSteaks, Sophia Genetics, Revolut and Writer. Most importantly, I owe Hiroki Takeuchi, my friend and CEO of GoCardless (another Balderton portfolio company), a huge debt for first introducing me to venture.

I'm very fortunate to work with some of the finest minds in venture capital across the globe and am grateful to everyone at Balderton for their support on this project, our investors, and my partners past and present who put up with my musings every day. I would like to thank Magda Lukaszewicz, Adrian Rainey and Rachel Bremer for reading early drafts. I'm also very grateful to the brilliant team at The Entrepreneurs Network for engaging with and challenging many of my policy ideas in the book.

I'd like to thank the whole team at Bloomsbury, in particular Ian Hallsworth and Allie Collins, for their support and the trust they put in a naive, first-time author. I couldn't have written any of this without the support of my family and friends, who have shown great patience with me while I was working on *Start-Up Century*.

The people I grew up around epitomize the hardworking, *everyday-everyone* entrepreneurial spirit for which this book is an advocate, even if they would never describe themselves in such terms. It was written with all of them in mind, and in loving memory of Andy Sawer.

Finally, thank you to my wife Elizabeth, who makes all things possible.

Index